Accounting Software and the Microcomputer

Accounting Software and the Microcomputer

A Practical Guide to Evaluation and Implementation

IRWIN WINSTEN

John Wiley & Sons

New York • Chichester • Brisbane • Toronto • Singapore

Library of Congress Cataloging-in-Publication Data

Winsten, Irwin, 1925–
    Accounting software and the microcomputer / by Irwin Winsten.
      p.   cm.
    Includes bibliographical references
    ISBN 0-471-85312-7
    1. Accounting—Data processing.   I. Title.
  HF5679.W56   1990
  657'.028'5536'20—dc20   89-29833

Printed in the United States of America

10 9 8 7 6 5 4 3 2 1

Preface

What, another computer book? Well, not exactly a book about computers. This book concentrates on one important computer application: accounting software. Is there really a need for such a book? Libraries are filled with computer books. The number of titles is overwhelming. And the shelves of magazine stores that cater to business are crowded with computer periodicals.

If you have made a serious search for suitable accounting software, you already know the answer. Despite all of the books and magazines that flood the market, it is nigh impossible to find good practical information and advice. In fact, there are very few books on the subject, and most of these are outdated and limited in perspective. A few magazines print software reviews from time to time, but they rarely provide the critical coverage that is important to the serious reader. One reason is that there are few reviewers with a background in computers, accounting, and business practice. Additionally, an in-depth software review requires many hours of time, and reviewers are rarely paid for this kind of effort.

Accounting software is one of the least understood products in the computer marketplace, even though the proper selection and use of such software is a vital concern to anyone responsible for enterprise management. Many people are disappointed with the accounting software products that they have purchased. A 1986 survey reported that more than 70 percent of responses were from readers who were not satisfied with their accounting software. Nearly 50 percent stated that programs did not meet advertised performance, and another 30 percent felt that they had been misled as to a program's capabilities.

Writing in *Business Software,* Sheldon Needle noted that "more than 50 percent of the micro-based accounting packages purchased by businesses over the past five years were either not installed successfully or were abandoned after a short period—mainly because of easily avoidable user and product problems."

Computer and Software News reported on a survey in which one-third of the larger small businesses complained their systems were either "too big or too small." Inadequate software presented problems to 31 percent of the larger firms.

PC Magazine stated (September, 1987) that "Americans spent nearly $6,265,000 on 28,400 PC accounting packages in the first quarter of this year. And nearly 40 percent of these packages will remain on an office shelf, never seriously implemented by the companies that purchased them."

Some accounting software is offered at $70, while other products, seemingly similar, cost over $2,000. Is any other group of products, claiming to do the same thing, offered at such a wide range of prices—in a scale of 1 to 30? How can the uninformed shopper understand and justify this huge difference in price?

Accounting Software and the Microcomputer has been written to address these concerns. You do not have to be a programmer or computer expert to understand this book. It is written in plain English and explains the technical jargon that is often used to confuse and intimidate information seekers. In fact, the book provides a good working vocabulary of the computer terms that will help you when dealing with salespersons and others in the computer industry. As you will learn from the very first chapter, the entire industry suffers from a language problem, and there is every reason to ask for an explanation when unclear expressions and words are used.

The book explains what accounting software can and cannot do, so that performance expectations are realistic and not exaggerated because of advertising hype. It addresses the situation that might be too small for accounting software as well as the situation that might be too big for the microcomputer. It describes in practical business terms how these programs function and offers practical advice about finding the software that will provide satisfactory results. It explains how to match hardware and software and discusses the advantages and pitfalls of networks. The book presents realistic guidelines for starting up accounting software and provides checklists, so that potential users will have a better idea of time and cost requirements and avoid later disappointment.

The text is generic: it explains concepts and functions. It is not a compilation of product reviews, although many examples are drawn from software that is currently available. Most examples originate from DOS-based accounting software, because at the time of writing, this is the most popular environment in the microcomputer world, although many good Macintosh programs are entering the marketplace. Sample screens from nationally distributed software products are displayed together with critical notes highlighting features and limitations. This unique presentation gives the reader an opportunity to compare and evaluate different approaches to software design.

The book addresses the interests and concerns of four important groups of readers:

Software users will save time and money, because the book sets forth practical alternatives; provides the information necessary for good planning and decision making; and guides the reader past many pitfalls that could result in unnecessary expense, time loss, and disappointment.

CPAs, accountants, and business consultants will improve their effectiveness in dealing with client accounting software applications, thereby enhancing their success and profitability.

Business educators will find a useful resource that explains the applications, capabilities, and limitations of accounting software and provides practical guidelines for use.

Accounting software publishers and designers will improve their competitive edge because of the many practical suggestions about software functionality and control.

Accounting Software and the Microcomputer is intended to raise the understanding and awareness of the reader who wishes to fully comprehend and deal with this important and challenging computer software product.

IRWIN WINSTEN

Scarsdale, New York
February 1990

Acknowledgments

I wish to thank the following publishers for permitting the inclusion of selected screens from their software products:

Advanced Business Microsystems, Inc.—Platinum Series software, version 6.0.

Charterhouse Software Corporation—Charterhouse Accounting Systems, version 2.1.

Computer Associates International, Inc.—Accpac Plus, versions 5.0 and 5.1. The screens are © 1989, Computer Associates International, Inc.

Microfinancial Flexware—Flexware, version 6.02.

Great Plains Software—Great Plains Accounting Series, version 5.0. The screens are © Great Plains Software, Inc.

Open Systems, a division of Convergent Business Systems—Open Systems Accounting Software, version 3.2.

RealWorld Corporation—RealWorld, version 5.0.

State of the Art, Inc.—MAS90 Evolution/2, versions 1.10 and 1.11.

TLB Inc.—Solomon III™, version 6.0.

TRADEMARK ACKNOWLEDGMENTS

The following products are trademarks of the indicated companies

Accpac Plus	Computer Associates International, Inc.
Apple	Apple Computer, Inc.
Appleshare	Apple Computer, Inc.
Certiflex	Certiflex Systems
Corefast	Core International, Inc.
CPA-11	Franklen Computer Systems, Inc.
DacEasy Accounting	Dac Software, Inc.
Excalibur	Armor Systems Incorporated
Flexware	Microfinancial Flexware
4-in-1	Realworld Corp.
Harmony	Convergent Business Systems, Inc.
IBM	International Business Machines Corp.
IBM PC	International Business Machines Corp.
Lotus 1-2-3	Lotus Development Corporation
Macintosh	Apple Computer, Inc.
Macola	Macola, Incorporated
Mas90	State of the Art, Inc.
MCBA	MCBA Corporation
Myte Myke	MDS Associates, Inc.
New Views	Q.W. Page Associates, Inc.
Novell	Novell Inc.
Open Systems	Convergent Business Systems, Inc.
OS/2	International Business Machines Corp.
Peachtree Complete	Peachtree Software
Pick	Pick Systems
Plains & Simple	Great Plains Software
Platinum	Advanced Business Microsystems, Inc.
Profitwise	TLB, Inc.
Realworld	Realworld Corp.
Solomon III	TLB, Inc.
Sourcemate	Sourcemate Information Systems, Inc.
TCS	TCS Software, Inc.
The Accounting Partner	Star Software Systems
The Assistant Controller	Lake Avenue Software, Inc.
The Shoebox Accountant	Cyma/McGraw Hill
3Com	3Com Corp.
Unix	Bell Laboratories
Visicalc	Lotus Development Corporation
Xenix	Microsoft Corp.

We have tried to supply information about company trademarks. Trademarks indicated were derived from various sources. However, we cannot attest to the accuracy of this information. The absence of trademark identification does not necessarily indicate an absence of the trademark.

Contents

1

Helpful Perspectives

INTRODUCTION

What are people looking for in microcomputer accounting software? What help can it provide for business operators and managers?

Some are simply looking for ways to computerize routine bookkeeping activities. Those who have worked in an office know how much time goes into entering, copying, and looking up detailed information. They also know how easily errors can be made when information must be copied from one record to another. Tremendous amounts of time can be spent in totaling, proving, and tracking down errors. Seasonal industries may not have enough trained personnel to do this work during their busy periods. In many offices, backlogs are the norm rather than the exception. This results in stale business information, a situation that can lead to serious adverse consequences. Customer service deteriorates, sales are lost to competition, wrong purchase decisions are made, inventory becomes unmanageable, and vital documents affecting cash flow (such as customer invoices and statements) are late.

The difficulties of recruiting and keeping competent bookkeeping personnel provide an additional motivation for seeking alternatives to manual methods. It is not always easy to find people who are willing to perform routine clerical tasks. Many who do this work become bored, fail to pay attention, and contribute to the error problem. Even those who usually perform well will occasionally make troublesome mistakes.

Computer systems offer the promise of providing information that has been needed but lacking. Effective business management requires a great deal of information. However, costs and other problems associated with producing this information prevent many managers from obtaining much of the data that they really need. Some businesses find it virtually impossible to maintain accurate inventory records with manual methods. Others would like to have detailed sales histories presented in a variety of ways: by customer, salesperson, product, and territory. Frequent aging of receivables is desirable yet often waived because of time constraints. Others find it difficult to track incoming orders and control backlogs. Cash management and cost control may be poor. Production may be inefficient because of late efficiency reports. However, the cost of additional personnel may be a deterrent to developing useful and timely management information.

Frequently, detailed information is produced in formats that are difficult to use. Detailed lists, many pages long, require a patient search by the user to find the exceptions that require action. This kind of laborious review is burdensome and discourages use of the information. Many managers look for computer programs that provide well designed exception reports that remove a great deal of the review drudgery.

Some seek computer systems that will permit the application of management techniques to provide more effective use of capital and optimize the application of resources. They look for accounting software that will improve inventory management, provide better control over job-type operations, assist in sales forecasting and budgeting, and provide timely financial and statistical data that will highlight the exceptions that demand management attention.

In summary, business managers turn to accounting software to

- ☐ Minimize manual functions
- ☐ Provide more information
- ☐ Speed the production of documents and information
- ☐ Organize information into meaningful reports
- ☐ Become more competitive and make better use of their resources.

Unfortunately, anyone wishing to obtain useful information about accounting software faces a tremendous challenge. Some readers will turn to this book because they have had little success in obtaining helpful information from other sources, information that is necessary in order to make intelligent decisions about using business software. Many people who sell accounting software do not understand what they are selling. Many who purchase it become discouraged because they have difficulty getting started, or become disappointed as they discover the limitations of the software. (Some statistics on this subject appear in the preface.) Magazine articles that purport to evaluate new products are shallow and frequently written by people who do not have the background required for a useful analysis.

Why so much confusion? This chapter offers some explanation by presenting historic and economic perspectives of the accounting software industry. These perspectives explain many of the attitudes and policies of software publishers and dealers. Those who are aware of them will be able to deal more effectively with software publishers and vendors.

The chapter also discusses a major industry problem, the lack of standardized terminology. Basic bookkeeping and accounting terms have been given new definitions by many software publishers; frequently such terms have very specific meanings that are not generally understood. Therefore, potential users must make certain that terms and expressions employed in software manuals and screens will not cause confusion and disappointment.

HISTORIC BACKGROUND

The computer age is very young. Developed during World War II, business computers were first introduced in the late 1950s. In the early days (until the early 1980s), most installations were confined to large organizations. Hardware and software costs started in the $50,000 range and could reach into the millions. Hardware required a sheltered environment and was often treated better than human beings, with temperature, humidity, and other environment controls. Computer operations required a large amount of space. Special flooring and electrical service was required to deal with the large amount of power and numerous cables that had to be fed to each machine. Many installations required the full-time presence of maintenance personnel because of frequent breakdown. Very few off-the-shelf programs were available. Very few companies were in the business of publishing and distributing accounting software. Programs were written under contract with software houses or by a staff of programmers, an expensive and time-consuming procedure. Many installations were sold on a "bundled" basis, meaning that whatever software existed was thrown into the deal in order to sell the hardware.

Companies considered their computer operations to be important status symbols and incorporated computer operations into their public-relations program. The computer room was equipped with glass windows so visiting functionaries could marvel at the sight of tape and disk drives whirring and white-smocked attendants moving industriously about their chores. This kind of image-making also conveyed a sense of awe and a feeling that working with computers was something special and required a great deal of technical ability and knowledge. Many people working in computer installations as programmers and operators fostered this attitude. The computer room and its personnel were often viewed as a special arcane operation. This attitude interfered with good communication between programmers and users. In turn, poor communication frequently led to disappointing results.

Vestiges of this era continue to make many people wary of computer operations. The problem of poor communication persists, exacerbated by the advertising hype of the young software industry.

The road to the microcomputer was laid in the 1970s when huge technological leaps were made in computer design—leaps that resulted in faster performance, lower cost and smaller size. The massive computer of the 1950s and 1960s, which required special air-conditioned rooms and dedicated power lines, was outdistanced by smaller units that were much cheaper to produce. Today's microcomputer has more than ten times the memory and speed of its 1950s' ancestor, yet it requires much less power and space and costs one-tenth the price. A report appearing in *Datamation* magazine shows that a byte of data storage, which cost four dollars in 1950, has dropped to a few pennies. The original PC (personal computer) microprocessor speed of 4.77 MHz has already been increased 600% to over 30 MHz. It may be hard to believe, but today's microcomputers can perform millions of instructions per second.

The original microcomputer appeared on the scene in the late 1970s. Using an eight-bit microprocessor (the heart of the computer), the first PC was designed for personal use, instruction, and playing games, and was too limited for serious business applications. However, one important product called VisiCalc®, the first popular spreadsheet program, caught the attention of managers.

Shortly thereafter, in 1981, the IBM PC® with a 16-bit microprocessor was introduced. This machine offered enough speed and capacity to open the doors for a new industry because it provided enough power for true business applications. By the end of 1983 almost 1.5 million PCs had been shipped. In 1984 the shipments more than doubled. By the end of 1987, almost 30 million PCs had been installed throughout the world.

Many saw a golden opportunity in the new breed of microcomputers. Some introduced competitive machines offering greater capability or lower price than the IBM PC. Others began developing and merchandising software for the micros. People who had written contract software for minicomputers began to rewrite their programs for the micro. Others who had written for the original PC (which was not too successful in the business community) decided to upgrade for the new microprocessor. Those with specific industry knowledge wrote software for special applications such as medical practice or construction. Hundreds of programmers set to work, consulting with accountants and other specialists and writing and rewriting software using a variety of programming languages. Some were employees of large companies; others toiled at night in their homes—all hoping to tap a bright new market and become millionaires.

There was a big rush to get product to market, to beat competition. Hardware manufacturers provided an additional push because they did not want to lose sales attributable to a shortage of software to run on their machines. Some software was written for specific computers; other programs were written for a variety of hardware. There were no standards. The degree and quality of testing were determined by each publisher. Many products were touted with exaggerated promises. "User friendly" was the watchword until many realized that most products were difficult to learn and often fell short in performance. Eventually "user friendly" became a tarnished catch phrase.

Today, the result of this disordered and uncontrolled effort continues to be felt. The hope of finding a mother lode in the microcomputer software market still lures software designers and publishers. A few millionaires have been able to find the lode—but not in accounting software. The market is crowded by many competing products that appear to offer very similar performance, often at very dissimilar prices. Appendix A lists more than 120 accounting software products that have been mentioned by a number of leading publications. New accounting software is announced almost every month, while uncompetitive products quietly disappear from notice. Some software publishers have attracted enough attention to attain national recognition. Others survive in local or regional markets.

The accounting software industry still has a long way to go. One industry magazine, *Computer Product Selling,* reports that as of late 1987 only 14% of small businesses are using accounting software. Sales for 1987 were forecast at 159 million and are expected to double in the next three years.

The success of the IBM PC and its associated system, DOS (disk operating system), has begun to create a de facto set of standards that provides some stability in this amorphous industry. But new technologies continue to emerge and challenge methods of operation. As of this writing, a new operating system, OS/2®, is promising better performance than DOS, while other systems such as Xenix® and Pick™ are attempting to obtain a better share of the market. Apple Computer, with its Macintosh® line, is also interested in serving the business community. Each operating system plays by a different set of rules. Accounting software that works with one operating system may not function with another.

Many who have resisted the computer now wonder whether they have missed out on improved business performance. Those who have tenaciously worked at uncovering the arcane secrets of the microcomputer have come to rely heavily upon it as a vital operating tool. Their success, indeed the meteoric rise in the use of microcomputers in the business world, beckons the resisters to join them.

DIFFICULTY IN OBTAINING PRECISE INFORMATION

Promotions of software products that offer to provide marvelous benefits for the business executive get heavy exposure. Such products are advertised on television, through the mail, and in newspapers and magazines. Most of these advertisements are general and vague. Those who wish to determine precisely how these products function in order to decide whether they will be truly beneficial are faced with a dilemma. The industry does not provide an easy path for those seeking specific information. Here are a few case histories to illustrate the point:

Case One. A potential customer entered a large computer store in midtown Manhattan and asked for information about software that was prominently displayed in one of the showcases. The salesclerk who responded to the inquiry looked a little embarrassed, and then started rummaging around the store, looking on a number of tables and shelves, and then disappeared into a back room. Finally he returned, downcast and empty-handed. The clerk stated that he had been unable to locate the manual. He surmised that it probably had been taken by a former employee who had been dismissed the prior week. The software product remained in the showcase but there was no one in the store who knew anything about it.

It is unrealistic to expect salesclerks to have the accounting and computer expertise to fully understand and explain accounting software. They have enough of a problem dealing with new hardware products.

Case Two. During her lunch hour, the owner of a small business spotted a notice in the window of a computer store inviting interested parties to sign up for a demonstration of accounting software. The manager made an appointment for the demonstration. A number of people arrived at the scheduled time and waited over half an hour for the show to start. They were then told that the people providing the demonstration were delayed en route. When the demonstrators finally arrived there was a lot of fussing around the equipment. Eventually it became evident that the demonstrators were unable to get the software to run the printer! By this time, most of the audience had lost interest and wandered out of the store.

Software demonstrations are often disappointing. Most computer retailers are ill-equipped to support such demonstrations, especially when hardware is not properly configured and the software must be loaded for each demonstration.

Some retailers recognize the special problems associated with accounting software and turn to outside specialists for help in demonstrating and explaining such products. But the choice of such specialists must be made with great care.

Case Three. A prominent computer retailer referred a customer to an outside consultant when the customer inquired about a specific accounting package that was prominently featured in the store. A week passed before the consultant responded. It would have been better if the consultant had remained silent: The weak, hesitant voice on the line quickly stated that he was in no position to demonstrate the product and that, anyway, the customer would not like it!

EXPLAINING THE DIFFICULTY

Why is it so hard to obtain information about accounting software? There are three important explanations. One lies in the nature of the product. The second arises from the economics of the industry. The third comes from the lack of standardization.

The Nature of Accounting Software

Accounting software is complex. One must have a wide knowledge base that includes business operations, accounting theory, and some computer technology in order to understand the functions and limitations of each software package. The organizations that design and program accounting software frequently are unaware of some of the requirements of the business community. This results in unbalanced programs. Some software provides excellent controls but is limited in function. Other software provides much greater functionality but fails to provide important controls.

The complexity of accounting software requires extensive testing in order to eliminate program errors. The degree of testing varies with each publisher. Many new releases contain program problems or "bugs"; many months may pass before they are detected and corrected. An article in *Business Software* magazine referred to companies that "send 'green' software out the door . . . to be first with a 'next-generation' program, to meet a pre-announced delivery date, or to follow the cynical policy of letting end-users help remove any bugs that remain." Some publishers have released corrections for as long as a year after the software entered the market.

The terms "business software" and "accounting software" are often used interchangeably yet they have different meanings. Business software refers to any software that can be used in business, from personal productivity products such as word processors and spreadsheets, to work aids such as calendars and electronic note pads. Accounting software, as used in this book, has a much more limited meaning and refers to the records, documents, and reports produced and maintained by enterprises to record and report business and business-related transactions. These records generally consist of ledgers and journals together with data concerning customers, vendors, products, and services. The production of business documents such as invoices, statements, and checks, as well as management reports, are important functions of the software. The product usually is sold in modules broken into operational segments such as general ledger, accounts receivable, order entry, inventory, purchasing, accounts payable, job costing, and so on.

Accounting software is significantly different from personal productivity products. This latter group is more likely to be used on an individual basis. Accounting software must be used by many people and requires interaction among persons with different functions. This imposes a challenge to those designing the software screens and manuals, the challenge of communicating instructions and explanations in clear language that will be understood by people with a wide range of skills and responsibilities. Rarely do the publishers devote the necessary degree of time and skill to this effort.

Accounting software addresses business operations in a very specific manner. It provides for records of a specific size containing predetermined fields of information, each field limited in size. The techniques for entering information, locating and correcting errors, providing reference information, and designing and printing reports are all precisely defined. Yet most manuals fail to provide a complete list of these vital performance requirements and specifications. Often one must search slowly and carefully through the entire manual to obtain this information. At times even this is not enough, and one must actually use the program to find out exactly where the limits lie.

Accounting software comes in two varieties. One variety consists of generalized software designed for general business use. The second variety consists of software designed for use in a specific industry. There is software for doctors, dentists, veterinarians, building contractors, retailers, property managers, and those in many other professions and industries. Industry-specific software is referred to by the term "vertical package." Some vertical packages provide meaningful functions that apply to their specific industries. Others are generalized packages with a few changes in terminology.

The Economics of the Industry

Publishing and selling accounting software involves much more than writing programs. In order to meet competition, programming objectives are constantly changing even as programs are being written. People who perform the first program tests may not have complete manuals and may omit tests of important functions. The information learned from these preliminary tests may lead to additional program changes. The entire effort of programming, testing, and rewriting often will be done under great time pressures because of fear that competitors will release enhancements and grab the market.

Additionally, publishers must devote some of their resources to dealing with rapidly changing technology. Today's microcomputers are made with a variety of microprocessors and operating systems, each requiring different programming. New microprocessors are constantly being introduced, with ever greater speed and capacity. Today, the IBM PC dominates the microcomputer market. However, the IBM OS/2 and the Macintosh II are challenging that dominant position.

Programs must be able to function with a number of different monitors and printers. Some monitors are monochrome; others offer color, but with a wide variation in the color image. Monitors are called workstations, when they provide a larger viewing screen. Printer technology is also changing. Daisy-wheel printers, once used for high-quality images, are being replaced by 24–pin-dot matrix and laser printers. The demand for multiuser and network operations involves additional programming effort. It is important to remember that each type of monitor and printer, and each network program, requires special program routines.

The business of writing clear and simple manuals and keeping them updated remains an industry challenge. Publishers face major problems in creating and updating their manuals. Some may change program specifications until close to the release date. The result is that manuals often are prepared at the last minute. The listing of performance specifications, such as the maximum size of data fields or the maximum number of accounts, may be hard to find without reading the entire book. Even then, important specifications, particularly severe limitations, may be undocumented. Frequently the language is so poor that one must actually sit down and run the software in order to understand what the software is doing.

In most situations software should not be selected on the basis of the quality of the manuals. A poor manual may require more training than a good manual, but the quality and performance of the software itself are much more important considerations.

The industry recognizes these difficulties by providing support to end users. Publishers may offer telephone support lines and software updates, or they may work with consultants who provide more direct on-site help. (Support is discussed in Chapter 9.)

The product must be advertised and promoted in order to find a niche against a host of competitors. A brief look at a few computer magazines and trade newspapers will demonstrate the degree of promotional effort that the industry seems to require in order to stay in business. However, advertising and promotion usually will not lead to a consumer sale. Because of its complexity, accounting software requires a third party, such as a retailer or consultant, to demonstrate and explain the product.

There are no specific channels of distribution. Some accounting software is sold through software distributors who, in turn, sell to retailers. Publishers who choose to distribute in this fashion provide training sessions for retail personnel, in an attempt to make them comfortable in explaining and selling the product. Retailers who purchase the software for resale face problems when new versions are offered. Some publishers will allow the retailer to exchange the old version for the new one. Others leave the retailer with outdated software.

Another source of software distribution are industry consultants called VARs (value added resellers). Some VARs specialize in specific applications such as medical, construction, and manufacturing. They may limit their efforts to software sales and support or try to sell a combination of both software and hardware. Once the product is sold, the publisher must make arrangements to support the sale by helping customers with their problems, tracking down and correcting "bugs," correcting errors in manuals, and improving and enhancing the product in order to stay ahead of competition.

In sum, the software publisher must have sufficient financial strength to provide programming, testing, manual writing, printing, publishing, distribution, sales promotion, advertising, dealer training, and customer support. When financial resources are limited, priority frequently is given to sales promotion and advertising. Some publishers may be more concerned with the appearance of their ads than the legibility and clarity of their manuals.

Is it any wonder that so many products reach the market before they are fully tested and documented? Many popular products have become successful because of the skill and resources invested in advertising and distribution, and not necessarily because they are superior products.

Lack of Standardized Terminology

As explained, the history of the microcomputer industry and the economic pressures on software publishers have contributed to difficulties in assessing software products. There is one additional source of confusion: the lack of standardization, particularly in the use of language.

Advertising hype has introduced confusion and misunderstanding into the minds of many who must deal with software products. Copy is often written by people who have little knowledge of office operations and accounting terminology. The confusion exists in large part because accounting software originates in a highly decentralized cottage industry with virtually no technical or quality standards. Each publisher, distributor, and retailer must try to get the attention of potential customers and convince them that their product will do the job and can be painlessly installed.

The product is sold without clearly recognizable and distinguishable trade names. Some brands are sold by product name, others by the name of the distributor or publisher. Products with similar names but different functions are offered by different publishers. How is one to distinguish software with names like CPA, CPA+, and CPA11™, or companies with names like Business Systems Group and Small Business Systems, Inc.? Some publishers distribute a number of software products under different trade names. Some purchase the distribution rights to programs written by others and may then give a new name to the software.

The confusion in names is compounded by confusion in bookkeeping terminology. Three important bookkeeping terms are frequently misused by software designers. The effects of the misuse are best understood from a brief review of the bookkeeping process.

1. Each transaction is recorded, generally in chronologic sequence, into a **Journal**. Separate journals are used to record different classes of trans-actions, such as cash receipts, cash disbursements, and sales. A separate set of journals is maintained for each **Accounting period**.

2. The chronologic data, which has already been entered into journals, is then copied into ledgers. The process of copying from a journal into a ledger is called **posting**. The accounting ledger is called the general ledger. Other ledgers, known as subsidiary ledgers, are maintained to keep track of customers, vendors, inventory, etc. Frequent postings are made to the subsidiary ledgers during each accounting period in order to keep information current.

3. Journal pages are closed and summarized at the end of each accounting period (also called **fiscal period**). Accounting periods are usually a calendar month. The accounting-period data is then posted to the general ledger.

4. Although separate journals and ledgers are maintained for each busi-ness entity (such as a corporation or partnership) there are times when the accounts of two or more related corporations are brought together into a single set of financial statements. The result is called a **consolida-tion**. Consolidated statements are usually prepared for a parent com-pany and its subsidiaries and require sophisticated accounting adjustments. **Combinations**, on the other hand, usually refer to the bringing together of the accounts of different departments within a business entity. For example, a retail store may operate a number of departments, each selling a different type of merchandise. Manage-ment may wish to see separate operating statements for each depart-ment, as well as a combined statement for all departments. A combina-tion, in its correct accounting sense, can also refer to the bringing together of the accounts of business entities that are not related by ownership, such as brother and sister corporations.

One would think that such common and well-accepted terms as "jour-nal," "posting," "accounting period," "consolidation," and "combination" would cause no problem with designers of accounting software. Unfortu-nately, this does not hold true.

The term "journal" is abused in a number of different ways. Some software does not use the term at all. Instead a similar term, such as "register," is substituted. However, this substitute terminology might disguise the fact that the software cannot produce a true journal—that is, a chronologic list of all transactions entered for the accounting period. Instead, a separate register must be printed for each batch of transactions. Another abuse applies the term "journal" to a list of transactions in account-number order, not chronologic order. Such software might be unable to produce a list of transactions in chronologic order. Since journals are important for both information and audit trail, users should place a high value on software that provides this important record.

It would seem that the concept of posting would be simple and clear-cut to any person with a bookkeeping background; not so to some designers of accounting software. In a few instances, the term "post" is incorrectly used to refer to the original entry of transactions. Other software may use the term "update" instead of the more correct term "post."

Why do some publishers cause so much confusion about dates and accounting periods? Accounting programs use different methods for assigning transactions to accounting periods. The easiest method lets the user enter the number of the accounting period at the time of transaction entry. Other software confuses the process, for example, by determining the accounting period from the transaction date. This is an awkward limitation, because transactions that arrive after the books are closed, such as late vendor invoices, must be misdated on the books in order to apply them to the appropriate accounting period. Other software determines the accounting period from a date that appears on the screen at the start of the entry session. This date might be called the "system date," "current date," or "record date"—a very confusing procedure that leads to accounting errors. The term "consolidation" is also much abused by software publishers. Most manuals use the term to mean the merging of the accounts of a number of departments—in other words, a "combination." The unwary user who requires true consolidation may purchase the wrong product and be disappointed.

In addition to the inappropriate use of basic bookkeeping terms, other words are misused in an effort to exaggerate the capability of the software. Consider the concept of "integration." Most of the accounting software coming on the market today claims to be integrated, which means that the software can transfer information from one module to another without the need for reentry of data. However, the method for transferring information may not be as simple and automatic as expected. Full integration is accomplished by very few software packages. (For an expanded discussion, please refer to Chapter 8.)

Other problems arise from the lack of standard accounting and computer terminology. How is a novice to deal with such terms as "building files," "video forms," or "unprocessed journal entries"? Even the basic term "password" is not sacrosanct: For instance, publisher uses the term "security code" where most users use "password," but uses the same term "password" to signify company code.

CONDITIONS ARE IMPROVING

Intense competition has forced publishers to pay more attention to many of the problems just discussed. New software versions are being introduced that provide, among other enhancements discussed in later chapters, manuals that are easier to understand, lists of specifications, and other materials that help a potential customer understand the software. These improvements are creating renewed interest in accounting software. Although the search for suitable accounting software continues to be a challenge, many successful installations prove that the search can be rewarding.

This book will provide specific answers to questions about finding, evaluating, installing, and effectively using accounting software. The following overview will direct the reader to the chapters of greatest concern and interest.

Chapter 2 will explain important differences between manual and computer accounting methods and indicate why noncomputer operations and internal controls may require change once computers are introduced. Long-term success with accounting software requires knowledge of these concepts. The chapter also discusses the degree of technical computer knowledge required for successful installation and use.

Chapter 3 discusses the differences in management and organization style that affect computer decisions. These differences will affect both the choice of accounting software and the timing of installation.

Chapter 4 talks about the matters to be considered before searching for software. It describes the circumstances that point to computerization, as well as those that do not. The choice of minicomputer versus microcomputer is discussed. Twelve important software attributes are introduced; they will be discussed more fully in succeeding chapters.

Chapter 5 explains the nature and functions of the various modules offered by accounting software publishers. It describes functions that are common to all accounting software and also illustrates some important differences among the products of different publishers.

Chapters 6 through 12 explain software attributes in detail: capacity, functionality, costs, and control. Readers who have completed these chapters should have the information and knowledge required for the successful choice of accounting software.

Chapter 13 provides guidance for the software search.

Chapter 14 discusses installation planning, a vital step in the successful installation of accounting software.

Chapter 15 offers views and ideas about future improvements in accounting software. It should provide some food for thought for those who are interested in this fascinating and fractured industry.

SUMMARY

In this introductory chapter, four major reasons why business managers use accounting software have been presented:

- ☐ To computerize manual operations
- ☐ To provide more information than is produced by manual systems
- ☐ To speed up data processing
- ☐ To organize information into more meaningful reports

All of these reasons can be summarized in reason number five:

- ☐ To become more successful.

However, the search for suitable accounting software is difficult. An important explanation of this difficulty lies in the historic development and economics of the industry. Accounting software products by and large are the result of a cottage industry that has evolved in the last few years with little control and standardization. Many publishers have limited funds that must be carefully allocated among a number of important business functions. In some instances this limitation has resulted in inadequate testing, confusing operator manuals, vague screen prompts, and poor user support. Channels of distribution vary from product to product, making it difficult to locate software that meets specific needs.

Exaggerated claims and poor terminology add to the sense of uncertainty. Users must verify performance and read manuals carefully to determine exactly how the software will perform. Fortunately, the recent industry trend points to improvements in these conditions.

In conclusion,

□ Purchase software that is published by a company with proven stability. Minimize the possibility of loss of support should the publisher go out of business.

□ Recognize the possibility that the software may not be error free. Determine how the publisher distributes corrections to end users.

□ View advertising claims with a healthy skepticism. Verify performance.

□ Determine how traditional accounting and bookkeeping operations are performed by the software. Understand how accounting and computer terminology is used by each publisher.

2

Comparison of Manual and Computer-Based Systems

INTRODUCTION

Anyone thinking of using a computer-based accounting system should understand and appreciate the profound difference between such a system and a manual one. Many users mistakenly believe that computer accounting systems are a simple enhancement of manual systems. In their view, the computer merely serves to speed things up and insure greater accuracy. They think of the computer as a big calculating and copying device. Do not fall into this trap! Such a view can lead to disappointment and serious operating problems. Successful software selection and installation requires clear recognition of important dissimilarities between the two systems.

DISTINGUISHING CHARACTERISTICS

Eight important characteristics of computer systems distinguish them from manual systems, and these characteristics must be recognized when planning computer operations:

☐ Lack of flexibility
☐ Lack of initiative
☐ Anonymity
☐ Reliability

☐ Compressibility of records

☐ Speed

☐ Vulnerability

☐ Need for special body of knowledge

The first two characteristics demand that potential users make a careful list of their data processing requirements and check this list against the performance of candidate software.

The next four raise questions about internal control, both controls provided by the software and controls that must be separate from the software.

The vulnerability of computer operations gives rise to the need for operating disciplines to protect against equipment damage and failure.

Concern about the special skills required to work with computers often stands in the way of an installation. While some knowledge is required, these concerns frequently are exaggerated.

One should also be aware of the fact that there are significant differences between accounting and other categories of application software; the final section of this chapter will address such differences.

Lack of Flexibility

It may come as a surprise to start this discussion by warning that computer systems are more rigid than manual systems. Newspapers and magazines are filled with articles describing how computers are being taught to "think." We read of chess matches in which computers beat human competitors. Artificial intelligence, the capability of computers to reason like experts, is discussed at cocktail parties. A battle rages in academic circles as to whether computers will eventually be able to think as well as, or better than, humans. This is fascinating speculation, but today's business manager is concerned with cost-effective performance and not academic theory.

Accounting programs are designed to fulfill a set of business requirements. Each accounting software product attempts to satisfy these requirements in a very specific manner. Yes, the programs can be changed if they are not satisfactory. But the cost of such changes can be prohibitive and involves a substantial amount of time and money. Unfortunately, some users have learned through bitter experience how rigid accounting programs can be. The fact remains that nothing can beat pencil and paper for flexibility!

For example, consider someone trying to prepare a budget by analyzing disbursements from a checkbook. A logical approach would be to take a sheet of columnar paper, select column headings to represent various expenses (such as rent, food, and utilities), and then enter each check. The chances are that after a few entries, the preparer would have to add a few more columns that were omitted from the first try. Suppose there are so many checks that the entries run off the page—no matter, additional pages can easily be added. In a similar fashion, if there is an insufficient number of columns, additional columns can be added by pasting pages onto the original worksheet. There is really no limit to the number of columns or rows that can be added. Even the dollar capacity of each column is flexible. If the amount of a check exceeds the digit capacity of the ruled column, the numbers can always be "squeezed in."

A computer "worksheet," particularly one that is part of an accounting program, does not work that way. The number of fields in a record (comparable to the columns in a worksheet) is predetermined by the program. The number of records (comparable to the rows in a worksheet) is limited either by the program or by the capacity of the storage medium. The size of each field is also set by the program. If the limits on the number of fields, number of records, or field sizes are too low, the task of increasing these limits is much more complex than with a paper worksheet. Reprogramming may be prohibitive in time or cost, or could even be totally impractical.

Consider another example from a popular accounting application, accounts receivable. Many accounts receivable programs can handle the needs of a simple business. They maintain a single accounts receivable file. One cash receipts journal and one sales journal are provided to record all receivable transactions. Cash receipts are deposited in one bank account. All sales are credited to a single sales income account. Sales reports list all customers as one group and show, by month and year-to-date, sales in dollars.

But what about companies that have different needs? Perhaps, because of divisional operations, they require two or more accounts receivable files. What if they would like to deposit cash receipts into two or more bank accounts? Perhaps the accountants advise setting up a separate journal for customer credits and allowances. Suppose sales management requires grouping customers into classes and reporting units as well as dollar sales? Perhaps sales should be assigned to different income accounts.

There is no assurance that an accounts receivable software program can meet all of these requirements. In fact, many cannot. Some programs permit only one accounts receivable control account per company. Some assume that all cash is deposited in one bank account. Some do not provide a separate journal for customer credits. Many are limited in the number of sales accounts. Almost all are limited in the content and scope of the reports that they can produce.

Functional limitations can also be very serious. There are wide dissimilarities in the way businesses deal with a host of matters such as sales commissions, sales terms, and pricing. Every software program differs in the way it deals with these functions. In fact, there are accounts receivable programs that ignore some functions altogether. Some will compute sales commissions; others will not. Some provide very limited pricing formulas or ignore due dates when aging the accounts.

Accounting programs generally are fixed in the terminology and design that appear on monitor screens. They require stepping through many fields of information, even if some fields are useless. The layout of forms, such as invoices, statements, and checks, may also be limited by the software.

This lack of flexibility applies to all computer programs. It applies to the amount and type of information that can be stored about customers, inventory items, vendors, and other important files. It applies to the functions that the software performs, whether it is programmed to compute finance charges, determine sales commissions, figure percent markup, and perform a host of business computations and verifications that are part of daily business life. Most important of all, it applies to the reports generated by the software. The fact that an accounting program provides for the storage of specific items of information does not necessarily mean that that information can be presented in the format, sequence, or scope desired by the user.

Be prepared for this. Take the time to determine and list your data processing needs in specific terms of capacity and performance.

Lack of Initiative

Good managers train their people to notice exceptions, to question the unusual. They complain about people who work mechanically and do not recognize information that is obviously wrong, or do not question results that are obviously false.

Do not expect this from accounting software! The ability to question seemingly false data or atypical results must be anticipated and built into the program. Any wrong condition that is not tested as part of the program will be processed without question.

Take a look at the following information about alcoholic beverages:

HARD DRINKS

	Serving Size (fl oz)	Calories Per Serving	Calories Per Ounce
Brandy	1.0	69	69
Cordials, liqueur	1.0	97	97
Daiquiri	3.5	122	35
Gin, rum, vodka, whiskey (80 proof)	1.5	97	65
Gin, rum, vodka, whiskey (86 proof)	1.5	105	70
Gin, rum, vodka, whiskey (90 proof)	1.5	111	74
Gin, rum, vodka, whiskey (100 proof)	1.5	124	83
Tequila (80 proof)	1.5	36	24
Manhattan	3.5	252	72
Martini	2.5	152	61
Whiskey sour	3.5	185	53

Do any of the preceding data look questionable?

Normally, if the copy were made from one computer file to another, it would be assumed that an exact copy would be made. But chances are, if it were hand-copied, there would probably be some question as to whether the calorie content of tequila (as shown in the table) is correct. The same idea should be applied to accounting software. Will the program accept a date that is remote from the current date? Will entries be accepted for accounts or customers that are not on file? Will the program accept weekly payroll hours or dollars, no matter how high? Can a limit be set on hourly rates? Will processing continue if entries do not balance?

Some programs are more helpful than others in pointing out conditions that require attention. This may be expressed in an inventory reorder report, or by flagging customers that exceed credit limits. However, in general, accounting software tends to provide extensive lists of information rather than highlight exceptions. Some publishers provide separate modules that permit users to design their own reports, including tests for exception conditions.

These two important characteristics of accounting software—the lack of flexibility and lack of initiative—make it imperative that potential users carefully assess their own requirements in detail. Never assume that the software will perform a specific function in an acceptable manner. Check out each requirement against the actual performance of the program.

Anonymity

Four characteristics of computer technology are essential to good computer performance, yet raise critical concerns about data protection and control. The first of these is the relative anonymity of computer operations. People who work on manual records leave clues as to who actually performed the work. The person who made a specific entry generally can be traced by examination of the handwriting. A secondary resource is the memory of coworkers. Manual operations take time and require access to bulky records. People in an office frequently remember who was present on a particular day and have a general idea of what they were doing. Typewritten records are a bit harder to trace, but there are ways of identifying the typewriter used to make specific entries. The examination of the paper or of the ink provides another means of tracing the source of manual entries.

None of this applies to computers. Information that gets into computer records carries no trace of the person making the entry. Computer files carry anonymous electronic bits. There is no telltale script, unusual erasure, overwriting, or any other indication of the person who made the entry. No amount of detective work can be applied to a hard disk to determine exactly who made specific entries.

Many programming techniques are used to control and track computer users. Passwords are the most popular. There may be a special password just to get into the computer, and another one to get into the accounting program. Different passwords may allow individuals access to specified portions of the program.

Another technique is the use of logs to record the name of each user, together with time of entry and lists of programs accessed. There are file encryption programs that rewrite files so that they can be read only by someone who has access to the encryption program.

Experience has shown that there are no foolproof program techniques that prevent the unscrupulous from accessing computer files. All of these safeguard techniques are useful, but it is still important to recognize that there is no way to establish, with absolute certainty, when entries were made and who made them.

An interesting example of the anonymous nature of computer files is a news story that appeared recently about the sale of surplus government electronic typewriters. Some of the officials involved in the sale were embarrassed to learn that the typewriters still contained government reports encoded on the typewriter disks. Nobody had erased the files!

And, in a letter to the *New York Times*, the writer reported renting a computer loaded with proprietary documents that had not been erased by a previous user.

The implication is quite clear. Controls must be established over vital computer records and files. Some of these controls must be maintained outside of the computer. Never rely completely on the computer to police itself. (For an expanded discussion, refer to Chapter 12.)

Reliability

As just noted, computers lack initiative. The converse also is true. Computers, in some respects, are much more reliable than humans. They can carry out a complex set of instructions an infinite number of times without changing a single step or slowing down. This ability to follow instructions to the letter, no matter how long or complex, and to work at a constant speed, is one of the great features of electronic data processing. Computers are not plagued by fatigue, absenteeism, or any of those unexpected human lapses that seem to be inevitable. When computers break down, the results are so unintelligible or illogical that the evidence of a problem is very clear.

The benefit of this characteristic is that computers can be asked to perform a very long and involved sequence of steps, and management need not be concerned whether the instructions will be executed perfectly every time. Not only that, but there is no need to train new personnel in these involved procedures because of absenteeism, vacation, or turnover. For the computer, there is no practical limit to the number of instructions that can be incorporated into a single program. Often, when humans must pursue a complex task, the work must be broken down into small segments because the overall task is too much for one individual to remember.

But this inexorable quality does carry a few problems. Computers are very literal. Users may introduce new conditions without fully anticipating how the computer will react. Our minds are much more flexible and often make adjustments to accommodate changes without realizing that such adjustments have been made.

When is this a problem?

First, some simple examples.

When tabulating the results of a questionnaire that calls for yes or no answers, humans would readily understand that the following answers are the same:

☐ YES ☐ yes

☐ Y ☐ y

To a computer, each of these answers is different, unless the program specifically directs the computer to treat them all the same.

Consider the way that dates can be written. To a human, the following all have the same meaning:

☐ January 1, 1989   ☐ 01/01/89

☐ 1/1/89   ☐ 1-1-89

Not only do computers interpret each of these dates as different, but many programs will refuse to continue if the date is entered in the "wrong" format.

Computers are just as fussy about the way that numbers and names are entered. Humans can add and sort a column of numbers even if the digits are not correctly lined up in each row. They can find a customer name even if slightly misspelled. Computers are much more rigid. This means that one must pay careful attention to the design and entry of account names and codes. The number 1 is not the same as the number 000001. The name McNeil is not the same as the name Mcneil.

Many computer programs are written by naive programmers who do not anticipate the possibility that users might press the wrong keys. Users know very well that beginners will almost certainly do just that. When a wrong key is pushed, there is no way to anticipate the results. In some cases, the program jumps to another subroutine. At other times, the program accepts information from the keyboard, even though the information is meaningless. Still worse is the software that leaps right out of the program back to the operating system. An unexpected leap of this kind can cause the loss of hours of work and even gum up the files. (One key that can cause a major disruption in some programs is the "escape" key.)

Some programmers refuse to recognize the possibility that printers can run out of paper or jam. If printing is interrupted, the program goes into a tailspin.

Computer programs include many decision points that branch to a different sequence of processing steps. It is very difficult to verify the performance of a program under every possible program path. This is the reason why an illogical or unexpected result (commonly called a "bug") may turn up weeks or months after the program has been in use. Users who require changes to off-the-shelf programs must realize that seemingly minor program changes can create unanticipated results.

Accounting software must be carefully reviewed to determine that it will function well under normal working conditions, not just in the hands of an expert demonstrator. Additional care is necessary if program modifications are required.

Compressibility of Records

Computer records are much more compact than the pen-and-ink or type-writer variety. One 5$\frac{1}{4}$-inch double-sided floppy diskette can hold the equivalent of 200 typewritten pages. A 10-megabyte hard disk can hold almost 30 times that amount, or 60,000 pages. New developments are constantly coming onto the market that provide for even greater storage capacities. The 3$\frac{1}{2}$-inch diskette introduced in 1987 has more than 4 times the storage capacity of the older 5$\frac{1}{4}$-inch diskette.

The storage medium itself is small, lightweight, and quite rugged (provided it is kept away from magnetic fields and liquids). Thus it is easy to carry about large amounts of information. People can copy files onto diskettes in order to take the information to other offices, or to work on at home or during a trip (using laptops or portables). What a difference from precomputer days, when the same information was stored in bulky folders and binders that were heavy and clumsy to move from place to place.

But this compressibility should place the user a little more on guard. At times, moving, or removing, information may be a bit *too* easy. Few copies were made of manual records because they were difficult to copy and to handle; today, there often is little or no control over the number of copies made of sensitive files, and certainly no assurance that the copied files are destroyed or returned after they have served their purpose.

Most businesses have a number of confidential files without realizing how easily this information can be copied and used by unauthorized employees and others. Just think what can happen if a salesperson is contemplating a change in employment and copies customer lists, cost computations, and sales statistics. Or think of the effect on the staff if a disgruntled employee is able to obtain payroll information.

Electronic records can be copied without leaving a trace, and the copies are so compact that they can be slipped into a pocket without detection. Users must give serious thought to arranging for proper controls.

Speed

The great speed of computer operations creates another control challenge. Manual files and records are bulky and difficult to remove or copy without detection. Nearly everyone has seen a spy movie in which secret agents slip into private offices late at night when there is less risk of detection and ample time to make photographic copies of secret papers. The spy story of the future will probably show the culprit entering as a computer repair person who copies the secret information in the time that it takes to pick up a screwdriver from the floor!

Computer technology permits voluminous data to be copied quickly. While this is an obvious boon to the authorized user, the important control issue cannot be ignored. Short lapses in control can create serious breaches in security.

Vulnerability

Picture office personnel writing at their desks when suddenly the lights go out. What would they do? Perhaps they would sit back and hope that power will be restored in a few minutes. Perhaps a few would look for candles or a flashlight so they could put their work away and make an orderly exit. In any event, when electrical service is resumed, people can retrieve the records and continue on with their work. The loss of power might be a nuisance, but will not seriously affect the files. It would take a major catastrophe such as a fire, flood, or explosion to destroy manual records so that they are unusable.

Not so with computer records. Any major change in electrical service, even for a fraction of a second, can cause a major record-keeping headache. The change can be a power interruption, or just a quick spike in voltage. Power interruption need not be caused by an electrical storm or other catastrophe. There are much simpler and more frequent causes such as someone tripping over an extension cord or the popping of a fuse.

Today's computers are so reliable, and are so much less sensitive to environmental conditions than their forebears, that it is easy to forget how vulnerable they are—until a costly "glitch" occurs. Many computer functions cannot be interrupted without creating problems. These functions may involve expanding files, posting, writing to disk, performing internal computations, or other tasks. Once power is interrupted, all information in RAM (random-access memory) is wiped out. The computer, literally, does not know exactly at what point it was interrupted and therefore cannot resume the way a human can. Instead, the files may be filled with errors or, in computer terminology, they are "corrupted."

Computers are sensitive to other conditions that rarely cause problems for paper systems. Voltage variation, particularly spikes of high voltage, can cause damage to electrical components. Some of these spikes come over the electric wires, others from static electricity. Dust and cigarette smoke can wreak havoc on disk drives. And, of course, spilled liquids such as coffee or tea can do much more harm to an electronic component than to a paper record.

In short, computers are much more vulnerable than manual systems to a number of conditions ranging from a sudden interruption of electrical service to someone smoking near the computer. And when computers are knocked out of service, the recovery of files and resumption of daily routines can be a nightmare.

Preventive measures and disciplines can minimize these hazards.

1. If power interruption is frequent or hazardous, use a special device that provides some form of assured continuous power.

2. Use nonstatic mats and surge suppressors to protect the computer from destructive voltage surges.

3. Establish policies that discourage eating, drinking, and smoking in the computer area.

4. Require users to make frequent backups of computer files.

Need for Special Body of Knowledge

How much computer knowledge is required to successfully use accounting software? Are programming skills important? Must computer specialists be hired to manage the operation?

Many managers are concerned that they will have to spend a lot of time learning arcane computer skills before they can work with accounting software. Some are fearful that they will be unable to absorb these new concepts, or that they will look foolish in front of others who have greater experience. Beginners usually face a period of three to four weeks in which they feel very clumsy at the keyboard and make a number of mistakes that require advice and correction from others. Every keystroke is made with caution, and every error message gives rise to a sense of anxiety and even anger.

This wall of knowledge is usually penetrated after the first month or so. Anxiety and tension are replaced with a sense of satisfaction that increases as skills grow and performance improves.

Successful computer operations entail learning a limited amount of specialized computer knowledge. However, at least one person in each user organization should have sufficient knowledge to establish reasonable policies about computer use and control, check the computer periodically for unused capacity and outdated files, and teach elementary computer skills to beginners. A greater body of knowledge is required for people who must manage networks. Most essential computer management skills can be obtained by learning basic operating system commands, either from one of the many courses that are available or from books and manuals.

What is *not* required is the ability to program. Although a number of programming languages are in use today, most users do not know which language is used by their programs, because this information has no effect upon the way they use the software.

The amount of knowledge required to manage a small computer installation is limited to learning a few operating system commands and understanding messages that may appear on the monitor from time to time. (All computers work with an operating system that acts like a traffic cop in coordinating files, disk drives, printers, monitors, etc. DOS is the most popular operating system in use today for microcomputers.)

However, there is a problem in knowing exactly which commands to learn, and understanding the subtle differences in format (often referred to as syntax), differences that result either in a properly executed instruction or in frustration. One must learn where spaces are important and where they can be ignored. For example, in DOS there is a distinction between a colon and a semicolon, and between a backslash (\) and a forward slash (/).

Additionally, the knowledge of special terminology cannot be avoided. The computer meaning of key words such as "drive," "default," "file," and "directory" must be learned. Macintosh users must learn how to recognize icons and work with a mouse. Additionally, one needs to learn the conventions for naming files and disk drives.

The problem is that while this information is really quite easy to learn, most courses and texts are much too generalized and cover far too much ground for any specific user. For example, today many different types of floppy diskettes are in use: single- and double-sided diskettes; diskettes that are hard sectored and soft sectored; diskettes with single, double, and high density; even diskettes with different physical dimensions—$5\frac{1}{4}$ inches and $3\frac{1}{2}$ inches. Training courses and texts attempt to explain the different treatment required by each of type. Most users have to know only how to deal with one or two, and discussions about all of the others cause confusion. Learning can be expedited by making certain that training is oriented to the specific hardware and software in use and is not generalized.

Training does involve sitting and working with the computer, becoming familiar with the keyboard, and memorizing the form and operation of computer instructions. People who attend training courses without having access to computers for practice soon forget what they have learned.

Some basics are common to all computer operations. Every user must know how to start up the computer (there is more to it than simply turning on the power) and the proper way to use diskettes so that they will not be damaged. Additionally, every user must learn a minimum set of commands in order to use the operating system. (A command is an instruction that is given to the computer by the user.)

At a minimum, those who manage computer operations should learn the following computer skills:

- ☐ How to format diskettes (Diskettes cannot be used until they have undergone a process known as formatting. Since different systems require different formats, the formatting operation must be performed by the user.)
- ☐ How to copy files
- ☐ How to back up and restore files
- ☐ How to check available disk capacity
- ☐ How to work with directories (Required when working with hard disks.)

Computer installations that involve connecting a number of workstations (a network) or communicating with other computers via telephone lines require knowledge of additional commands that assign facilities to different users and limit access to programs and files.

Some accounting software attempts to avoid the need for learning any operating system commands by providing the ability to perform all or most of the functions just described, with special routines (called utility routines) that are included with the software.

Of course, there are many other commands that provide additional functions for dealing with computer files and programs. Interested users learn these additional commands as new situations and problems arise. Others prefer to rely on dealers and consultants, because the most important skill of all is knowing when to call for help.

Those who prefer to limit their computer skills to a bare minimum usually can acquire this capability in a day or two. The lack of basic computer knowledge is not a reasonable basis for avoiding computer applications.

DIFFERENCES BETWEEN ACCOUNTING AND OTHER SOFTWARE

In addition to recognizing the important distinction between manual and computer accounting systems, one should be aware of three important differences between accounting and other categories of computer software:

1. There is a greater probability of programming errors (or "bugs") in accounting software than in most other software.

2. Many application software products can be used without requiring much background in another technical discipline. Effective use of accounting software requires some knowledge of two disciplines: computer usage and bookkeeping.

3. Most software can be learned and applied in small increments. Accounting software requires a greater knowledge of the product in order to get started.

Greater Chance of Program Errors

Because of its complexity, accounting software is more prone to errors than are other programs. Accounting software programs must be able to perform diverse business and computer functions under a wide set of operating conditions and circumstances; they must work with many files and hardware components. A program must be responsive to a variety of business transactions that may be entered by different people in a different sequence of steps. The reliability of performance necessitates a great deal of testing under different business environments and circumstances. It may take months, even years, for all program errors to be detected and corrected.

Potential users may face a difficult choice. One product may have proven reliability because it has been on the market for many years but may show signs of age in poor screen design, vague prompts, and clumsy operations. The alternative may be a newcomer offering improved functionality and ease of use, but with limited field experience. One must find a balance between reliability and meaningful but unproven design enhancements.

Training Must Cover Two Disciplines

People who work with accounting software must learn how to operate the software, but they must also understand the accounting effects of the entries that they make. They must be able to set up the chart of accounts and deal correctly with accounting periods and closings. They must be able to create reliable reports and effective working documents such as sales invoices and disbursement checks. Successful installation and operation places a greater demand on accounting and business knowledge than on computer skills.

Greater Knowledge of the Software Is Required To Get Started

Most people learn word processing and spreadsheets in small doses. The software does not ask up-front for users to make selections among a number of options. Beginners can start with simple tasks and slowly build up a repertoire of skills.

Not so with accounting software. Right from the beginning, users must understand many operating decisions demanded by the software: how to set up the files, enter data, correct errors, and print reports. They must be able to make informed decisions about coding structure and the method for carrying balances forward from the old system to the new. (This start-up process is explained in more detail in chapters 5 and 14.)

Accounting software requires much greater planning and training prior to installation than does other software.

SUMMARY

This chapter has made two important points:

☐ Computer systems involve characteristics that are quite different from manual systems and place different demands on users. The choice of software demands careful assessment by the potential user, to determine that the software will function successfully. Controls under a computer system differ from manual systems. The vulnerability of computer operations points to the consideration of special devices affecting power supply, as well as the importance of backup disciplines. The need for computer skills has been exaggerated in many instances, but cannot be ignored.

☐ Accounting programs are different from general business programs, necessitate some bookkeeping knowledge, and require greater care in installation planning and training.

3

User Considerations

INTRODUCTION

The previous chapter discussed characteristics of accounting software that distinguish it from manual systems and from other business software. It stressed the importance of preparing precise detailed specifications of data processing requirements, because computer programs lack the flexibility and initiative capability that are inherent in manual systems. Additionally, accounting software programs give rise to a whole new set of control considerations.

The determination of data processing requirements is more than a rational exercise because it must take into account two very important human considerations:

☐ Management style
☐ Working environment

This chapter will discuss the affect of these considerations in determining software requirements.

MANAGEMENT STYLE

Most people are aware of the fact that many of their decisions, both personal and business, are based as much on emotional as on rational considerations.

Indeed, applying pure economic theory to every business decision would make life very dull and stifle innovation. Many successful ventures have started with ideas supported as much by hopes and dreams as by cash flows and return on investment computations.

Every business organization has a style, and many a business thrives because it is successful in one or two areas of operation, such as selling or styling or financing. Every facet of a profitable business may not operate by purely rational design. One can always find, even in the most successful venture, some weakness or idiosyncrasy in management. In many cases, the very factors that have created success are also associated with some significant nonrational management attitudes and foibles. Attempts to use accounting software to improve a weak control system or provide sophisticated business tools for a resistant management will result in frustration and failure.

Effective selection of accounting software involves considerations of management perceptions and operating style that go beyond purely logical assessment of business requirements. One unusual characteristic of the accounting office is its close relation with top management because the reports that it produces are used to guide business decisions.

Decision makers have different ways of reacting to proposed office innovation because of their perceptions of the following important decision determinants:

- [ ] Costs and benefits
- [ ] Risk
- [ ] Change
- [ ] Status and power

Costs and Benefits

All management, when faced with proposed operating changes, is concerned with costs and benefits. Before the arrival of the microcomputer with its relatively low cost, computer installations required extensive outlays for hardware, software, and environment control. Because of this large investment, few installations were given serious consideration without the preparation of a feasibility study that attempted to set forth the costs and benefits of the proposed installation. Such studies in themselves required a sizable investment in time and cost. Nevertheless, because of the limited pool of experience, many early studies tended to understate costs and overstate benefits. A major source of poor guesswork lay in forecasting payroll reductions that never were achieved.

Today's economic environment is quite different. Costs of hardware and software, particularly with respect to microcomputers, are much lower. In contrary fashion, personnel and professional costs have gone up. The change suggests a less formal review of costs and benefits than a full-blown feasibility study, particularly for smaller businesses. Managers are more inclined to invest in computer solutions that offer the possibility of improvements that cannot easily be quantified, such as higher inventory turns, improved customer service, faster information, or better use of management time. Of course, the degree of attention given to costs and improvements will vary with the amounts involved in relation to available cash resources.

Risk

A number of risk elements are related to the contemplated introduction of accounting software:

☐ Understated costs and overstated benefits

☐ Software not performing as expected

☐ Poor vendor support

☐ Deterioration of performance and morale during the changeover period

There are many costs associated with accounting software, as will be elaborated on in chapters 9, 10, and 11. It is easy for many cost elements to be understated or overlooked. Hidden costs, such as time spent in training, file conversion, and parallel processing, can mount up quickly. It may be difficult to turn back when costs become excessive. However, in light of the great reduction in hardware and software prices, as well as the widening pool of experience, there is less concern today about severe cost overruns, particularly with respect to microcomputer applications.

The selection of accounting software is a time-consuming and painstaking process. Unfortunately many executives are not aware of the shortcomings of the software products offered to them. The result is a high degree of customer dissatisfaction. Many potential users hear about these problems and become fearful.

Another dimension of risk relates to vendor support. How reliable is the software? What happens if the publisher goes out of business? Despite the plethora of accounting software products on the market, many users have specific needs that are met by a limited number of software packages, if at all. An extensive search may be required to find the one product that can do the job. And this product may be new and untested or may be provided by a fledgling organization.

Obviously, one prefers to obtain software from a publisher who has been in business for some time and has a good performance record. (Since this is a young industry, anyone in business for more than three or four years demonstrates some stability.) However, if a newcomer's product appears to provide a better solution, or perhaps the only solution, one must assess the risk and decide whether to proceed.

At times the only solution is to arrange for custom programming or extensive modification of an existing product. In this situation, the software provider might be the publisher or an outside programmer. Custom programming carries its own risk. Frequently there are serious communication gaps between user and programmer. Time and costs may be seriously underestimated. Program modifications, often performed by companies not associated with the software publisher, may void support by the original publisher and may also result in unanticipated problems. Publisher upgrades may not be compatible with custom modifications. The risk of poor software performance and support may be higher with custom programming than the risk associated with a standard off-the-shelf product.

Any major change in operating methods can seriously affect performance and morale. The effort required to plan the change can consume a great deal of management time, thereby diverting attention from other matters. Operating personnel are placed under pressure because of the need to produce while learning new procedures. A parallel operation places additional burdens on the organization. Personnel changes may be required to implement the new system. There is a risk that the combination of (1) time pressures, (2) the need to learn new methods, and (3) uncertainty about changes in job definitions and responsibilities can seriously undermine morale. Management must be sensitive to the needs and perceptions of its employees in order to minimize this problem.

Change

There can be both rational and emotional reasons why people resist or promote innovation. Concern about risk in change is a legitimate concern.

However, there may be resistance to change even when it produces beneficial results. Some people do not like to change habits and are irritated by the thought of doing things in a different way. Perhaps they find security in repetition, or are fearful that they might have difficulty in learning and adapting to new methods. Some feel that continuing the old ways is a kind of tribute to the past, a tribute to the ownership and management that created a successful operation. How often is the phrase "We've always done it this way" used as a justification for resisting change?

The desire to improve performance is a legitimate reason for seeking innovation. A more personal motivation is held by those who look to change as a source of stimulation and escape from boredom. Or perhaps they feel that new procedures will permit them to learn new skills, even if the overall benefit is minimal.

Status and Power

Innovation, with its attendant costs and benefits, risks, and changes in methods, is bound to have some effect on organization and power structure. The very acts of investing in new hardware and software, installing new procedures, and altering work assignments can provide opportunity. Those who perceive a threat to their status and areas of influence will resist such change. Those who see an opportunity for themselves will tend to support it.

DIFFERING PERSPECTIVES

In what way will differing management perspectives of these important determinants affect decisions about accounting software? Some executives push for change. Some wish to proceed slowly and cautiously. Some are fearful and will procrastinate and delay. One executive may be willing to take responsibility for decisions whether they prove successful or not. Another may always seek to blame others when results are poor. The selection of accounting software and timing of installation must recognize these differences in attitude and management style.

Innovative Management

Generally, innovative managers will be the least critical about cost projections and most optimistic about benefits. Such managers are not fearful of risk and change. They view successful innovation as both a positive reflection of personal image and a status enhancer. They take pride in being the first, in applying new techniques and ideas to operations. They may be upset if they have not kept up with the latest management theories and techniques. Such managers will push to try new unproven methods. They may wish to install software that is new and innovative, even though it may not have been subjected to a reasonable period of field testing. They may also press for more advanced configurations such as the use of networks, even though not required in the foreseeable future.

Some managers, in their search for the latest and best, will continuously inquire about new products because of their concern that something even better may be "just around the corner." These managers must be brought to realize that the search for the very latest and best software package is time consuming, expensive, and counterproductive. There are well over 100 publishers offering accounting software for microcomputers. New products are announced almost every day. In this dynamic atmosphere, the search for the latest and best can never end. Finding the very best software product can be an exercise in futility.

Innovative management is most likely to favor new, unseasoned products that appear to offer useful enhancements not available in older products. Managers willing to try the new must be willing to take greater risks, to gamble on success. The software may prove to be useful, but the effort and cost of successful implementation may be high. The probability of discovering program bugs and of misunderstanding documentation is much greater than when dealing with a seasoned product. At worst, the product may prove to be unworkable and the project will have to be abandoned. Some innovators have been seasoned enough to recognize the possibility of disappointment and are willing to take the risk. Others may lose their enthusiasm at the first sign of trouble and very quickly turn to critical and negative attitudes.

The relatively easy "sell" to such a manager can lead to subsequent problems if the rush to new technology results in faulty programs and excessively complicated hardware. Care should be taken not to let the enthusiasm of the innovator create an unnecessary risk of success. Recommended software should have been seasoned in use and offer meaningful enhancements. Software that offers functions that look good in the ads but are of little real benefit should be avoided. The interest and support for innovation should not be allowed to lead to excessive pressure for rapid change. Installations must be carefully phased to minimize disruption and provide for the correction of planning errors.

Conservative Management

Conservative management will approach software proposals with guarded interest. Conservative managers require carefully prepared cost projections and will be inclined to move cautiously. They probably will have a greater concern about the possibility of failure and the negative impact of computer operations on organization and morale than will the innovative manager.

Conservative management, particularly executives with little computer experience or limited interest in and patience with office operations, must be approached in a slow and deliberate manner. Make certain that technical concepts and ideas are clearly explained and understood. Allow time for suggestions to be considered and evaluated. Ideas that are resisted at first may be reconsidered if properly presented and given time for study and review.

When dealing with conservative management, it generally is preferable to find software that will offer useful benefits that require minimal changes in operating methods. Programs that offer additional useful, but not vital, functions at the cost of greater change should be avoided. It is best to select hardware that has been time-tested and to develop an installation timetable that will minimize organizational stress and have maximum probability of success.

STATUS QUO MANAGEMENT

There are many reasons for managers to oppose change. Some may resist computerization altogether because of a bad computer experience in the past. Others may remember the computer problems of business associates or friends. Negative stories tend to live longer in memory than positive ones.

Some management feels hard pressed for time. These people look to accounting software to solve specific problems, but are nervous about making substantial and far-reaching changes in operations that will require a large time commitment from them and their subordinates. These managers will be more responsive to software that answers immediate needs and will resist attempts to make more than minimal changes in operating procedures. At times, they will not agree to change until working conditions have deteriorated to a crisis stage marked by serious problems with errors and backlogs. Unfortunately, the decisions made under such conditions are often made in haste and result in quick remedies that turn out to be shortsighted and expensive.

Procrastinators often lack confidence, particularly when dealing with unfamiliar areas of knowledge. Many are afraid of making the wrong decisions, or being "shown up" as incompetent by underlings who know more about computers than they do. They may be awed by the current speed of technological change and fear that a hasty purchase will forestall adopting something better that will be available tomorrow. Or they may feel that the numerous decisions that attend every computer installation—decisions about coding, timing and training, hardware selection, personnel changes —are too overwhelming. Some may hope to retire before working with computers becomes a necessity.

Another important source of resistance to change is the perception by some managers that they are in a "no-win" situation. They believe that their superiors will take all the credit if changes are successful and blame them for failure.

A common technique for masking indecision is to seek extensive cost justification for every change and question every premise underlying the computations. A full-blown feasibility study may be more costly than the situation warrants and may rely on assumptions that cannot be proven. Many successful computer installations are started because of a belief in the intangible benefits that will accrue. Cost justification, measured in improved cash flow, reduced investment in resources, or personnel reduction, is often very difficult to document. The important objectives of improved management reporting and decision support, vital as these may be, are intangibles that cannot be readily forecast and measured.

Successful installation of accounting software requires management support. Therefore, it is most important to be aware of resistance and determine its cause. The way to deal with resistance arising from poor prior computer experience is quite different from dealing with a manager's fear of criticism or concern about overwork.

A bad computer experience can be overcome if it can be shown that the situation occurred years ago, when computer technology was vastly different from today, or that the circumstances surrounding the perceived failure do not exist in the current situation. Some executives who have lived through a troublesome computer ordeal are ambivalent, because they recognize that many technological changes have occurred in the interim and feel that perhaps it is time to try again. Undoubtedly the best way to seek approval is to recommend changes in small increments and slowly win back confidence in the computer approach.

Executives who feel hard-pressed for the time necessary to implement change can be a challenge. They may be poor time managers or may have limited capabilities for organizing and delegating work. Caution should be exercised when working with these people until there is clear evidence of their support. It is important to find software solutions that will provide relief in as short a timespan as possible.

Frequently it is easier to satisfy the limited objectives of such a manager than to meet the requirements of an innovator. However, with the passage of time, top management may become aware of the missed opportunity to make substantial improvements, and may regret the cautious approach.

Managers who are concerned about their lack of computer literacy can also pose difficulties. One wonders why they choose to avoid acquiring a skill that has become so fundamental. Some may be persuaded to attend training sessions and discuss their perceptions with opposite numbers in other offices who have successfully faced similar challenges. Hopefully this will give them enough confidence to give serious consideration to software recommendations. Others may continue to oppose the introduction of any software and may be difficult to convince otherwise.

The selection of accounting software for a management that delays the decision process, or seeks a provable return on its computer investment, should be limited. The best approach is to identify one serious problem that can be markedly improved with appropriate software, such as improved cash flow, faster billing, speedier processing of vendor invoices, and improved inventory turnover. It is advisable to proceed slowly; avoid major changes; and select software that is least likely to promote controversy, has proven reliability, and is easy to install. It is best to avoid innovation and keep things as simple as possible. Installation should be limited to one application or module. Success in that one application may create interest for expanded use.

When middle management resists change because of an overly critical top management, there is a need to change this attitude before proceeding with any contemplated changes in operation. The installation, if agreed upon, should progress cautiously, with frequent review and evaluation of results so that corrections, if required, can be made before serious problems arise. Managers who fear criticism will quickly turn on others if they perceive their situations to be in jeopardy.

Political Management

It is necessary also to consider the management that does not openly and directly express its real objectives. These people give lip service to rational business aims, but their decisions are based on personal benefit. They have little interest in procedures that will improve the performance of others, or reduce their personal power base. They are quick to take the credit for success, and just as quick to blame others for failure. They shirk commitment and responsibility until they are certain that there will be a positive result that will redound to their benefit.

Working with the political manager requires the utmost caution. This includes making certain that all recommendations are clearly understood, and that all decisions have been approved. Results should be tracked frequently because the tolerance for error may be very low.

Some organizations have a number of top managers, each with a different operating style. A frequent example in a small company is the contrast in attitudes between first- and second-generation management. Those of older management are more likely to be resistant to change. They may remember the losses and stress associated with an earlier aborted computer installation. On the other hand, the next generation may be more willing to take risk and be enthusiastic about computerization.

The different management styles within an organization may result in a compromise, perhaps a cautious plan that will not create a major upset. Sometimes the result is inaction, with very little opportunity for change. At times, the more innovative executive may prevail, but at the cost of a constant clash of personalities during installation of the new system.

MANAGEMENT QUALITY

Two important aspects of management quality affect the probability of success:

☐   The commitment of top management to the new system

☐   The ability of management to enforce the required disciplines

Almost all change is stressful. Certainly the installation of accounting software, which requires careful planning, attention to detail, accurate data entry, and the learning and implementation of new procedures, is bound to create some strain in the organization. Deficiencies in planning and unfamiliarity with new procedures are certain to give rise to errors and mistakes. The burden of parallel operation during the installation period contributes another source of pressure.

Signals given by management indicating its degree of support are very important during the critical installation period. Before starting such a project, management must be made aware of the possibility that stressful times lie ahead and be prepared to see the project through to success. Expressions of uncertainty on their part can quickly destroy morale and diminish the organizational incentive to learn and function effectively with the new system. The seeds of failure grow quickly when there is poor management support.

One important signal of management commitment is the manner in which staff is provided the opportunity to learn the new system. Installation plans must involve adequate provision for training. New procedures are difficult to learn when the student is under time pressure or is constantly interrupted. Finding the time for training may be difficult. Parallel operation increases time requirements. In some fashion—perhaps by timing training during a seasonal lull, perhaps by using temporaries or providing incentives for overtime—time for training must be found.

If management foresees difficulties in training, the choice of software may be limited to products with reduced functionality that provide good documentation and screen prompting. Functional objectives may have to be subordinated to simplicity.

Another important signal of management commitment arises when errors are discovered, or when there are problems using the new procedures. A positive approach is most important. Unjustified criticism and the tendency to blame others and put them on the defensive can undermine the chance of success.

What is the case for a committed management that lacks the ability to enforce organizational discipline? This may occur in an organization that is successful because of strengths that lie outside of management skills—strengths in product design, engineering, or selling. Some managements of this genre recognize their weaknesses and hire good managers. However, if this is not done and procedural controls are poor, accounting software probably will not work. Personnel may not take the trouble to learn the new system or to pay attention to the necessary detail. There is a serious danger of error and loss. Without good organizational discipline, the installation of a computerized accounting system can have serious problems.

It should now be apparent that management style affects the answers to several important questions related to the choice of accounting software:

- ☐ Is the degree of innovation and change that will be introduced with the software within acceptable limits?

- ☐ Is there an acceptable risk with respect to the reliability of the publisher/programmer?

- ☐ Is the difficulty in learning and installing the system within acceptable limits?

☐ Will management exercise the proper degree of supervision and discipline?

WORKING ENVIRONMENT

Another major human consideration affecting the choice of accounting software is the working environment. Applicable to this are four critical factors :

☐ Nature of the work force

☐ Recognition of exceptions

☐ Supervision and control

☐ Negative attitudes

Nature of the Work Force

The nature of the work force must be considered when planning the installation of accounting software. Consider an office in which almost every employee has been with the company for less than a year. How should this affect plans for installing accounting software? The answer depends on the reasons for the lack of experienced workers.

Perhaps the cause is poor personnel policy. Whatever the reasons for such turnover—poor recruiting and selection, low pay scales, faulty management, extensive work pressures—the result is bound to be low morale, which leads to poor attention levels and resistance to responsibility and change. This onerous situation spells trouble, trouble in training, trouble in maintaining adequate systems, and trouble with computer operations. The outcome is a never-ending succession of errors, poor performance, and unacceptable results.

The introduction of a computer into a work environment subject to high turnover and low morale can spell disaster. It is better to delay installation until there is strong employee motivation to stay on the job and succeed with new tasks. Software selection should weigh heavily in favor of simplicity of operation and clarity of documentation and screen prompts. Because of the unseasoned staff, good supervision is required to insure the continuous application of proper control and backup procedures. Additional safeguards, such as writing and maintaining procedure manuals and training several employees in the same tasks, should be adopted.

Other reasons for a relatively new work force are not so serious. The business may have moved to a new geographical area, or a rapid growth in operations may require a sudden increase in staff. A seasonal business usually maintains a skeleton crew during the off-season and expands as the season advances. Under these circumstances, two important factors affect the choice of accounting software and the timing of installation. (1) One must proceed slowly with an untried work force. (2) If the business has grown rapidly, business requirements may not be clearly perceived because management does not have the time to think carefully about its needs or because the character of the business is changing. Management definitions of software requirements must be critically reviewed and questioned. Provide adequate time for thoughtful discussion and planning before determining software objectives.

A start-up situation provides a special challenge. The nature of some businesses is such that they require computer support from inception. Software selection must be made before the business gets off the ground. In other cases, a young enterprise finds that it is swamped with paperwork and feels the need to computerize, even though business objectives and methods of operation have not yet stabilized. The business organization and its operating procedures are new and unfamiliar. Management often finds it difficult to define data processing requirements, particularly when it is uncertain of its market niche and feels that it is still experimenting with resources, products, and operating policies.

The challenge posed by a fledging organization is to find software products that can meet current needs and still be flexible enough to accommodate to changes in operation that may be required in the near future. A few alternative strategies should be considered. One is to select simple products that are inexpensive and easy to use, with the expectation that they will be replaced as objectives become clearer. An alternative is to limit the software search to those products that provide functions or modules that cover present and anticipated future needs. Some thought should be given to selecting publishers who provide source code, which means that their software can be modified, if necessary. Hopefully, with this approach, there will not be a need to change software in the coming years. A growing organization may wish to limit selection to products that can run on a network. Some thought should be given to the effect of growth on the capacity and speed of the software. Unanticipated capacity limitations can render a package unusable. A program may be fast when files are small, but serious slowdowns can occur as files increase in size and printouts get longer. (Capacity is discussed in Chapter 6; speed, in Chapter 11.)

With new and growing companies, or with enterprises in a rapidly changing environment, software selection should lay great stress on flexibility, capacity, and speed.

Recognition of Exceptions

The previous chapter listed a number of characteristics that distinguish computer from manual operations. The first two points in the chapter referred to the lack of flexibility and initiative in computer programs. Most business operations must cope with exceptions, with unusual conditions and requirements that fall outside the orbit of routine. People try to provide for these exceptions when planning computer installations. Frequently, many exceptions are overlooked or may be totally new. What is to be done when such conditions arise?

The first question is whether the unusual condition will be detected at all. A well-trained and motivated staff will question an unusual transaction before attempting to proceed. Good supervisors will train their people to be alert for unusual conditions and to ask questions. Poor supervisors may stifle initiative, and the exception may not even be recognized. If not detected at an early stage, a problem may surface when management reviews journals or reports. Loss of confidence in information produced by a new accounting system can seriously affect the success of the project. Even worse, if undetected, the end results can be misleading information and wrong decisions.

What should be done when the unanticipated situation is detected? Sometimes it is possible to find a way for the software to process the transaction. Often, one can make a program perform in a manner not anticipated by the manual. Other transactions may require manual processing followed by introduction into the computer work stream at an appropriate time.

Delay in recognizing the need for special processing increases the time and effort required to correct the error. Faulty corrections compound the problem. Effective responses to unanticipated exceptions require alert and capable supervision.

Supervision and Control

Three characteristics of computer software discussed in the previous chapter increase the possibility of unauthorized tampering with and copying of information. These characteristics are the anonymity and compressability of electronic records, as well as the speed of computer operations. Many safeguards are available (as discussed in Chapter 12).

However, these safeguards can quickly become ineffective. Unattended workstations soon remain open, files remain unlocked, clerks may not care who stands behind them when they are working on confidential matters.

Passwords may be bandied about like popcorn. Logging procedures are abandoned, or the logs not reviewed. Diskettes and backup tapes may lie exposed on tables, and obsolete manuals carelessly thrown into waste bins.

Computer vulnerability places great stress on the importance of backup. During periods of high production, backup may be required every few hours. Active files usually are backed up daily. Backups must be rotated in a logical manner, which includes careful handling with regard to labeling and storage. All this takes time out of the regular workday.

Constant and vigilant supervision is required to maintain computer safeguards because compliance is a necessary nuisance.

In addition to all of the safeguards and controls specific to computer operations, there are other controls inherent in good office procedures. These involve the division of duties and effective assignment of authority, the use of control totals, the review of documents for approval and proper coding, the protection of confidential information, and the timely resolution of problems.

Computer operations impose new supervision and control requirements into the office routine. Adequate supervision and control must be in place before attempting a computer installation. Without this important ingredient, computer operations will probably add to existing problems with disastrous results. A company that operates with poor supervision and control will do better investing in good management than buying hardware!

Negative Attitudes

Another consideration that relates to the work environment is the situation in which there are key employees who have had a prior negative computer experience. An experience of yesteryear, particularly a poor one, may have implanted a negative attitude that can be very difficult to overcome. If there are such individuals, and they are important for successful installation, a special effort must be made to win their cooperation and support.

SUMMARY

This chapter has explained why the choice of accounting software must take management style and work environment into account. Examples were given showing how these factors affect the selection of suitable software.

In conclusion, the selection and installation of accounting software will vary with management style and the work environment in the following manner:

☐ When working with innovative management, one is more likely to select new software, or software provided by a small, unproven vendor. However, it is wise to guard against the unnecessary risk of selecting software because of trivial enhancements.

☐ Management's willingness to take risks affects both software selection and the rate of installation. Some managements are more comfortable proceeding at a slower pace than others. Some press for too rapid a rate of change. Custom programming should be avoided if management is not willing to recognize the risk. Consider both the needs of the business and management perceptions when setting installation schedules.

☐ Management under stress may look for quick solutions that are shortsighted. The need for quick relief should be balanced with meaningful long-range objectives.

☐ It is important to assess the political environment. It makes good sense to proceed very cautiously with managers who are overly concerned with failure and criticism. Representations regarding system objectives should never be accepted at face value without an independent evaluation. Performance should be monitored frequently.

☐ Recognize conditions not conducive to computer applications, such as poor management, poor controls, low employee morale, and high turnover.

☐ Software selection criteria should include consideration of the stability of the work force. Greater value should be given to good documentation and ease of installation when there is high turnover.

☐ The special needs of a start-up situation must be recognized. At times, a short-range solution using simple software may be the best way to begin. An alternative is selecting software with a high degree of flexibility.

4

Getting Started

INTRODUCTION

The preceding chapters offered important background information that should inform the prospective user of accounting software with basic perspectives. Chapter 1 provided background information on the accounting software market, information that explained the difficulties in obtaining information and the high degree of buyer dissatisfaction. Chapter 2 explained the difference between manual and computer accounting software systems and stressed the importance of determining specific and detailed operating and control requirements. Chapter 3 explored the relationship between accounting software and the organizational environment.

INITIAL DECISIONS

With this background in mind, attention can be given to the basic decisions that must be addressed when considering the possible installation of accounting software. Before starting a serious software search, five fundamental questions must be answered:

- ☐ When is it time to computerize?
- ☐ Are microcomputers the correct arena for the search?
- ☐ What are the costs and benefits?

☐   How should the effort be organized?

☐   What functions should be computerized?

Assuming that a search is warranted, this chapter stresses the importance of preparing a detailed list of performance requirements. This is followed by a discussion of three basic criteria that must be addressed by accounting software. The chapter concludes with a brief overview of the attributes of accounting software that relate to the three basic criteria, attributes that will be explored in detail in later chapters.

When Is It Time to Computerize?

Should the decision be based on sales volume, profitability, or other indicators? Should the decision be deferred because of anticipated new technology? There is no simple guideline for determining when an operation is ready for accounting software. Many small businesses, with volumes well below $500,000, benefit from the use of accounting software if

☐   The owners enjoy working with computers and are willing to spend the time and effort required for successful installation

☐   Management is interested in computer applications that look beyond immediate business needs

☐   Computerization promises to free up valuable management time.

In many cases, the decision to computerize, particularly with a smaller business, is made at a gut level without much of a formal effort to consider costs and benefits. The decision may be triggered by the exacerbation of some of the problems just listed or by a feeling that computerization will improve performance. A small business may not be a good candidate if the principals have no interest in learning computer operations and must rely on others to operate the computer. Such a business could become too dependent on one employee for its office operations. The replacement of a computer accounting system bookkeeper could be more difficult than finding a replacement under a manual system.

Most operations with sales exceeding $500,000, or with two or more people heavily involved with paperwork, are good candidates for accounting software. A survey conducted by the Touche Ross Enterprise Group conducted in 1986 reported that 85% of the respondents (526 companies with sales from $1 million to $75 million) said that their computer systems made a significant difference in business operations; 76% used their computers for accounting and record keeping.

There is also a place for micro accounting software in large organizations, particularly for doing general ledger work and financial consolidations. *Computer Decisions* magazine quoted one VP of finance as saying that he would rather process accounting information in the accounting department rather than relying on a computer center. "Micros give us control over priorities and deadlines."

Should one wait for new technology that promises better performance at lower cost? In most situations, the decision to wait for something better is counterproductive. There are many reasons for this.

1. An organization and its management must learn computer disciplines and capabilities. Deferring computerization merely postpones a learning effort that will have to be sustained at some future time before the benefits of computerization can be achieved. Computer proficiency requires training and experience.

2. Many promised technological improvements take longer to reach market than expected. An example was the long industry wait for IBM® networking software. The decision to delay can result in a greater time lag than anticipated.

3. After reaching market, many improvements require many months of field experience before they are problem free. There have been problems with new disk drives and new computer chips. Jumping on the bandwagon may lead to troublesome performance.

4. The benefits of some improvements sometimes prove to be highly exaggerated.

There are situations in which current technology is so costly or unwieldly that postponement is justified. An example of this would be a small company with complex functions that require minicomputer performance but cannot justify the cost.

Are Microcomputers the Correct Arena for the Search?

Are the processing demands too large for a microcomputer? How is one to choose between microcomputer and minicomputer software and hardware? The technical boundary between microcomputer and minicomputer is rapidly becoming more difficult to define. The ever-increasing speed and storage capacity of microcomputers, as discussed in Chapter 1, is an important reality. New operating systems on the horizon will further expand microcomputer functionality. One bit of evidence of this is a report in *Datamation* magazine (November 15, 1987) showing 5% new minicomputer sites in the past year, compared with a 12% compound growth over the past eight years. Later, in June 1989, the same magazine estimated that the microcomputer market had overtaken the minis in dollar volume and was rapidly overtaking the mainframe market.

The line of demarcation between micro and minicomputer remains a little clearer with respect to accounting software for two reasons: the availability of industry tailored programs, and differences in capacity and speed.

The microcomputer world has spawned a plethora of general-purpose accounting packages resulting in a wide array of software choices. However, some highly functional industry-specific software is offered on minicomputers that is not available on micros. Some of these programs were designed to take advantage of the higher capability of the minicomputer. In time, as micro capability improves, these programs may be brought into the micro world. For the present, potential users who require the functionality may find it cheaper to go with the minicomputer than attempt to program for the microcomputer.

There are some capacity and speed attributes that require careful timing evaluation before deciding between micro and mini. Large files and lengthy printing requirements may prove much slower in one environment than in the other. For example, some printers that work with minicomputers are much faster than microcomputer printers. Even though microcomputers are getting faster and increasing in storage capacity, accounting software often lags in technology because of the time required for reprogramming.

Minicomputers also offer much greater experience with networks, particularly multiuser systems that tie a number of inexpensive terminals into a central computer.

What Are the Costs and Benefits?

Will the benefits of computerization justify the time and expense involved in installing and operating accounting software? Obviously, accounting software cannot be cost justified for all organizations. An inexpensive canned program may be a good fit for one operation, even though very small. Another enterprise with the same sales volume and profitability may need a more complex program that is more expensive to install and maintain, and that requires costlier hardware.

The exercise of cost justification can lead to uncertain results, because it is difficult to place a dollar value on the benefits of generating information that can lead to faster and better decisions. A business that refuses to computerize because it cannot see a reasonable return on its investment may find itself outdistanced by competitors. On the other hand, a business with limited resources may not have sufficient funds to finance all of the computer applications that can improve profitability.

Assuming that an organization appears to be a candidate for the application of accounting software, how carefully should costs and benefits be forecast?

The classic approach is to prepare a fairly precise cost/benefit analysis by performing a feasibility study (sometimes called a needs analysis). Such a study sets out to specify data processing requirements in terms of function and capacity—what has to be done, how much has to be done, how quickly it must be done. Alternative solutions are reviewed in order to arrive at the best solution for optimizing results based on cost/benefit computations. The best solution is stated in specific hardware and software requirements that are given out to potential vendors for competitive bidding. The scope of the feasibility study can cover an entire organization or be limited to specific departments or phases of operation. A wide-ranging study often involves considerable time and cost. Frequently outside consultants are engaged to perform these studies.

A full-fledged feasibility study can be overkill and even unsuitable for small or rapidly changing organizations:

- [ ] The cost of an exhaustive study may be prohibitive.
- [ ] Management and organizational style (discussed in Chapter 3) may be dominating factors in software decisions.
- [ ] Instability in the organization or business environment may indicate that forecasts of future needs can be wide of the mark.
- [ ] The measurement of intangible benefits can be difficult and subject to a wide range of error.

An alternative to the feasibility study is a more limited study that focuses on finding solutions to operating problems. Among the problems frequently mentioned by management are the following:

- [ ] Late financial statements
- [ ] Excessive work backlogs
- [ ] High clerical costs; too much overtime

☐ Too many clerical errors

☐ Poor gross profit

☐ Poor inventory control

☐ Slow collections

☐ Poor expense control; desire to reduce outside data processing costs

☐ Weak cash management

☐ The need for better data analysis in order to deal with competition

☐ Poor sales management

☐ Poor customer service

☐ Personnel problems; difficulty in hiring qualified bookkeepers

There is a danger in accepting management perceptions of problems without an objective review. Petty annoyances can be exaggerated. Difficulties may arise from causes not easily corrected by computer programs. In some situations, management may be the problem. For example, a top executive who procrastinates in making decisions can be the major cause for late financial statements. Or an officer who is careless about recording inventory withdrawals contributes to poor inventory control.

However, most of the problems just cited are susceptible to improvement through accounting software. In that case one can frequently arrive at successful results in a shorter period of time and at lower cost than through a feasibility study. The shorter approach can lead to faster results. However, beware of superficial answers that do not address fundamental problems.

Most people with a limited knowledge of computers have a great deal of difficulty in setting cost objectives. Many people think only about acquisition costs and pay little attention to all of the other costs that are involved. Many have unrealistic concepts of costs and find that they must revise their cost projections a number of times. (Chapters 9, 10, and 11 discuss costs in detail so that the propective user will have a clear idea of what is involved and can arrive at realistic cost projections.)

How Should the Effort Be Organized?

If a tentative "go" decision is reached, how should the effort be organized? What role, if any, should be played by accountants, consultants, and others? Once a decision is made to look seriously into accounting software, what is the next step? How should this study be conducted?

Small organizations rarely have the expertise to make a serious evaluation of accounting software. Remember that a number of disciplines are involved. Decisions must be made that relate to accounting and bookkeeping, as well as computer hardware and software. Management and outside accountants and consultants may all have a role to play.

Top management must set the stage by stating performance goals and cost boundaries. Management perceptions about correcting operating problems have already been discussed—perceptions that must be considered when planning a new system. Operating changes may be contemplated that can affect operations. Perhaps there are plans to expand the scope of operations, offer new products or services, or change the way of doing business. A new pricing structure or sales commission plan may be under consideration.

In addition to stating the objectives of the contemplated system before the start of a serious study, top management must be prepared to pay careful attention to the recommendations that result. Frequently the broadbrush statement of objectives made at the outset of the project fails to cover a number of requirements that surface at a later time. Communication problems and the lack of knowledge of the detailed workings of accounting software can lead to misunderstandings about expectations. Sometimes it takes the review of a specific software product to focus management attention on critical performance requirements.

Accounting software rarely provides a total solution. In most cases, users are willing to compromise objectives in order to arrive at a feasible solution at an acceptable cost. However, in order to avoid disappointment, top management must be made aware of the compromise built into the recommended solution and must be willing to accept this.

Middle management frequently has the task of translating broad objectives into specific performance criteria. Accounting personnel may have the most detailed knowledge of data processing needs. Sales and service people may have similar insights with respect to their responsibilities. Middle management is usually good at spelling out existing requirements and spotting performance problems. However, they usually are not in a position to comment about contemplated changes in broader objectives.

Outside accountants have an important role to play in the search for computerized accounting solutions. Their familiarity with the company and its personnel makes them a valuable resource for reviewing the objectives set by management and making their own recommendations. They should review the adequacy of the chart of accounts contemplated under the new system, together with the accounting entries that will be generated. Once specific software is under serious study, the accountants should be called upon to comment on the audit trail and the controls, or lack thereof, provided by the program. They are in the best position to recommend an overall plan of internal control that will work both within and around the computer.

As already discussed, there are difficulties in finding and reviewing accounting software. A qualified consultant can save a tremendous amount of time and effort. However, in order to be qualified, the consultant should have a knowledge of accounting, business, and computer operations and be familiar with a number of accounting software products. He or she should also be a good communicator and teacher and be truly objective in arriving at a solution.

Many so-called consultants are limited in one or more of the areas just listed. Few consultants have in-depth accounting knowledge or a deep understanding of internal controls and office operations. Some have had experience with one or two accounting products and are not qualified to conduct a professional search. Sometimes the search for a consultant is as difficult as the search for software. Here are some suggestions:

☐ Many retail computer stores work with consultants and can supply recommendations.

☐ Some accountants provide consulting services or work with outside consultants.

☐ Word-of-mouth recommendations from friends and acquaintances can be helpful.

☐ Software publishers maintain lists of qualified consultant/installers.

A good consultant can be invaluable in providing the following services:

1. The consultant will assist in formulating practical objectives. For example, the consultant should know which functions are easy to find and which are difficult. Many first users assume that their requirements are easy to fulfill. This may not be so. Transaction volumes may be so low that a computer solution may not be warranted, or so high that a microcomputer may be impractical.

2. The consultant can speed the search for software because of his or her knowledge of many of the products that are available.

3. The consultant can advise management on the best way for using accounting software, techniques of account coding, information processing, and integrating information.

4. The consultant can also advise on the purchase of hardware and related items for maximum effectiveness.

5. After purchase, the consultant can provide practical suggestions regarding installation and training, perhaps providing the training personally.

Many people are fearful of hiring consultants. One reason is the fear of engaging the wrong person. Finding someone with all of the required qualifications, both technical and emotional, is not easy. Even with the most careful checking of credentials and references, many mistakes have been made. The possibility of error can be minimized by preparing a list of qualifications before an engagement interview. For example, detailed questions about education and work experience should be asked. Determine the products the candidate is familiar with and whether he or she has any interest in the sale of these products. Follow up with a well-prepared set of questions to be used when checking references.

Cost is a second reason for avoiding consultants. In many cases this concern is unreasonable, because, if the effort is properly organized, the cost of the consultant will be a very small part of the overall picture and may very well save expense and avoid serious error. Cost estimates should be obtained before starting an engagement. It must be made clear that the client expects to be notified ahead of time if consultant costs will exceed the estimate. Determine exactly who will be assigned to each engagement and whether the assigned personnel will remain on the job until completion.

A frequent cause of excessive fees is misuse of the consultant's time. A clear statement of engagement objectives is a must. The scope and cost of an engagement will depend on the time availability and knowledge base of in-house personnel. Communication problems can be avoided by assigning one person to act as liaison with the consultant. Schedule conferences and training time when there will be no interruptions. See that assignments are carried out without waiting for the consultant to act as a monitor. It is also wise to arrange as many tasks as possible to be performed by company personnel, not by the consultant.

How Should Computerized Functions Be Selected?

Must one consider all possible computer applications, or can the effort be directed to a limited set of functions? How should the functions be selected? These questions are as important for the small startup business as they are for the large experienced organization.

If accounting software appears to be feasible, an important decision is the selection of the functions that will be computerized. Accounting software generally is sold in modules such as general ledger, accounts receivable, accounts payable, and so on. (A description of the various modules will be found in the next chapter.)

Some situations call for the installation of a single module. One phase of operations may lend itself to computerization because manual operation is troublesome and a packaged program is available that provides a practical solution. For example, a financial organization may find that general ledger software is sufficient for its needs. Some service organizations are content with accounts receivable because their other accounting needs are simple.

Most organizations require a number of modules. Many of these modules must work together for effective use. A frequently used combination is accounts receivable, order entry, and inventory. Accounts payable and purchase order is another combination that is often linked together.

Users frequently start with a few modules with the expectation of adding others at a later date. Since each module requires time for training, setting up computer files, and parallel operation, modules are usually phased in one at a time. The overall installation can stretch over many months, particularly if a number of modules are being installed and numerous computer records must be set up.

The five critical questions just discussed may not be laid to rest until the software search has been completed. Cost estimates are usually optimistic and must be revised upward as a result of the study of needs and costs. The search for a feasible solution may start with microcomputers and end with a program that runs on a minicomputer. Increased cost estimates may necessitate reducing the scope of the installation or deferring computerization to some future time. Difficulties in finding the time or in-house expertise may change the decision regarding the engagement of consultants. The knowledge gained by studying software may lead management to change the accounting modules selected for installation.

PERFORMANCE REQUIREMENTS

Once a decision has been reached to computerize one or more accounting functions, management must determine, with great precision, exactly what is to be expected from the software. The need to establish specific performance requirements cannot be overstressed. Much of the disappointment with accounting software arises from assumptions about performance that are not fulfilled.

There are a number of reasons why many people fail to prepare precise performance specifications:

☐ The task is time consuming and requires a detailed knowledge of operations.

☐ A lot of software advertising stresses flexibility and ease of operation. Naive users are lulled into believing that the software is more flexible than it really is.

☐ Someone unfamiliar with accounting software may have difficulty determining the specifications that are required.

Usually a number of people are involved in the process of evaluating needs and planning procedures. Some of these people may be part of the organization. Some may be outsiders such as accountants and consultants. It is surprising how much confusion and misunderstanding can arise when a number of people have to communicate with each other about detailed clerical operations. A written list of performance requirements is an important step in clarifying ideas and creating a common frame of reference for all responsible parties.

An Overview of Software Evaluation

In order to do its job, accounting software must be able to satisfy three important questions:

1. **Can the software do the job?** In other words, is the software capable of performing the required functions?

2. **Can the software do the job at reasonable cost?** Will the costs of installation and operation fall within acceptable cost limits?

3. **Can the software do the job at reasonable cost with an acceptable degree of risk?** Will the controls provided by the software together with other procedures outside of the software provide adequate accounting control?

In order to explore the answers to these questions, one should be able to evaluate the software in relation to twelve important attributes. The following chart shows the relationship between these three software questions and their related attributes. The chart also indicates which chapter explains these attributes in detail:

	Chapter
Do the Job	
Capacity	6
Functionality	7
Integration and connectivity	8
Cost	
Acquisition	9
Installation	10
Operation	11
Control	
Control features and problems	12

The relative importance of each of these attributes will vary from user to user. For example, one user may place more stress on ease of learning than another, and care little about internal control. Others may place great value on the quality of the controls provided by the software. Flexibility will be very significant for an organization anticipating change. A stable organization may be less interested in this feature. Prices and costs may be critical for a small struggling organization and less important for another. Because the search for software can be very confusing, it is suggested that the attribute be written on a chart and a degree of value from one to ten, be given to each. In turn, each software product that appears feasible should also be rated. The resulting comparison is most helpful in comparing one product against another.

Now, of course, many initial objectives change during the course of the software review. At the start, some are impressed by software performance that soon appears to be humdrum because similar performance is offered by many competing products. A certain sales manual, for instance, advised demonstrating the power of the software to post to the general ledger because the speed and accuracy of posting (as compared with manual procedures) would be impressive to a would-be purchaser. That particular sales manual obviously was directed to an unsophisticated user because the posting function is performed by all general ledger programs.

Many functions that are time consuming and troublesome in a manual environment are performed at lightning speed by many accounting software products. However, the positive impression created by demonstrations of these functions can lead to the dangerous assumption that accounting software will be able to improve on all manual functions. Many are surprised to discover that functions considered simple in a manual system are performed with some difficulty under a computer system. For example, some programs keep general ledger detail for only one accounting period (usually one month). Some billing programs assume that the same sales commission rate applies to every item on a sales invoice. Many payable programs assume that all checks are drawn on the same bank. Users who look for the ability to handle split sales commissions, or to print comparative profit-and-loss statements showing one department per column, are in for a difficult search.

A major source of disappointment is the belated discovery that forms and reports generated by the software are inadequate. The fact that certain specific fields of information are maintained in computer files does not necessarily mean the information is reported out in a satisfactory manner. Often there are serious limitations in the way the data can be rearranged, or in the use of subtotals and group totals. At times, report design wastes a lot of heading space with the result that reports run on for many pages and are difficult to handle. Some software limits report width to 80 characters across in order to accommodate narrow printers. In order to pack in a lot of information, reports can require two or more lines of information per item, a very confusing form of presentation.

Rarely does one find software that meets all requirements. Expect some compromise and change of direction. Try not to lose sight of original requirements and the reasons why changes are made in performance specifications. Be aware of the compromises and modifications to original plans that are made in order to achieve practical results. There is a danger that important operating details will be forgotten by the time final decisions are made and the time-consuming effort of setting up computer files has started. The significance of these oversights may become apparent when computer operations commence and it is found that a wrong system of code numbers has been entered, or that wrong information has been entered in the computer files.

SUMMARY

This chapter has explained the matters that should be considered before spending the time and effort on a serious search for accounting software. Five basic questions should be answered. If the responses indicate a "go" situation, the search must be properly organized. A detailed written list of objectives and specific performance requirements is vital. The chapter concluded with a brief overview of software evaluation, including 3 questions that software must address, and the 12 software attributes that relate to the questions.

In conclusion,

☐ There are no simple guideposts indicating when an organization is ready for accounting software. Under some circumstances, small organizations with annual sales under $500,000 can benefit. At times, much larger organizations will be unable to find suitable software at an acceptable cost.

☐ The choice of microcomputer versus minicomputer will depend on speed of performance and the availability of software. Applications with large files (over 5,000 records), many workstations (more than 8), and complex functional requirements may find more acceptable performance with minicomputers. However, these guidelines are changing rapidly as new microprocessors and related software come into the market.

☐ Cost justification, although important, can be applied too vigorously because of the difficulty of evaluating the intangible benefits of computerization. Practical time limits should be set on feasibility studies. The potential buyer must be aware of all of the cost components of a computer installation, and set cost limits, but should also expect them to change.

☐ If a computer study is warranted, think carefully about how the study will be conducted. Many people should be involved, including top management, middle management, accountants, and (frequently) outside consultants.

☐ Do not assume that successful computerization requires putting all operations on the computer. Accounting software is modular.

☐ Clearly state the objectives of computerization in detail and put this information in writing. Reconcile different objectives and perceptions as much as possible before the serious study begins.

☐ If the services of a consultant are contemplated, plan how to get the maximum benefit of such services.

☐ Expect a change in plans before a solution is adopted. The search for accounting software involves dynamic reactions to the different products that are studied.

__ 5 _____

A Tour of Accounting Software

INTRODUCTION

Chapter 4 stressed the importance of preparing a detailed list of performance specifications prior to searching for software. A person with intimate
knowledge of the needs of the business may find the preparation of such a
list to be difficult and frustrating if he or she has very little knowledge of
how to express these specifications in terms that relate to accounting
software. Anyone who has tried to buy an item without any knowledge of
what is available and what experience people have had with the item will
recognize the dilemma. The situation is aggravated when it comes to
accounting software because there are so many products to choose from
and it is very difficult to obtain significant information about any of these
products.

Many chapters of this book explain significant features of accounting
software that will provide a prospective user with sufficient knowledge
and understanding to be able to develop a clear picture of accounting needs
in terms related to the products designed to meet these needs. This chapter
presents an overview and is organized in two parts. Part one describes the
different modules generally offered by accounting software publishers.
Part two describes the major components common to accounting software.

All accounting software follows a similar structure. The software tries to
provide the accounting procedures and services in general use whether
applied on manual or machine systems. It does not offer anything that is

conceptually new. Instead, the computer is used to improve on manual operations through speed and reliability.

The fact that most accounting software is structured the same way is obscured by the lack of standards in language and program organization. Each publisher uses different language and presents a different sequence of screens to accomplish similar results. Anyone who looks at a number of software products can easily be confused by these differences in language and presentation.

SOFTWARE MODULES AND TYPES

Most accounting software is sold in functional segments or modules. The less expensive software usually combines a number of modules into one product. The modules are usually designated as follows:

- General ledger
- Accounts receivable
- Order entry
- Accounts payable
- Purchase order
- Inventory
- Payroll
- Job cost
- Professional time and billing
- Bank reconciliation

(A few publishers offer additional modules such as fixed assets, bill of materials, and estimating.)

Certain modules may have to be installed before additional modules will work. Many publishers require the installation of a separate "master module" that provides functions that service all other modules. Some require the installation of the general ledger before any other module can be used. Order entry modules may not function without accounts receivable. Purchase order may require accounts payable.

The number of modules, and the functions performed by each module, varies from one product to another. The more expensive software usually offers a broader line of functions than do cheaper products. Some modules enhance the capability of the basic accounting software; examples of such modules are

☐ Report writer

☐ Sales analysis

☐ Import and export facility

There is a lot of confusion in identifying different products. In Appendix A alone, there are six companies listed with names beginning with "Micro." Some companies offer more than one product line. Different products often have similar names, such as "Business Management Series" and "Business Management Systems," or "MCBA®" and "MCBS."

There are two major classifications of accounting software: software designed for general use and software designed for a specific type of business or application. The latter, called vertical software, is designed to meet the requirements of a specific industry. Among the many business environments addressed by vertical software are

☐ Medical practice

☐ Dental practice

☐ Real estate management

☐ Construction

☐ Manufacturing

☐ Professional practice

Vertical software is provided in modules similar to that of general software.

Modules

The following is a brief review of the most popular accounting software modules. (More information about the functions of these modules will be found in Chapter 7.) Every specific program will deviate in some fashion from this generalized approach by omitting some functions and possibly offering some not listed here.

General Ledger provides a number of functions similar to, but not exactly corresponding to, a manual general ledger. General ledger usually is used to

☐ Enter journal entries

☐ Print journals

☐ Post to general ledger accounts

☐ Close accounts at year end

☐ Maintain comparative and budget data

☐ Print trial balances

☐ Display or print general ledger account detail

☐ Print financial statements

☐ If integrated, accept journal entries prepared in other modules and post them to general ledger accounts.

Some general ledger modules provide limited capabilities for accounts receivable, accounts payable, and payroll.

Accounts Receivable is used to

☐ Enter cash receipts and customer adjustments

☐ Enter sales (if order entry is not used)

☐ Apply cash

☐ Print cash receipts and adjustment journals

☐ Print sales journals (if order entry is not used)

☐ Compute finance charges

☐ Compute commissions

☐ Post transactions to customer accounts

☐ Maintain customer information. Some of this information is used by order entry.

☐ Print agings and cash forecasts

☐ Display or print details of customer accounts

☐ Print customer statements

☐ If integrated, transfer journal entries to general ledger

☐ Perform sales analysis.

Different modules provide sales analysis information, depending on the product. Sales analysis might be provided by accounts receivable, order entry, inventory, or even a separate sales analysis module.

There are major differences in the types of sales analysis provided by different products. Among the types of analysis provided are

☐ Dollar sales by customer, item, sales territory, state, and sales-tax region

☐ Dollar sales by customer class and item class

☐ Item sales by customer and customer sales by item

☐ The preceding data expressed in units and/or gross profit.

Order Entry is used to

☐ Screen customer orders for credit limit

☐ Enter quotes and customer orders including the calculation of extensions

☐ Print order acknowledgments and pick tickets

☐ Print sales invoices and credits including the computation of sales discount, sales tax, and sales commission (some vendors provide this function in the accounts receivable module.)

☐ Prepare back orders

☐ Print sales journals

☐ Post sales and credits to receivable and job cost accounts (if integrated)

☐ Maintain open order information

☐ Print unshipped order reports

☐ Perform sales analysis

☐ If integrated with inventory, price orders, reserve inventory for unshipped orders, and reduce inventory for shipments.

Some products provide the invoicing function in accounts receivable. **Accounts Payable** is used to

☐ Enter purchases

☐ Select vendor invoices for payment

☐ Compute discounts

☐ Print disbursement checks

☐ Process hand checks

☐ Print purchase and cash disbursement journals

☐ Post transactions to vendor accounts

☐ Maintain vendor information

☐ Print agings and cash requirements

☐ Display or print account detail

☐ Print 1099 forms

☐ If integrated with other modules, increase inventory for receipts, costs in job cost, and transfer accounting transactions to general ledger.

Purchasing Order allows the user to

☐ Enter purchase orders
☐ Print purchase orders
☐ Maintain open purchase order information
☐ If integrated, increase quantities ordered in inventory
☐ Permit comparison of quantities and prices between purchase order and vendor invoice.

Inventory is used to

☐ Enter inventory transactions
☐ Maintain perpetual inventory records
☐ Compute costs
☐ Compute inventory valuations
☐ Print inventory transaction journals
☐ Display or print inventory item detail
☐ Print physical count sheets
☐ Print price lists
☐ Print other lists, such as items to reorder, excess inventory, and old stock
☐ Maintain information for order entry, such as item descriptions, prices, and availability.

Payroll allows the user to

☐ Enter payroll transactions
☐ Maintain payroll records
☐ Compute gross pay for hourly employees
☐ Compute payroll tax deductions
☐ Compute other deductions
☐ Compute tax and other payroll related obligations

- [ ] Print payroll journals
- [ ] Print payroll checks
- [ ] Maintain employee payroll data
- [ ] Display or print employee payroll data
- [ ] Distribute gross payroll by department for accounting purposes
- [ ] Distribute gross payroll by job for job cost purposes
- [ ] Print data for payroll tax reports
- [ ] Print W-2 forms

Job Cost provides the capability of maintaining estimates, costs, and billings by jobs and phases within jobs. Some modules provide for overhead and other allocations and provide worksheets for billing. The modules frequently are integrated with payroll.

Report Writer permits users to design their own reports. Some report writers are limited to recasting information already captured by the accounting software and cannot mix data from different modules. Other report writers permit users to add new data and combine information from different modules.

Import/Export Facility allows users to transfer data to (import) and from (export) the accounting software. The import feature is helpful for capturing information required by the accounting software that has already been entered in other computer programs. The export facility allows users to transfer results to spreadsheets for analysis purposes, or to word processors in order to improve the presentation quality of reports.

It can be noted from the preceding review that in most instances it is possible to transfer information between modules. This capability can save time and reduce error. The installation of systems that plan to use this transfer capability generally requires more careful planning, testing, and training than do modules that will stand alone.

This brief overview is designed to give the reader a general understanding of the functions of accounting modules. But a word of caution should be repeated: There are no standards. A function appearing in the accounts receivable module of one publisher might be provided in the order entry module or sales analysis module of another. Or the function might not be available at all.

More important is the fact that the manner in which these functions are actually executed varies considerably from one product to another. Virtually all programs will carry statements to the effect that they provide complete audit trails, or that users can define their own formats for financial statements. In fact, the adequacy of the audit trails, or the flexibility in the design of the financials, will be very different from one product to another. (The following chapters can be consulted for more detail.)

THE ANATOMY OF AN ACCOUNTING PROGRAM

Accounting software consists of a set of programs that are stored in program files. The program files, in turn, create sets of data files that contain user information. There are three types of data files. Master files contain information that is retained by the system such as customer or vendor records. Transaction files store transaction detail. Working files contain transient information that is erased after the information has been transferred to transaction and master files. Many programs use working files to store input temporarily until the user accepts the input as correct and instructs the program to transfer the information to transaction and master files.

Originally, many accounting programs were designed for floppy disks. Operation was clumsy because of the need for a lot of disk interchange. Today, most programs take advantage of hard disks because of their greater convenience and low cost. However, the programs are not consistent in the manner in which the program and data files are stored on the hard disk. Some require that all program and data files be in the same directory. This arrangement creates more difficulty in file maintenance than do programs that place each company's data files in a separate subdirectory.

All accounting software tends to follow a similar structure, although differences in language and screen design tend to obscure this similarity. The structure consists of a set of routines for different functions. The major functions are

- ☐ Utilities
- ☐ User options
- ☐ Entering passwords, reporting units, and accounting periods
- ☐ Adding and changing information in master files
- ☐ Initializing information in master files
- ☐ Entering and editing transactions
- ☐ Posting transactions
- ☐ Closing accounting periods
- ☐ Printing forms

☐ Printing reports

☐ Transferring information between modules and programs

Some functions require more accounting knowledge than do others, and some should only be entrusted to reliable persons. The manuals that come with accounting programs do not make these distinctions clear and may confuse the reader with odd terminology.

The first three functions just listed generally must be used when the software is installed and may never be used again. They can be baffling to the uninitiated.

Utilities

The word utility is one of many computer terms that causes confusion because the meaning is far from clear. A function that is listed under "utilities" in one program might be listed by another program under "user options" or some other place. In general, "utilities" are routines for telling the software what hardware it will work with and organizing computer files.

Accounting programs require preliminary information before they can function properly. One important piece of information is a description of the monitors and printers that the software must work with. The accounting program uses this information to set up special files called "drivers" that contain the specific operating instructions that permit the software to display and print information. Like almost everything else in the computer world, there are no standards for device drivers. Many accounting programs provide driver files for the most popular monitors and printers. Users with unusual equipment, particularly unusual printers, may face a challenge in providing the correct instructions for the program. Printers can be quite a nuisance, especially for beginners, and some programs make life easier than others when it comes to getting them to behave properly. A pertinent comment in the 1988 brochure for the AICPA Microcomputer Conference reads as follows: "Printers will cause you more aggravation than any other piece of microcomputer equipment."

The possibility of having difficulty with printers and monitors is one reason why the selection of software should precede the selection of hardware. Most software vendors will supply information about the devices that work easily with their software.

Accounting programs set aside disk space for data files. Many programs do this by reserving this space when the programs are installed. Such programs must be told how much space to reserve. They do this by asking the user to answer questions that relate to file sizes. The programs usually compute the amount of required space and display this amount for the user to review. If the computation is acceptable the program then blocks out the files. (A good example of computer double-talk—this process is often called "building the files.") The program may refuse to function until this process has been completed.

The answers to file size questions are not always simple. Users must decide whether to base them on current transaction volumes or to think about future needs. Some programs are capable of storing more transaction detail than others and let users decide how much detail they would like to store. For example, should individual checks be posted to the general ledger? How many months of invoices should be stored?

Users may worry about the importance of precise answers. What happens if they guess wrong, and the space blocked out is too small? Some programs automatically increase files when required, a process called "dynamic sizing." Some provide a file utility that displays for each data file the amount of reserved space and the percentage utilized. Warnings flash on the monitor when files are getting crowded. File utilities must then be used to expand the files. Trouble will follow if the warnings are ignored. Some programs allow users to reduce files sizes if they are too large, thus saving file space.

A program may provide a utility for backing up and restoring files. The idea of providing this facility within the accounting program sounds good because backups are important and should be used frequently. Unfortunately, the utility frequently cannot be used because it relies on the DOS BACKUP routine, and many systems use other backup programs that are more flexible, or because they are required for running their backup hardware.

Other useful file utilities are "file purging" and "file compression." These utilities are helpful when disks are full and something must be done to make more space available. File purging is the process of deleting detail information. For example, a program might store all accounts receivable transactions until users wish to purge the file. At that point, users usually are able to instruct the program to erase all transactions older than a date given to the computer. File compression is similar, except that the program continues to store transaction totals after the details are erased. One example is the purging of general ledger transaction details but keeping account totals.

A recent innovation is a utility for designing the printing of forms such as sales invoices and disbursement checks. For many years, few accounting programs gave users any control over the appearance of the forms printed by the program or over the information printed on the forms. Programs that offered this flexibility were rather difficult to learn. Today, a number of newer programs give users a great deal of flexibility over the size of printed forms, as well as the selection and location of the information to be printed.

User Options

After dealing with device drivers and file sizes, the user frequently must answer questions that control the operation of the program. Often the user is unprepared for these questions and, worse, does not understand their significance. You will get some of the flavor of these choices by looking at the sample screens in the appendix.

The software may present these questions in a number of ways. Some software asks these questions automatically when the program is used for the first time. Other software lists this function, along with many others, at the main menu of the program. If the confused user fails to go into this routine, the program probably will stop when the operator tries to do something else in the program. At that point, the prompt may or may not show that the option menu requires answers before operations can proceed. The option screen may guide the user by displaying preset answers called "defaults" that can be changed. Or, alternatively, there may be no answers, and the user must decide both the answer and the precise format in which the answer must be entered.

Programs that offer user options usually are more flexible and adoptable than software that does not do this. Yet for some mysterious reason, users often get very little help in understanding how their answers will affect results. The questions themselves may be obscure. Additionally, there may be no clear indication as to whether wrong decisions can be changed. User options vary in their complexity and significance. Some questions affect both the amount of disk space that will be used for data files and the amount of detail information that will be available. Software questions may be asked about integrating different modules. Some give the user a choice in designing codes. Code design affects the way information will be grouped and totaled in reports. Some software provides choices that affect controls. The answers to control questions require accounting expertise. Some questions can be straightforward, such as one that lets the user decide whether commissions will be computed at the time of invoicing or cash receipt.

Option screens are good sources of information about the functionality of the software. Potential users should be sure to look at them before purchasing the software and take their time about answering them at the time of installation. (Options are further discussed in Chapter 10.)

Controlling Passwords, Reporting Units, and Accounting Periods

Most accounting software provides a password function. This function may not be in use when the software is installed, or initial passwords may be assigned by the publisher that can be changed by the user. The decision to use passwords may be one of the option questions asked at start-up. Passwords assigned by publishers are printed in the manual, sometimes buried, sometimes easy to find.

The way passwords can be assigned varies from one software product to another. Some programs assign passwords by company and module (a two-level system). Others add another level by providing for the assignment of passwords by function within each module (a three-level system). One program allows password protection for separate fields on each screen. Networked systems provide their own password controls through the networking software. Network password systems usually provide more flexibility than do the systems provided by the accounting software. Decisions and procedures related to password control are important and should be given careful consideration prior to software installation. (They are discussed in greater detail in Chapter 12.)

The designation of reporting units must also be given some thought. Will the software deal with more than one set of books? Multicompany operations require following setup procedures for each company, particularly the procedures applying to file management and options. The software for starting a new company may be included in utilities or require the use of a separate diskette.

Will the operations of one company require a breakdown by location or division? If so, thought must be given to coding the master files in each module so that information will be processed in the appropriate manner.

The designation of accounting periods can be troublesome to people with little bookkeeping or accounting experience. All general ledger modules ask users to enter the number of accounting periods in the accounting year, as well as the first and last dates of each period. All accounting programs provide for 12 accounting periods per year; some provide 13. Users are usually asked at start-up to enter the current accounting period. Accounting periods usually are given a number that is used by the software to designate each period. A calendar-year company would use the number one to designate January, number two to designate February, and so on.

Most software products require entries regarding all three functions—passwords, reporting units, and accounting periods—before the programs can be used. The order in which the entries must be made may vary. (The preceding discussion follows the usual entry sequence.)

Adding and Changing Information in Master Files

After completing the routines for blocking out files, answering questions about options, and providing basic information, the user is ready to create the information files. (Different programs give various names to these files; in this text they are called master files.) Once set up, the information entered in these files may remain unchanged for long periods of time except for summary data that is compiled and updated by the software itself. The most frequently used master files store information about general ledger accounts, customers, vendors, and inventory.

Procedures for entering and changing information in master files is different from the procedures used for entering transactions. Separate routines are used for adding new records, modifying information already on file, and deleting records. Most accounting software uses a number of code files to facilitate the operation of the program. For example, an accounts receivable master file might require the entry of codes for billing terms, salesperson, sales tax, and territory. Users establish the codes by making entries into special code files that keep track of the code numbers and their associated descriptions. The programs often limit the number of characters and the number of codes that can be used in each code file. These limitations cannot easily be determined from brochures and manuals. There may be limits on the number of salespersons that can be used for sales analysis, the number of sales terms used to forecast cash flow, or the number of jurisdictions available for sales-tax analysis.

Many people have difficulty at first in understanding the relationship between code files and master files. The files must be set up in the appropriate sequence, or the system will lock. Usually, one cannot set up master files until all of the code files have been established that must be referred to by the master files.

Master files often require the entry of information that must be gathered from a number of sources. Some of this information is not time sensitive and can be entered prior to active use. For example, information that can be entered ahead of time into an inventory master file can include item code, description, unit of measure, alternative unit of measure, vendor name, alternative vendor name, vendor item code numbers, minimum quantity, reorder quantity, and bin location. The task of assembling all of this information for an inventory of a few thousand items can take a considerable amount of time and must be carefully planned.

In most instances, the master files must be created before the user can start entering opening balances and transactions. New records are routinely added to the files for new customers, vendors, or inventory items.

Initializing Information in Master Files

Information that is time sensitive should be entered and verified just prior to active use. In general ledger, this could be the trial balance at the beginning of the accounting period. In the case of inventory, time-sensitive information would be the quantity on hand and cost. Some software provides special routines for entering this kind of information. These routines permit the entry of information without distorting information in other modules. Initializing routines, at times, are simple and straightforward. In other software, the routines can be complex and difficult to follow. They can be used only once.

There is a significant difference between accounting software products in the way the software deals with changing and deleting master files. Most software will not permit records to be deleted if the record shows a balance. Some programs provide better control by not permitting deletion if any transactions remain on record. However, many packages permit users to make entries, even alter balances, without going through routines that create proper audit trails. This lack of control is serious.

Entering and Editing Transactions

The software functions that have been described up to this point are used most frequently as part of the start-up process and are referred to very rarely once the installation becomes active. From this point on, the functions for entering and processing transactions are the ones that are used most often and take up most of the time.

Accounting software usually functions in "batch mode." In batch mode, all transactions are entered in groups and are not available for processing until (1) the entries pass programming verification (such as verifying that code numbers are valid and that entries balance) and (2) the operator presses a key to indicate the batch is ready for processing. Batch mode permits correction of errors at inception and also allows a review by a second person before transactions formally enter the system.

There are different ways in which the programs work the batches. The most limiting approach permits only one batch per module before processing and does not permit placing the batch on hold for review. A second approach still limits each module to one batch, but allows entries to be added to the batch until the batch is accepted for processing. The most flexible approach allows each module to hold a number of batches before they are processed.

Some software functions in "real time." Under this method, each entry is accepted and processed at the time of entry. Real time is most useful when users must refer to the files for current information, such as in an active order entry situation in which clerks must know current inventory status in order to process customer orders.

Generally, batch processing is preferable to real time because it provides a better degree of control and detects errors at an earlier stage of processing. The notion that real time provides faster accounting information is fallacious because meaningful financial statements usually require adjustments such as accruing unpaid bills and making inventory computations that must be performed after the end of the accounting period.

Methods used for entering transactions are tied very closely to cursor movement and the design of input screens. There is a wide variation in the ease of entry, ease of correction, and degree of control provided by different publishers. Since transaction entry consumes so much time, potential users should look carefully into these different methods. (See Chapter 11.)

Important computations may be made by the program during transaction entry, particularly in relation to customer orders and inventory. For example, the software may select prices; compute extensions, discounts, and commissions; and adjust inventory costs and balances. As will be shown later in the book, each software product has its own unique set of capabilities and shortcomings. For example, there are wide variations in methods for selecting prices and for computing discounts and sales commissions.

Certain transactions may be initiated by the software itself after prompting by the user. One example is the computation and billing of interest on past due accounts. Another example is the creation of recurring bills, such as rent bills for an apartment house.

Posting Transactions

After transactions have been entered (and corrected if necessary), the next step is to process the transactions by posting to the related master records and updating related balances. This is a complex procedure. The software manual should explain the specific steps taken by the program during this operation. Because posting can take some time, many programs warn users to back up their files before they start, because any disturbance in the power supply during posting can damage computer records.

For purposes of control, some software automatically prints journals at the time of posting. Many programs that integrate general ledger with other modules do not post the general ledger at the same time as posting is done in the other modules. These programs usually transfer data to the general ledger from the other module and then require a separate posting function in the general ledger to complete the process. (See Chapter 8 for more details.)

Closing Accounting Periods

Generally speaking, accounting software is less flexible in dealing with accounting periods than are manual systems. Users must understand when periods should (or should not) be closed, and what happens if closing is not done in the proper fashion.

Period-end closings have two meanings in accounting software. One meaning relates to general ledger accounting periods and related financial statements. The other relates to starting a new statistical period for purposes of computing period-to-date sales, purchases, or similar data.

As with all other functions, the flexibility associated with accounting periods varies from one package to another. The most limited software permits only one period to be open at a time. Once a period is closed it cannot be accessed again, and all entries after closing must fall into a subsequent period. This rigidity usually forces users to "hold the books open" into subsequent periods in order to be certain that income and expense are properly associated with the correct accounting period. The worst case arises at year end, when months can pass before all closing adjustments are available.

Other software permits access to a number of accounting periods. This software requires the user to enter the accounting period for each transaction or batch of transactions. Period closings may not be required at all, since the software can sort out data for each period from the transaction files. In some instances, accounting periods can be placed "in suspense" and can be accessed only by special password. This feature is useful at year end when the accounts are awaiting the final adjustments.

Some software even permits entry into closed years and updates the accounts for the intervening period. The closing date need not be the same for all modules. Some users prefer to close some modules such as billing and accounts payable much earlier than closing the general ledger.

Most software provides a special function for year-end closing. This function sets year-to-date data fields to zero. In the general ledger it closes out nominal accounts to the appropriate equity accounts.

Printing Forms

The facility for printing business forms such as sales invoices, customer statements, and disbursement checks is one of the important attributes of accounting software. Unfortunately, many prospective users do not pay enough attention to the details of the printed output, usually because they are not aware that most accounting software is quite rigid about this. Modifications frequently are required in order to satisfy user requirements. Sometimes there is need to place information in a different location on the form, or there is need to add more information or delete data that is confusing. The format of an invoice for a retail, service, or consulting business is quite different from that of a manufacturer or distributor. Some software will suit one industry more than another.

Most software provides screens for selecting the forms for printing by range of customer numbers, date, or some other means of selection. Many provide a previewing function so that users can review the items selected and change the selection before printing, a function that is most useful for the printing of disbursement checks.

Provision is also made to print test patterns in order to insure the correct alignment of the forms in the printer. Reprinting may also be available, a function that is useful when forms jam in the printer, or when additional copies are required. (The number of legible plies ranges from four to six.)

Printing Reports

The numerous reports produced by accounting software are among its most important features. However, the usefulness of a report cannot be determined by its title. Reports by different publishers may have the same name yet present very different information.

Some software requires all reports to be printed. This can be quite a nuisance when looking up one account record. The trend is to permit users to choose between the printer and monitor or even allow reports to be queued on disk for printing at a more convenient time.

Many reports are designed to look good in sales brochures but may not be practical. A design that uses many lines for headings increases the number of printed pages, a serious problem when large files are printed. A design that uses two or more lines of information per record can be very confusing to the reader.

Early software was designed to work with printers that are limited to 80 characters per line. Today's software prints reports up to 132 characters across. This number accommodates wide dot-matrix printers at 10 characters per linear inch. The software usually will automatically print smaller characters (16.5 per inch) for narrow printers when wide reports are to be printed.

Report design varies in rigidity. Generally speaking, lower price software provides fewer options than do more expensive products. As mentioned earlier in this chapter, some publishers provide special modules that permit users to design their own reports using information stored in the other modules.

Transferring Information

Accounting software transfers information in three different modes:

☐ Integration between software modules
☐ Networking
☐ Transferring information to and from other programs

Most accounting software today claims to be integrated, meaning that the modules can transfer information from one to another without the need for the reentry of the data. In fact, the amount of effort required to transfer information between modules varies from one product to another. Some of the information required by different modules may not automatically pass from one to the other. For example, many programs do not fully integrate job costing with payroll, accounts payable, and billing. In some cases the degree of integration is limited to a fixed number of accounts. There may be a limit on the number of general ledger accounts that can be accessed from accounts payable.

The simplicity of information transfer varies from one product to another. For example, some software does not verify the correctness of general ledger accounts referred to in other modules until the user attempts to post from that module to the general ledger. An error message appears if the program detects an invalid account number at the time of posting. This might occur days after the original entry was made and require spending time to track down and correct the error. Better software design detects and reports an invalid account number at the time of original entry.

Many publishers provide network versions of their products. These network versions are programmed to work with specific network software. Users who require their accounting software to be networked must (1) be certain that a network version is available for the software that they have selected and (2) install the correct network software. Users with an existing network may find that compatability will limit their choices of accounting software. (Chapter 8 includes a discussion about different software techniques used in posting and transferring data between software modules.)

Some accounting software products increase flexibility by allowing users to bring in (import) information created with other software and to export accounting information to other software products. The import function is useful for entities that need special programs for one or two aspects of their businesses, such as inventory control and billing, but can use general purpose software for other functions. The function also is useful for bringing in start-up information that has already been created by another program.

The export function permits users to enhance results by (1) dressing up reports with word processing software and (2) analyzing data in a database or spreadsheet.

Import and export functions are usually designed by sophisticated users who understand how to accomplish the desired results. Beginners who need to use these functions should engage qualified consultants to set up the required routines.

SUMMARY

This chapter presents a general description of the functions provided by the different modules of accounting software such as general ledger, accounts receivable, order entry, inventory, and many others. The text describes, in general, the way that accounting software is organized, from the setting up of files, through data entry and posting, to the creation of forms and reports. This overview should provide the reader with a common frame of reference for viewing and evaluating competing software products.

In conclusion,

☐ There are no industry standards. One result is that there is no assurance that any module of a particular software will provide the functions that one might expect to find in such a module. One product line may offer a different modular breakdown than its competitors. Never assume that they are the same.

☐ Although all accounting software must follow a similar logical organization, this similarity is masked by differences in language and screen presentation. These apparent differences add to the difficulty in comparing one product with another.

6

Capacity

INTRODUCTION

This chapter begins an in-depth discussion of the 12 important attributes of accounting software referred to in Chapter 4.

Many readers may wonder why there is a need to discuss capacity. The marketplace is offering larger and larger disk memories for microcomputers, memories that exceed 100 million bytes (100 megabytes) of memory. While the amount of available memory has been increasing, the cost of this memory has been dropping. With the availability of tremendous amounts of low-cost memory, a memory unheard of just a few years ago, why should capacity be a problem? If the hard disk gets crowded, why can't one simply purchase a larger one?

Unfortunately, the capacity of accounting programs is not a simple question of disk size. Many purchasers have had the misfortune of learning this fact when they discovered that the software they purchased was unworkable because of its capacity limitations.

People who are accustomed to working with productivity software such as spreadsheets and databases can readily determine their capacity limitations before purchase from sales brochures and other literature. Spreadsheet limitations are expressed in the maximum number of columns and rows. Database specifications include the maximum number of records and fields and maximum field sizes that the program can accommodate.

Unfortunately, it takes a lot more time and effort to get similar information about accounting software. Some publishers print lists of capacities, but the lists usually are far from complete. Size restrictions about accounting software frequently are buried in manuals, or may not be stated anywhere at all. There are occasions when the first inkling of a capacity limit is a beep from the computer or a cursor that refuses to move. Frequently the only way to get all of the required information is by trying out the software.

Between the software and the hardware there are various limitations:

- ☐ The number of workstations that can operate with the software
- ☐ The minimum amount of RAM (random access memory) required to run the program
- ☐ The amount of RAM and disk storage that can be accessed by the operating system
- ☐ The amount of disk storage that can be used by the software
- ☐ The number of records that can be placed in a data file
- ☐ The size of information fields
- ☐ The type of information that the software can store

Some of these limitations are not significant for a smaller business. However, most people find that one or two limitations are significant when searching for suitable software.

This chapter will explain each of the preceding limitations and give examples from various accounting software modules.

LIMIT ON THE NUMBER OF WORKSTATIONS

Some users plan on having a number of workstations work with the accounting software at the same time, a capability called "networking." While this will be discussed in more detail in Chapter 8, it is worth noting here that it cannot be assumed that a particular accounting software product can be networked. Some products are designed solely for single station use.

Publishers that have designed their accounting software for networking specify the required network software. In turn, some network software is limited with respect to the number of workstations.

If the need for multistation access to the accounting software is anticipated, either at inception or at some future time, the software chosen should work with network software that handles the required number of workstations.

LIMIT ON AVAILABLE RAM

Accounting programs are requiring larger amounts of RAM. Many early DOS programs operated without a murmur with only 128K. RAM requirements started to increase as enhancements were added to the software and the price of RAM plummeted. Programs today reach as high as 512K (640K on a network), although many can work with 256K or less.

Most users will have no problem with the RAM requirements of the accounting software that they select. Virtually all DOS computers on the market today come with 640K RAM, which exceeds the needs of the software. People wishing to run some of the newer software products on older machines may have to upgrade their equipment.

However, the greater size and sophistication of accounting software has been paralleled by other programs that share RAM. Operating systems (such as the famous DOS COMMAND.COM) have grown in size, and memory resident calendars and message pads have become popular. Users of accounting software with high RAM requirements soon will have to watch for problems arising from RAM limitations, problems that may require an additional investment in hardware for an effective solution.

LIMIT ON STORAGE SPACE ACCESSED BY OPERATING SYSTEM

Presently, the DOS operating system is the most popular for micro business applications. More accounting programs will work with the DOS operating system than with any other. All DOS versions below 4.0 have one serious limit that affects the use of accounting software: They cannot work with a disk drive larger than 32 megabytes ("32 meg").

Until recently, this limit was of little concern; 32 megabytes seemed way beyond the needs of any user. Not so today. Many accounting software applications require files with storage requirements that exceed this limit.

This does not destroy the usefulness of the software. But it adds a complication if files must be stored on more than one logical disk drive. (Note: A physical disk drive can be broken down into separate compartments in such a way that the software thinks of each compartment as a separate disk drive. Thus a 40-megabyte disk drive can be divided into two logical drives: a C drive of 30 megabytes and a D drive of 10 megabytes.)

Most, but not all, DOS accounting software can function with multiple disk drives. Users who anticipate exceeding the DOS disk limitation should determine ahead of time whether the accounting software they select can do this.

RESTRICTION ON THE AMOUNT OF STORAGE SPACE

Accounting software works with three kinds of files: programs, data, and tutorial/reference information. All of these files must be stored somewhere—on floppy disks or hard disks. There are significant variations in the amount of space required for program files. Many are so large that they must be stored on a hard disk. Some require additional space for multicompany situations because separate program files are required for each company.

The amount of storage required for data files also varies from program to program. Some of the factors that affect data file size are the programming language, the complexity of the functions provided, and the amount of information to be stored.

Many programs come with learning aids such as tutorials, practice data, and help screens. This material increases storage requirements.

Most software publishers provide sizing calculation charts for computing disk requirements. The charts may be printed in user manuals, or provided to dealers in the form of printed charts or special sizing programs. Most people like to retain as much information as possible, provided they do not run out of disk space. Unfortunately, many sizing programs ask how long users wish to retain information but do not indicate how much space is required for each additional month of information.

Effective software selection requires that the user make reasonably accurate determinations of transaction volumes and the related file sizes that will be created by candidate software. Dealers should be able to provide sizing charts and explain any sizing questions that are not clear. The answers provided by the size calculations are important for

- ☐ Comparing the amount of disk space required by different software products. Question any large differences in results. They may not be truly comparable.

- ☐ Determining whether the DOS limit, as just discussed, will be exceeded (If so, prospective users must determine whether the software will permit data storage on multiple disks.)

- ☐ Determining the size and performance characteristics required of the storage medium, be it floppy disk, hard disk, or a combination (This is discussed further in Chapter 9.)

☐   Blocking file space on the hard disk.

Some programs incorporate a technique called dynamic file sizing, whereby files automatically expand if insufficient space has been allocated. Other programs flash warnings if there is a need to expand the files and provide special "utility" programs for file expansion. Very few programs warn if the entire hard disk is approaching saturation.

A number of techniques are available for freeing up storage space. Tutorial and help screens can be erased. Another technique is to reduce the number of time periods for which detail information is maintained. Some software provides a file compression facility that erases transaction details but maintains period totals. Before using this facility, many users transfer the details to diskettes for storage and recall if needed. If the software provides for file reduction, the operator can use software utilities to spot unused file space and reduce sizes where appropriate.

It is important to note that file size requirements, and the techniques for warning when files are getting full, modifying file sizes, and storing detail information varies from one software product to another. Prospective users should make a careful assessment of present and projected transaction volumes, as well as the need for maintaining historic detail, before beginning a software search. Once computer applications begin, one important supervisory function is the periodic review of unused computer memory.

LIMIT ON NUMBER OF RECORDS

The next item on the list of capacity concerns is the issue of limits on the number of records that are allowed by the program. The software may be limited to a maximum number of general ledger accounts. Similar limits may apply to the number of customers, vendors, or inventory.

Diskette-based systems and lower priced accounting software are more likely to place limits on the number of records they can handle. Most higher priced accounting software does not place any limit on the number of records other than the storage capacity of the disk itself. However, even some of the more expensive software is restricted in the number of inventory locations that the software can address.

The amount of storage available for transaction entry and processing may also be limited. Some programs restrict the size of journal entries. Many limit the amount of space available for temporary storage. These programs place transaction data into temporary storage files until the user tells the computer to accept and process the transactions. The use of temporary storage facilitates review and correction. Some programs unduly limit the number of temporary files, forcing users to process frequently in order to clear out the files and prepare for another batch.

LIMIT ON FIELD SIZE

The fact that handwritten large numbers can always be "squeezed" into a narrow column was pointed out in Chapter 2 as an example of the inherent flexibility of manual systems. Software is much more rigid.

Accounting software works with data files. Each data file contains a number of records. Each item of information in a record is stored in a section of the record called a field. Each field has a predetermined size, which means that there are a limited number of character positions in each field for storing information. This explains why computer-generated forms often display abbreviated names and addresses. Often the size of a field is critical. Perhaps it is the number of characters available for an account number, or the maximum dollar amount that can be stored for the balance in a ledger account. It may sound like a very fussy exercise, but prospective users must determine whether the field sizes provided by candidate software are adequate. This can be time consuming since one rarely finds this information without actually working with the software and counting the number of positions in important fields. (Note: Some sophisticated operating systems provide for variable field sizes, but very few micro-based accounting programs work with such systems.)

The most serious size limits are concerned with dollar amounts and codes.

Dollar maximums involve both the largest dollar amount that can be entered and the largest dollar total that the system can maintain. Most software provides for an input maximum of $10 million and for totals of $100 million. These limits should be checked into. Many users have found to their dismay that the software that they purchased did not provide for amounts large enough for their needs.

It may be important to check the limit on the number of decimal positions. Some people require three or more decimals when computing costs and selling prices. Some require decimals for quantities. There are wide variations between different products in their provisions for decimals.

Next consider the number of positions assigned for code numbers. People who are already using account codes may wish to simplify the complications of changing to a new system by maintaining the same account codes. Others may take the opportunity of installing new software to expand codes, particularly if installing an inventory system or extending the general ledger to cover branches and departments. There is wide variety in arrangements for account codes. Some software provides a single code number; other products provide one or even two sets of subcodes. Some permit the user to divide the code number into many segments. (Coding is further discussed in Chapter 10.)

The selection of a coding scheme has a significant influence on the effectiveness of the software. A properly planned scheme helps produce well-organized reports and reduce coding errors. Poorly devised schemes can lead to problems in organizing information for reporting purposes, excessive time for looking up and assigning code numbers, and numerous coding errors. Since the coding scheme and code size are related, it is most important to select software that provides code field sizes that will support the most benefical coding scheme.

At times, the size of explanation (or description) fields is an important consideration. Accounting software usually provides for an explanation field when entering transactions such as cash receipts, cash disbursements, purchases, and adjustments. This information is very useful in looking up information and analyzing accounts. Large fields are desirable because they facilitate clearer explanations. The size of these fields varies from one product to another, usually between 15 and 30 characters. Explanation fields that are smaller than 20 characters really limit the usefulness of the records.

A similar consideration relates to the size of description fields used for sales invoicing. Virtually all accounting software limits the number of characters of description that can be entered on each line of the invoice. There are significant differences in the number of permitted characters. Short description lines may be acceptable in some instances and troublesome in others.

On occasion, the size of other fields can be important. Since all fields are limited in size, it is advisable to check to see whether limits on the size of customer names or of product descriptions can create problems.

PROGRAM RESTRICTIONS

Another important restriction on capacity arises from programming constraints. These limits will vary from one publisher to another and may appear in one package without similar restrictions arising in others. Because they are program oriented, they are the most difficult to anticipate and therefore create unpleasant surprises.

Although the determination of field size restrictions can be difficult, the determination of program capacity restrictions can cause even greater frustration because it takes so much time to pry out this information from manuals and the program itself. These restrictions fall into a number of categories:

☐ Restrictions on field information

☐ Restrictions on the number of items in a reference file (such as a file of billing terms or sales tax entities)

☐ Other restrictions

—. General ledger
—. Accounts receivable and billing
—. Accounts payable
—. Payroll
—. Inventory

Restrictions on Field Information

The program determines the information that will be stored in each record. In most instances, the number and nature of the fields in each file are fixed and cannot be changed.

As an example, consider the master file for customers. These files normally provide a number of fields of information: customer name, address, telephone, contact name, salesperson, credit limit. Some, but not all, programs provide additional fields for telex number, usual sales terms, date of last order, date of last payment, preferred freight carrier, sales tax category, and so on. Some programs provide a category field that permits classifying customers for purposes of sales analysis, or include pricing code fields that simplify pricing orders. Some users require other fields indicating whether the customer will accept substitute items or is rigid about cancellation dates. There may be a field for special comments that can be used to note special shipping requirements or restrictions. There are major differences in customer sales data compiled by different programs, ranging from one year-to-date sales amount to information on orders and shipments over a period of years.

In a similar vein, there can be a wide variation in the fields provided for inventory master files. Some programs provide only one field for the name of a resource vendor; others provide additional fields. Some provide only one field for vendor part number; others provide two or three. Additional information fields that are useful to some users and meaningless to others are date of last inventory count, reorder points, reorder quantities, substitute part numbers, status (current or obsolete), category, and engineering drawing numbers.

Some software screens may not be quite so rigid. A few accounting programs provide a few optional fields that can be labeled by the user. In some situations, with a little ingenuity, one or two fields can be used for purposes not originally intended by the program.

What happens if someone begins using the program and finds that a new field is required in one of the master files? Once the program has been installed and is working, the addition of a new field through a program modification can be cumbersome and expensive. This can be prevented from happening by reviewing the fields provided to determine whether the information is adequate.

Restrictions on the Number of Items in a Reference File

Accounting programs frequently are limited in ways that are unexpected to new users. Many programs use reference files for a number of purposes. These files contain information that is combined with other files for information processing. Examples are files containing information about

- ☐ Salespersons and commissions
- ☐ Sales terms
- ☐ Bank accounts
- ☐ Sales taxes
- ☐ General ledger accounts
- ☐ Financial statement formats
- ☐ Departments
- ☐ Shipping methods.

Most accounting software limits the number of reference items that can be stored. At times, the limit is determined by the size of the provided code field. For example, a one-position numeric code for salesperson limits the number to ten. A two-position alphanumeric code increases the limit to well over a thousand.

In other cases the limit can be determined by examining the screen that is used for entering the reference information. For example, a screen that has ten numbered lines for entering sales terms may be limited to a total of ten. This can be a bit tricky because some programs allow additional storage by means of "scrolling," a technique that moves information up and down the screen. This makes more information available than can be seen in a single screen.

Companies, such as importers, that bill on many different sales terms that consider discounts, due dates, insurance, and freight costs should watch out for limits on the number of terms and on sales term terminology.

These reference files limitations often are difficult to review because they are buried in manuals, or may not be clearly stated at all. Users must carefully search for these limitations in light of their needs.

Other Restrictions

Some surprising limitations are found in many popular accounting software products. The prospective buyer must watch out for a limit on the number of general ledger accounts that can be accessed for distribution of sales, cash receipts, or cash disbursements. The software may insist that all sales be credited to a limited number of sales accounts, or that all sundry customer charges be credited to one general ledger account. There may be a restriction on the number of general ledger accounts that can be accessed from a vendor invoice. Some software limits the cash journal to receipts from customers; all other receipts must be entered in the general ledger module. Some software programs permit only numeric codes, while others accept alphabetic as well as numeric characters. Some are very clumsy if bank deposits or cash disbursements affect more than one bank account. In a similar vein, the buyer should watch out for restrictions on the number of formats than can be stored for financial statements and sales invoices, the number of sales tax entities permitted, and so on.

Most software places a limit on the number of accounting periods for which detail information is stored, and sometimes this limit varies from module to module. Many programs allow 12 periods, others 13. Some software erases all detail each period after the books are closed. Some programs will keep the general ledger detail for the year, but erase detail originating in other modules. Some "integrated" software limits the number of general ledger accounts that can be accessed by other modules. The following examines some of the additional capacity limits that are frequently encountered:

General Ledger

- ☐ A limit on the number of companies

- ☐ A limit on the number of reference journals. Some packages provide one general journal. Others provide for a limited number of basic journals such as cash receipts and cash disbursements. The use of different reference journals in the general ledger module provides a good method for segregating and processing similar transactions such as cash receipts and cash disbursements. Separate transaction listings by journal provide a much easier trail for tracing and analyzing transactions.

- ☐ A limit on the number of departments. Some software programs provide a maximum of ten; others go much higher.

- ☐ A limit on the number of financial statement formats. Software that relies on the chart of accounts to prepare financial statements usually will print only one balance sheet and profit and loss statement for each company. (The column headings may be changed, but the side captions are fixed.) Many companies are accustomed to varying formats for different purposes, such as condensed versus detailed presentations, and will find this restriction very burdensome.

- ☐ A limit on the number of accounting periods that can be presented in financial statements.

Accounts Receivable and Billing

- ☐ A limit on the number of accounts receivable control accounts. Although many businesses use only one account, there are circumstances in which the use of multiple accounts is preferable.

- ☐ A limit on the number of ship-to addresses that can be accessed for a customer. Many business operations, such as those dealing with chain stores and multiwarehouse distributors, must be able to work with a large number of ship-to addresses for each customer.

- ☐ A limit on the number of sales tax entities. Businesses that must collect sales tax for a number of jurisdictions (for example, a business shipping merchandise to a number of states) will be forced to perform additional steps in order to comply with sales tax laws.

- ☐ Restrictions on the format of sales invoices. Many accounting software products were designed for warehouse distribution operations. Invoice formats programmed by these products provide columns for quantities and unit prices. Such formats are not suitable for service billing.

☐ A limit on the number of line items that can be printed on an invoice page. Companies that require many-item listings per invoice must look for software that provides higher limits.

☐ A limit on the number of discounts calculated per sales invoice. If a business applies different discounts for different items, it must watch out for software that will only compute one discount per invoice.

☐ A limit on the number of sales prices that can be assigned to each product

☐ A limit on the number of aging periods

Accounts Payable

☐ A limit on the number of accounts payable control accounts

☐ A limit on the number of checks that can be printed on a disbursement voucher or stub

Payroll

☐ A limit on the number of payroll gross pay accounts, tax deductions, and other deductions. Since most payroll modules contain some limits on these payroll fields, users must be careful to select programs that can properly analyze gross pay and all deductions.

☐ A limit on the number of states that can be referenced for payroll taxes. Some payroll software provides for only one state tax and one local tax.

Inventory

☐ A limit on the number of units of measure

☐ A limit on the number of levels used to compute inventory costs

HOW IMPORTANT IS CAPACITY?

At this point, many readers who are looking into accounting software for the first time may be somewhat surprised and dismayed by the long recital of software capacity limitations. And no doubt many others who have worked with accounting software have experienced many of the problems posed by these restrictions. It is likely that much of the disappointment with accounting software referred to in the preface has occurred because capacity limits were not explored properly before the software was selected.

How serious are capacity limitations? How much time must be spent looking for them?

Experience indicates that in many applications, capacity restrictions are a nuisance but are not significant. The additional steps required to circumvent these restrictions are offset by other features of the software that are more important to the user. Some of the techniques used to deal with capacity restrictions are

- ☐ Abbreviating names and terms when they exceed the capacity of the field provided by the software. Some abbreviations must be carefully selected in order to avoid confusion.

- ☐ Printing detail information or storing it on diskettes or cartridges if the software does not provide storage of the data for future reference. Some programs erase monthly journals after postings are completed and the month is closed. In this situation, backup files can be created for future reference in order to supplement printed journals. The programs may erase data at year-end closing. However, the information can be saved by copying the data files.

- ☐ Making transfer accounting entries when the program limits the number of cash and control accounts in accounts receivable or accounts payable

- ☐ Using a word processor to format and print financial statements when the program is too limited in statement formats

- ☐ Supplementing accounting information using other software such as a database or spreadsheet

- ☐ Obtaining a program modification.

Serious capacity problems, if they exist, usually are critical in a few areas, perhaps three or four. However, they do occur frequently enough for prospective users to be aware of the potential problem and make a serious effort to identify capacity limits and evaluate their effects on operations before accounting software has been selected. Some limits may prove to be unacceptable, and the software must be rejected. Others limits may be acceptable if the software performance is satisfactory in other respects.

SUMMARY

Software capacity is not a simple matter of disk size. The capacity of accounting software must be considered in seven aspects:

1. The number of workstations
2. The amount of available RAM
3. The amount of storage that can be accessed by the operating system
4. The amount of storage available to the software
5. The number of file records that the software must address
6. The size of information fields
7. Other limits imposed by the program

Some limits, such as the first three just listed, are easily determined. Items four and five are usually available, sometimes with a little effort, from manuals, promotional literature, or special sizing programs. It can take a bit of doing to ferret out the data for items six and seven, but this must be done in order to avoid disappointment.

In conclusion,

☐ Accounting software is subject to a series of capacity limitations. Prospective users should understand the seven functional areas in which accounting software is limited and make careful determinations of their own capacity requirements with respect to:

—. The number of workstations that will be required
—. The amount of RAM required by the application program
—. The number of records that will be stored
—. The amount of storage space that will be required
—. The specific information that must be stored for reference purposes
—. The number of characters that must be stored in information fields.

☐ The user must also be aware that many programs contain additional limitations that do not surface without a serious study of the software.

☐ Capacity limitations, in some instances, can be circumvented without adding a serious burden to operations. However, there are many situations in which candidate software must be rejected because of this problem.

7

Functionality

INTRODUCTION

Chapter 6 discussed limits on software capacity, limits that are frequently overlooked by the software buyer with unfortunate results. The serious software buyer obviously must rule out for consideration any software that does not have sufficient capacity to do the job.

After passing this hurdle, the characteristic that usually attracts the most interest is functionality. Can the software perform the functions required by the prospective user? Many novices assume that most accounting programs perform in a similar fashion, that virtually all general ledger or accounts receivable modules do the same thing. The novice may check on the performance of a few critical functions. If the software passes that test, the assumption is made that everything else will be satisfactory. This can lead to trouble. A much better rule is to assume that no function is acceptable until its performance has been verified. It is far better to spend the time checking this in advance, than to face disappointment at a later time.

This chapter stresses once again the importance of determining one's specific operational requirements before searching for the right software, even though this task can be difficult and conclusions may change as greater insight develops into the nature of accounting software.

This chapter also briefly discusses three ways of obtaining information about the functional capability of different accounting software packages, software manuals, demo software, and demonstrations. These sources are useful for making preliminary determinations and obtaining some sense of the ways that the various software programs function. (A more detailed discussion about software research is found in Chapter 13.)

The rest of the chapter discusses the significant functions that are provided by different software products. First there is a discussion of global functions (functions that apply to all modules). This is followed by a discussion of the functions available in each of the major modules.

THE IMPORTANCE OF DETERMINING PRECISE USER NEEDS

The software of choice must be able to do the job. Unfortunately, the task of stating one's needs in precise terms and determining the relative importance of each function can be quite a challenge.

Functional requirements will vary from one organization to another. Are customer statements required? How much information must be printed on sales invoices? What method must be used to age accounts receivable? Must inventory be kept on a serial basis? What kinds of sales reports are needed? Some functions that are vital to one business may be "icing on the cake," or even confusing, to another business.

1. Business operations are dynamic and must change from time to time to meet changes in the business environment. How is one to know how long present operations will continue on the same course? How does one predict changes that will place new demands on the accounting software? For example, today a simple price system is in use. Tomorrow may bring the need for a more complex pricing plan. One warehouse may serve today's needs. Competition or changes in freight rates may lead to multiple warehousing. To what extent should the software be able to perform functions that are not needed today, but might be required in the future?

2. The choice of accounting software involves compromise. The chance of finding a product that meets every need is virtually impossible. The software search usually aims for finding a good fit, together with the acceptance of a few shortcomings in the software. The task of evaluating different software products usually includes considering the additional effort each product may require because of its shortcomings. The process may lead to reconsideration of what software functions are really vital as well as the willingness to perform some functions outside of the program.

3.   Examination of accounting software frequently discloses useful functions that were not considered when the search began. For example, a prospective user may be delighted to discover that the program can print customer labels or provide for special sales prices, even though these functions were overlooked when the software performance specifications were originally developed.

The interplay among (1) concern about future needs, (2) the perception of performance strengths and weaknesses in each software product, and (3) the discovery of new and useful functions can result in a frequent reevaluation of what one should be looking for in accounting software.

DIFFICULTIES IN DETERMINING PRECISE SOFTWARE FUNCTIONS

Some of the difficulties encountered when trying to evaluate the capacity of accounting software have already been mentioned. It is a rare experience to find manuals that list all capacity limitations. Most often the potential buyer must work with the software itself to obtain the required information; this can be a time-consuming and difficult task.

There is a different kind of problem associated with functionality, and this problem arises from the difficulty most people have in perceiving and communicating in precise terms the details of their routine activities. Just as a test, a group of accountants were asked to list the different types of journal entries that they use. This list is important because the software that they use should process each type of journal entry in a different manner. The one-time journal entry is most frequently used. Recurring journal entries are repeated every accounting period. Standing journal entries show the accounts to be affected but provide for the entry of different amounts every accounting period. In addition, there are reversing entries, closing entries, and report-only entries. The interesting point made by the exercise of asking accountants about these different types of journal entries is that most of them cannot recall all of them, even though they use every one in their practice and would be disappointed if they purchased software that could not process them properly.

The fact that a particular software package performs a specific function does not necessarily mean that the way it does this will satisfy all users. Consider the computation of interest on past due accounts receivable. One user might wish to compute interest at a single rate on all past due balances. Another might use an interest rate that varies with the amount of the unpaid balance. Some businesses charge a minimum amount regardless of the balance, others may not wish to charge interest on small past due amounts. One company might automatically charge past-due interest on all accounts. Another might wish to determine, customer by customer, which accounts to charge. Some may wish to record interest charges when they are computed; others may choose to book them when they are paid.

The significant point is to remember that most business functions can be executed in many different ways. Users must be very clear about their requirements and then check software performance in detail in order to determine whether the software will do the job in the required manner.

Coupled with this difficulty is overblown advertising copy that gives the impression that the software can do more than it really can. For example, people who are accustomed to designing financial statements with paper and pencil often assume that the same flexibility is available with accounting software. Many general ledger programs encourage this attitude. The ads for such programs may state that hundreds of financial statement formats can be produced by the software. The fact is that virtually all software is limited in some fashion when it comes to report design. Users who expect to use accounting software to print financial statements that fully conform with GAAP (generally accepted accounting principles) had better be very careful in their software selection.

Another example of exaggerated advertising copy is accounting software that claims to provide "complete audit trails." In fact, the adequacy of audit trail varies considerably from one product to another and rarely is complete.

At this point, the reader should be reminded about the confusion in terminology that was discussed in Chapter 1. Most accounting software literature and manuals are written by people who have little or no experience with bookkeeping and accounting terminology. The unfortunate result is that they misuse language or substitute new words for well-understood bookkeeping and accounting terms. This places an additional burden on the prospective user who is trying to evaluate the software.

THE NEED TO REVIEW SOFTWARE DOCUMENTATION

It should be clear at this point that even the preliminary determination of software suitability mandates a software review that goes far beyond reading promotional literature. It should include a review of the software documentation together with a demonstration that addresses the specific needs of the prospective user.

Software manuals can provide a great deal of useful information. Printed examples of critical screens, such as those used to display information about customers, vendors, and inventory items are good sources of information about the information that the software stores for reference. A quick source of information about processing functions is often found in the section of the manual that explains the screens used for selecting user options. These sections are often called "setup" or "option" screens. (For a more detailed explanation, see Chapter 5.) Manuals should also include sets of sample reports. (Report design is discussed later in this chapter.) Although most manuals are poorly indexed, look up critical functions to see if the software addresses these needs.

Sometimes a brief review of the manual is all that is required to determine that the software is not suitable. It may take a much longer time to verify the fact that the software will function in a satisfactory manner.

Many publishers sell demonstration diskettes at nominal cost. These diskettes are designed to stress the features of their products and rarely are full-featured. Review of this limited software without manuals usually is not satisfactory.

Software demonstrations can be useful when organized and presented to address specific needs of attendees. General purpose demonstrations frequently gloss over important specifics. Some demonstrations stress features that are commonly found in similar products. For example, one sales manual advised demonstrating account posting because the speed was impressive when compared with manual methods. In fact, all software performs this function, and posting speed is hardly the reason to be impressed with one package over another. The ability to distinguish a truly unique or unusual function over a run-of-the-mill one requires some experience.

GLOBAL SOFTWARE FUNCTIONS

Software functions can be divided into two groups. One group comprises functions that are available in all modules of the software. Some of these common functions may appear in a menu called "utilities" (discussed in Chapter 5.) The other group consists of functions performed by specific modules. The so-called global functions fall into the following categories:

- ☐ Information transfer between modules and workstations (discussed in Chapter 8)
- ☐ Password security (discussed in Chapter 12)
- ☐ Help screens (discussed in Chapter 10)
- ☐ Pop-up windows (discussed in Chapter 11)

- ☐   Information exchange with other programs
- ☐   Assigning transactions to accounting periods
- ☐   Provision for user-designed reports and documents
- ☐   Provision for viewing, printing, and storing information.

(The discussion here will start with the fifth category, since the first four are discussed at some length in later chapters.)

Information Exchange with Other Programs

Some accounting software provides routines for exchanging information with other programs. A popular use of these routines is to transfer (or "export") data from the accounting program to a spreadsheet. Once the data is transferred, the spreadsheet program can be used to analyze the information and display comparisons not easily developed within the accounting software itself, such as the preparation of budgets and projections. The spreadsheet approach can also provide greater flexibility in report design such as the printing of more columns in financial statements than can be handled by the accounting software.

Another popular use of the "export" facility is to transfer financial statement information to word processing software, particularly when the accounting software is limited in its ability to handle footnotes and other verbal material. The word processor can then be used to add footnotes and reposition contents in order to enhance the appearance of the printed report. The word processor may also deal more easily with printing different fonts on a laser printer.

Software programs use different file formats. A user who is interested in the export capability of an accounting program should determine whether the data is transferred in a format that is acceptable to the receiving software. Most export functions will create a file in ASCII, a format accessible to most word processors. DIF and WKS formats are used by databases and spreadsheets.

A small but growing number of accounting software products provide for information to be brought in ("imported") from other software. This function can save a great deal of time and effort when moving from one accounting software product to another because data files developed under the old software can be brought into the new software without the need for the time-consuming reentry of the information.

Another use is the linking of good application software with good accounting software. Frequently, vertical software packages provide very good operating functions but are weak in general ledger. One user, for example, may wish to use one publisher's accounts receivable but finds that the sales order processing software of another company is better suited to his or her needs. The import function can be used to transfer information from the order processing module to accounts receivable without the need to rekey information.

At times the movement of files between programs requires a number of file translations. Generally, importing is trickier than exporting because wrong file formats in accounting software can be difficult to correct. If the import function is important, it should be made certain that good technical support is available in the event the information transfer proves to be troublesome.

Assigning Transactions to Accounting Periods

The concept of accounting periods can be troublesome for many nonaccountants. Typically, a calendar month is adopted as an accounting period, although it is possible to adopt other time periods such as four weeks. All transactions falling within an accounting period should be assigned to that period. However, with a little thought, one realizes that the relationship between transaction dates and accounting periods can be a bit tricky. Consider the processing of vendor invoices. These documents may take many days to travel from the vendor's office to the customer's office. After the invoices are received, they may not be ready for data entry until someone verifies that the shipment was in good order and that prices and arithmetic are correct. As a result, purchase invoices dated in one month may not be entered until well into the next month.

This is just one example of the many circumstances under which an accounting period must be kept open long after the calendar says that a new accounting period has started. In some instances, businesses may delay the closing of their books until many months of the new year have passed.

People who plan to run general ledgers on their computers must determine whether candidate software provides sufficient flexibility and proficiency in dealing with accounting periods. Three specific time functions must be addressed:

☐ The ability to assign transactions to specific accounting periods
☐ The ability to post transactions to different accounting periods in the same fiscal year
☐ The ability to enter and post transactions in different fiscal years

It is surprising how many different ways software designers have provided for assigning transactions to accounting periods. At one extreme is the software that will not permit users to start entering information into a new period until the old one has been closed—an unwieldy restriction. Imagine not being able to print customer bills, update accounts receivable, or write checks because the old accounting period remains open.

A middle ground is provided by the software that determines the accounting period from the transaction date. Users of this software will find that all invoices dated in one month will be assigned to the accounting period of that month. This approach is troublesome to users who prepare monthly financial reports, because late entries can affect accounting periods that have been closed. Consider a company that prepares monthly expense reports for management on the tenth of the month. What happens if a late vendor invoice is received after the report has been prepared? In most cases, the practical answer would be to throw the late invoice into the subsequent period. Software that determines the period from the transaction date will not permit this (unless a false transaction date is used to make the entry).

Another approach is to ask the user to enter the accounting period at the time that transaction batches are transferred from other modules (such as accounts receivable or accounts payable) to general ledger. The problem with this method is that the transaction batches by themselves do not show the accounting period with which they are associated.

The best control and greatest flexibility is the software that permits the user to enter the accounting period at the time of transaction entry. The way to determine this is to examine the data entry screens and see if a field is provided for the accounting period. (Chapter 8 includes a more extended discussion on the designation of accounting periods.)

The number of accounting periods that can be accessed varies from one software product to another. Some software is limited to just one accounting period at a time. Usually there is a setup screen in which the user enters the current accounting period. A mistake in this screen means that all transactions will be posted to the wrong period. Most of the higher performance products permit access to any period within the current accounting year.

What about making entries in different fiscal years? Most users must have a way of keeping the old year open long after the new year has started because of decisions and other matters that delay the closing. Some users, particularly accountants and financial managers, require the ability to enter closed periods for making corrections and changes.

Very few software programs provide unlimited access to different accounting years. Some programs provide a fixed number of accounting periods—a period in the new year is obtained by losing access to a period in the old year. Some provide a limited number of periods in the new year that can be accessed while the old one is open. A few programs, particularly those oriented to accountants, provide means of reopening closed years and rolling forward any adjustments that affect the intervening periods.

Provision for User-Designed Reports and Documents

Until recently, most accounting software was fixed with regard to the format of the documents and reports that it could print. Users who required different output had to find programmers to make the revisions, no matter how small.

Now, many accounting software products allow users to design many of their own forms and reports. This is accomplished through two different types of subroutines: a routine for form design that comes with each module, and a report writer that usually must be purchased as a separate module.

Form design capability is used most frequently for sales invoices but also can be used for sales order acknowledgments, pick tickets, payment vouchers, and similar documents. This design capability has the following advantages:

- [ ] Users avoid scrapping blank unused forms
- [ ] Customers do not have to get used to new formats
- [ ] Users can select which fields of information are to be printed on the invoice

Of course, some form design programs are easier to work with than others, and they all have their limitations. But in general, these programs are very useful.

An important report function is the ability to prepare user-designed reports. An example of this could be the design of special sales reports combining sales and inventory data, or department operations reports that compute overhead expenses on a cost per unit basis. Persons who have computer smarts can accomplish this by exporting data from the accounting software to a database or spreadsheet. This may be too demanding for the ordinary user. Some software publishers provide a more limited solution in the form of a report writer module. The degree of flexibility in report design varies from one product to another. Some report writers limit reports to data available in master files and do not permit combining information from different modules. Others are more flexible and even allow adding fields of information that are not provided in the accounting modules. Varying arithmetic and logical functions are permitted by different report writers.

There are two important reasons why this report design flexibility becomes more valuable as users become familiar with their accounting software:

1. Users often wish to obtain new reports once they become aware of the information capability of their software.

2. Users can introduce new management reports to accommodate changing business needs.

Provision for Viewing, Printing, and Storing Information

The information that is accumulated in accounting software generally is made available to users by three different methods:

- ☐ Viewing on the monitor screen
- ☐ Reading printed reports
- ☐ Storing in special files for use at a later time

There are many situations in which the preferable method of looking at information is viewing the monitor. This is useful for checking the status of a customer's order or looking up the details of a general ledger account. In such instances, monitor viewing is much easier than tying up a printer and waiting for hard copy.

Printed copy is preferable for wide and lengthy reports and for a permanent record. A monitor screen is much more limited in size than paper. Additionally, the information on the screen is transient; printed reports remain available for review.

There are situations in which the ability to store information in special files is helpful. For example, some software provides the option of "printing" forms and/or reports to a file. If this option is selected, the program will create new files for this purpose. The new form files can be used to print the forms at a more convenient time. The new report files can be used to transfer the data to an outside program.

Accounting programs vary in the choices just described. Some programs provide very limited information via the monitor and require that virtually all information be printed before it can be viewed. This is a clumsy limitation that should be avoided. Some programs provide a greater degree of monitor viewing but still lack the flexibility of the programs that provide unlimited choice among monitor, printer, or file.

The design of the reports generated by many of these programs requires scrutiny. Management reports that are designed to look impressive in sales literature and manuals frequently result in a lot of waste because of elaborate headings. The potential user should beware of software that consumes a lot of unnecessary paper. A nice-looking inventory report that wastes an inch per page with headings is acceptable for a list of 50 items, but quite a nuisance with a list of 2,000 items.

Generally, each software module will provide a series of so-called audit trail and management reports. These report formats should be examined carefully to determine how well they meet the user's requirements both in terms of legibility and information. Ease of comprehension depends a great deal on report design. Prospective users should consider the following advice:

- ☐ Be on the alert for reports that contain a lot of useless information. For example, do customer lists contain a lot of fields that are meaningless? Does the trial balance list accounts with zero balances?

- ☐ Determine which reports will be lengthy, such as detail sales and inventory reports. (Most reports are printed on paper that is 11 inches long and print 6 lines per inch.) Compute how many excessive pages will be produced because of elaborate and unnecessary headings.

- ☐ Avoid lengthy reports with limited totals. Lengthy reports become easier to comprehend when information is presented and totalled in logical subgroups.

- ☐ Determine whether any reports will print more than one line per record. Reports that require double or triple lines of information are hard to read.

- ☐ Do not assume from the title that a report contains the information the user requires. The phrase "sales analysis," for instance, can mean many different things.

Aligning forms in printers requires some experience and skill. Software that prints business documents such as checks, invoices and purchase orders should permit the user to run tests that will verify that forms are properly aligned in the printer. The software should also permit reruns since many printers are limited to four clear copies.

Standard horizontal character spacing on printers is 10 characters per inch. Dot matrix and laser printers can change this spacing when given the proper commands. In order to accommodate narrow printers, some software restricts reports to 80 characters per line (thus fitting on paper that is 8.5 inches wide). This limits the amount of information per line and often leads to confusing reports. A better solution is provided by software that accommodates 132 characters per line but automatically selects compressed printing (16.5 characters per linear inch) if a narrow printer is in use.

A considerable amount of time may be required to print lengthy business reports. A number of techniques are available, using both hardware and software, that free up the computer for other uses while the printer is working. Some software provides for background printing and even for switching between printers. Some programs permit sending reports to disk files for printing at a more convenient time.

The ability to interrupt printing is also important. This may be necessary if the paper jams or if a long report is called for by mistake. Software that does not provide an easy way to stop printing can be quite a nuisance.

Many of the general, or global, functions may not be the same for every software module. Export and import functions may be limited to the general ledger. More open time periods might be available in the general ledger than in accounts receivable or accounts payable.

This text has discussed software functions that apply to all accounting functions. Some functions, particularly those applying to report design and open accounting periods, should interest all users. The importance of the other functions will vary with user requirements.

SPECIFIC FUNCTIONS

There has to be a limit to a discussion of the different ways in which various software modules perform—there are just too many publishers and products on today's market to cover them all. This section addresses many of the popular features and functions that are presently available. (The sequence that follows bears no relationship to the relative importance of each module.)

General Ledger

Many people consider all general ledger modules to be very much the same and spend less time on this module than on others that they consider much more critical such as inventory or billing. The fact is, general ledger modules deserve a more close examination.

Some differences in flexibility and treatment of time periods have already been mentioned. The ability to handle more than one business entity (without the need to store separate software programs for each company) has also been touched upon. But there are other functions in which one general ledger product may differ from another.

One important distinction is the manner in which the accounts in the general ledger are linked to financial statements. This is done in one of two ways. Some software links general ledger accounts directly to the financial statements through a modified chart of accounts that includes statement captions and format codes. The format codes provide instructions about printing columns, combining balances, computing totals, and other operations related to the printing of financial statements. The user must understand how to insert statement captions and codes before setting up the chart of accounts.

An alternative approach is to provide a special file that contains the instructions for printing financial statements. The report specification file references each general ledger account by its number. Either way, report formatting codes are among the most difficult procedures to learn when using accounting software.

Generally, software that sets up financial statements through a modified chart of accounts is easier to use than software that requires a separate specification file. Additionally, since all accounts are listed in only one place—the modified chart of accounts—there is no possibility that an account will be omitted from the financial statements.

However, there is a trade-off:

1. Users must give some thought to the form of their financial statements and must learn the format codes at the very inception of the setup process. This can be a formidable challenge to nonaccountants.

2. Only one form of financial statement can be produced without a lot of extra effort.

Software that uses specification files provides much greater report flexibility. For example, one could prepare both summary and detailed operating statements, or organize data that will easily flow into tax returns. Another advantage of the second method is that users can set up their charts of accounts and start using the software without concerning themselves with report formats.

For an application that requires a simple set of financial statements, the modified chart of account type of general ledger software should be used.

Users who expect to prepare sophisticated financial statements in a number of formats should look for the report specification type of general ledger.

Flexibility in the selection of columnar financial data varies from one product to another. Many general ledgers limit the financial statements to showing amounts for the current period (usually the current month) and year-to-date. People who require reports for other periods, such as for the quarter, or for a selected two-month period, will be out of luck. Some software cannot display budget and comparative data in the same financial statement. Very few products can line up different departments side by side on a financial statement. Users who anticipate the need for these types of reports must be careful in selecting their general ledger software.

In addition to the capacity limitations that have already been discussed, one limitation that can seriously affect financial statements concerns text printing. The number of characters that can be printed in a side caption varies from one general ledger to another. Some products make it very difficult to insert footnotes without the use of a word processor. Users who require financial statements that conform to generally accepted accounting standards (GAAP) face more challenges. Most software cannot select proper placement on the financial statement if the sign of an account should change. For example, an account designated as an asset account will be printed as a negative asset if there is a credit balance. Proper accounting treatment requires disclosure among the liabilities.

Most, but not all, general ledger modules provide for comparative and budgetary data. The entry of comparative data can be quite a nuisance and is often ignored during the first year of operation. Thereafter the software automatically transfers current data to comparative status when the books are closed. Purported budget capability can be misleading. The software might limit the budget data to an annual amount. Some software facilitates the entry of budget information by permitting the user to repeat monthly amounts, to divide annual amounts by 12, or to increment monthly amounts by a fixed percentage. This facility is most useful for heavy budget users.

As discussed earlier, many types of journal entries have been developed to simplify the process of preparing financial statements and closing books. Most general ledger software provides for the entries required to close the books at year end, but many do not recognize other types of entries. This may not be a serious limitation, particularly if financial statements are prepared infrequently. The use of recurring, reversing, standing, and report-only entries can be important for applications requiring frequent preparation of financial statements.

Another feature offered by some general ledger software is the use of memo accounts. These accounts are used to store statistical information that is incorporated into financial statements. For example, a hotel operation may wish to store information about room vacancies, or a textile importer may wish to store information about the number of yards of material purchased and sold. Information in memo accounts, such as number of rooms or number of yards sold, can be combined with accounting data to compute and report average room rentals, or average costs and selling prices per yard.

The availability of account information is another important variable among software products. Ideally, one should be able to use either the monitor or printer to look up account information. Account selection should be easy. The amount of detail should be selected by the user. Some software provides an option in each module to post transactions in detail or summary form. Some programs allow users to decide for each account whether the data should be in summary or detail form. Detail postings facilitates inquiry processing. Summary postings avoid cluttered accounts and excessive storage requirements. Some packages can only store account details for the current month; some cannot store any detail at all.

Flexibility in the choice of accounting period can be significant. Some software packages are much easier to work with than others when it comes to holding one accounting period open (such as the last month of the fiscal period) and making entries into subsequent periods. Additional functions, such as the computation of financial tables and the printing of financial ratios, may also be provided in the general ledger.

As mentioned, some general ledger modules provide a limited capability for processing accounts receivable, accounts payable, and payroll. This feature is useful in situations in which the number of subsidiary ledger accounts is very small and the limited set of functions and reports provided by the software is adequate.

It is likely that many of these differing attributes of general ledger software are more interesting to bookkeepers and accountants than to business managers. It is important to understand that some of these products are better than others in providing financial statements tailored to user needs, simplifying the accounting process, and providing account information.

Accounts Receivable

Software functions for managing accounts receivable are usually closer to the immediate interests of management. What follows are some of the most interesting features of such software.

1. Most, but not all, accounts receivable software handles both balance

forward and open item accounts receivable. Users should make certain that the software selected meets their requirements.

2. There is a wide variation in the methods that are provided for computing sales commissions. At one extreme is software that makes no attempt at all to compute commissions. Some software will accumulate sales by salesperson, but leaves the actual commission computation to the user. Many packages will compute one sales commission per sales invoice. Some programs (by referring to the inventory module) can compute a sales commission that varies with the inventory item. In most cases, split commissions must be computed outside the software. Some software provides the option of computing commissions on shipments or cash receipts.

3. The tracking of sales for sales tax purposes is another function that differs a great deal among software products. Some software programs facilitate accumulating this information; others provide no help at all.

4. Many products computate finance charges on past due amounts. Some products provide greater facility than others, including a two-tier rate system, setting minimum charges, determining customer-by-customer who shall be charged, totaling finance charges by customer for the current year, and other options.

5. Many modules are geared for a single accounts receivable control account and single cash account for deposits. While this satisfies most users, there are situations in which these conditions are too restrictive.

6. In some software the aging brackets are predetermined and cannot be changed. Other software lets the user set the age brackets. If dating is an important feature, aging by due date (rather than invoice date) is an important feature.

7. There are a number of choices for printing customer statements. Some software permits the user to limit statements to past due accounts. Some programs will print a one-line description for each transaction. Some will print messages at the bottom of the statement, or dunning messages that vary with the age of the balance. Some provide the user the option of omitting statements for customers with credit or zero balances.

8. Curiously, many accounts receivable modules do not provide for the entry of sundry cash receipts. This omission creates problems for users who must deal with this type of transaction.

9. Another frequent shortcoming is the clumsy treatment of credits and cash refunds. Many packages do not provide a separate journal for credits but print credits in the sales journal. What is worse, credits are

netted against sales and not kept separate for accounting purposes, thereby distorting sales information. Cash refunds usually must be processed by issuing debit memos.

10. The treatment of unauthorized customer deductions is another software variable. Some software will not permit deductions that exceed invoice terms. This can cause problems for users who are accustomed to such activity and are willing to allow unauthorized deductions at the time of payment.

11. The storage of transaction history is another variable. Accounting software varies in its ability to store customer invoices, credits, and cash receipts. Some software erases all paid transactions at month end. Some allows users to keep a transaction history file. Other software provides for an invoice history file.

12. An important issue is the type of sales information provided by the software and the modules required for accumulating this information. The term "sales analysis" is too vague to provide meaningful information about the information provided by the system. Sales information by customer may range from virtually no information at all, to a long list of data such as sales, credits, transaction dates, promptness of payment, and credit. Dollar sales analysis by salesperson, territory, or other criteria may be provided in a number of modules, such as accounts receivable, order entry, inventory, or a separate sales analysis module. Sales analysis by products, such as information by product line or gross profit, usually is provided by order entry or inventory.

    Lengthy sales reports require a variety of sorts and subtotals. In some cases, an extensive sales history may be useful. Other managers may work with quotas and sales targets. Some software packages provide reports that are too detailed and cluttered, thereby discouraging review. Some are very limited in sales reporting or flexibility in selecting and grouping sales data. Potential users should take the time to determine whether the sales reports produced by the system will meet their requirements.

13. Although virtually all accounts receivable modules provide an aging report, very few provide a cash flow report. This report shows when cash is expected based on sales terms, and is a very useful management tool.

14. People who are interested in printing sales invoices, but not concerned with order processing, should look for accounts receivable modules that include invoicing. (Most software provides this in the sales order module.) One publisher even provides a file for storing item descriptions and prices that facilitates the billing operation.

15. There are additional accounts receivable functions that can be helpful:

   ☐ Customer labels

   ☐ Cycle printing of customer statements

   ☐ Storage of customer preferences with regard to part-ships, back orders, and substitutions

Order Entry

Most general-purpose order entry and invoicing modules are designed for a jobbing or distribution operation. Consequently, order acknowledgment and billing forms printed by the software are oriented to selling products, not services. Columns are provided for stock numbers, descriptions, quantities ordered and shipped, unit prices, and extensions. While this format is fine for many jobbers and wholesalers, it will not do at all for many organizations that are service oriented. Therefore, it is very important to review the format of printed forms.

Most software limits the number of characters of description in the body of the sales invoice. This can be a troublesome restriction for service organizations and other businesses selling complex products. The maximum number of characters per printed line may vary from 25 to 60 or more. Some software programs allow only one description line for each dollar extension, others allow more lines. Some limit the number of lines; others do not. The ability to store and recall descriptions can be a big help in the billing function. Many software packages link invoicing with inventory. This permits calling up item descriptions from the inventory files. If inventory is not being used, some software provides for description files in either accounts receivable or order entry. However, some software does not permit any change in the description that is called up at the time of billing. If descriptions require many modifications, this restriction can be serious.

Some software insists on filling columns assigned for quantities and unit prices with numbers. This can be confusing on service invoices.

Some software addresses the need for flexibility in format by incorporating design capability into their products. Such software permits users (within limits) to determine the information that will print on such forms as sales acknowledgments, pick tickets, and sales invoices, as well as to determine where the information will print on the form.

After determining that the print format will be satisfactory, there are a number of important functions to review. (These vary so much from one operation to another that the following discussion will cover just a representative sample.)

1. Some software handles multiple ship-to addresses more easily than others.

2. Many products severely limit the size of the field for entering sales terms. This limitation may create problems for those who require lengthy descriptions of these terms. (Although is some cases the terms can be entered in the body of the sales invoice.)

3. There is a wide variety of pricing options provided by different software packages. Some of these options are customer oriented and are available through accounts receivable and order entry. These options usually provide different discounts to various classes of customers. Some options are item oriented and offer discounts based on quantities or ranges of items. Some software can print the amount of discount per item; others cannot. Some provide special sales pricing.

4. Some users buy in one unit of measure and sell in different units. For example, an item might be purchased by the gross and sold by the dozen. Some programs are better than others in dealing with this situation. A related requirement arises when different items are combined for a special combination sales pack.

5. Some businesses sell items in fractional quantities such as eighths of a yard. Some price in tenths of a cent or some other fraction. Many order entry products do not handle fractional quantities or prices.

6. Different credit limit controls are provided at the time of order entry. Some software will display the amount of unused credit. Other software will show the amount of unfilled orders on hand, or the maximum amount of credit allowed in the past.

7. UPS shippers can take advantage of software that stores UPS zones by customer and computes freight charges based on weight and UPS zone.

8. Various types of order and billing requirements such as quotes, standing orders, recurring billing, substitutions, multiple shipments, back orders and cancellation dates, are addressed by different packages, although no one product covers all of these processing needs.

9. Some software costs each sale from cost data stored in an inventory module (subject to override). While the capability of costing sales on a day-to-day basis is very appealing, the application of proper costing methods can be challenging and often requires professional advice.

10. Users who must generate back orders should ascertain that the software they select provides simple routines for this purpose.

11. Drop shippers must determine whether the software can identify drop ships and how drop ships appear in sales reports.

12. Some order entry software programs store and report sales statistics by item and customer.

13. In some industries, a report of open sales orders by cancellation date is important.

14. Most order entry modules require separate orders and invoices for each shipping location. This restriction poses a problem for some operations.

15. Some programs display more inventory data than do others at the time that orders are entered. Some programs show the balance on hand at the selected warehouse; others may also show unfilled customer orders and quantities open on purchase orders. A multiwarehouse operation may require display of quantities at all warehouses.

Accounts Payable

Accounts payable and purchase order modules usually are organized in a fashion similar to accounts receivable and order entry. Bear in mind that accounts payable software generally is used to process all invoices—invoices from vendors as well as expense bills. There are several significant features that can be important in meeting user requirements:

1. Most accounts payable software programs assume that users are on the accrual method of accounting. The software requires separate operations for the entry of invoices and the processing of payments. People accustomed to recording invoices directly from cash disbursements may find these separate operations to be cumbersome. A few products allow for direct entry of invoices at the time that payments are processed.

2. Similar to accounts receivable, many modules are geared for a single accounts payable control account and a single cash account for making disbursements, restrictions that can be troublesome.

3. Another parallel with accounts receivable deals with the processing of vendor debit memos. Some software programs make better provision for this than do others.

4. Just like accounts receivable, purchase information by vendor varies from virtually no information to a long list of statistics. Purchase data can be useful in negotiating prices.

5. A good accounts payable product should facilitate cash management. The user with adequate cash resources should look to the software to facilitate making timely disbursements to obtain maximum cash dis-

counts. Some software tracks both discounts earned and discounts lost. A user with limited cash should use the software to optimize selections for check writing. Such a user requires software that will print a report that analyzes unpaid invoices by due date (a report that is the opposite to an accounts receivable cash flow report).

6. Cash management is facilitated by simple methods for selecting invoices for payment. Different packages provide varying ways for selecting invoices for payment. The most common choices are by due date, vendor, discount date, and specific invoice. Prospective users should make certain that the selection choices agree with their method of doing business. Additionally, the software should provide a prelist for review before the checks are printed.

7. In order to guard against erroneous disbursements, some software provides for the placing of payment holds against vendors and against individual invoices.

8. There are times when checks must be handwritten or voided. Users who process many of these transactions should look for software that simplifies the process.

9. Some software provides for recurring charges. This capability simplifies the processing of routine payments that are required on a periodic basis such as rent and service contracts.

10. Many programs accumulate data for 1099 reporting.

Inventory

As indicated in Chapter 5, inventory modules generally provide two basic functions. One is to provide inventory information, and the other is to provide item data for order entry. Many noninventory applications use an inventory module to simplify billing. Because of the close association between inventory and business operations, finding a module that comes close to fulfilling the needs of a specific user can be a challenge.

Limitations on field sizes, discussed in Chapter 6, are frequently most critical in inventory applications, particularly the number of characters permitted in item codes and descriptions.

The number of decimals available for costing and pricing generally ranges from two to four, depending on the product. The choice of decimal positions may be global (applies to all items) or might be selected by item.

A number of methods are provided for item pricing. Some software provides fields for list price (which is printed on price lists) and sales price (which is the price actually used in order entry). Price discounts usually can be based on customer type or purchase quantities. Other pricing methods, such as markup on cost, negotiated prices, and broken case penalties are available with some software.

For those users who wish to track inventory costs, most inventory modules offer one or more of the following costing methods: first-in-first-out (FIFO), last-in-first-out (LIFO), average, standard, and last. The number of layers provided for inventory computations varies among the different accounting packages.

A number of information fields may be provided to facilitate purchasing such as reorder point, reorder quantity, the names of one or more source vendors together with their corresponding item numbers, and lead times.

Some software can deal with different units of measure, including purchase, inventory, and sales units.

Some modules provide a field for distinguishing among different types of inventory, such as obsolete items, sale items, regular items, and so on.

There are wide variations in the reporting of inventory status for purposes of fast inquiry. Status information may include such data as quantities in stock, on order, on unfilled customer orders, and reserved. For inventory in multiple locations, this information may show by location or be combined.

The ability to change all sales prices by a fixed amount, or fixed percentage (a so-called global price change), can be important to some users.

Some software provides useful statistical information by item, such as date of last receipt, quantity received, period and cumulative sales, and so on. Some users require lot number or serial number controls.

For inventories that comprise thousands of items, the software should provide the ability to sort items into useful groups and classes.

Item shipping weights, if provided, help in computing freight costs.

Multiwarehouse operations require an easy facility for handling warehouse transfers.

In some applications, a field for bin location assists the process for picking orders.

SUMMARY

This chapter has stressed the importance of making a very specific determination of required software functions and the need for careful inquiry to determine how well the various software packages fulfill these functions. Because of poor use of language and advertising hype, many purchasers expect software to meet their needs and are disappointed when they try to put the software to use. There is no alternative to carefully studying software manuals and reports.

The chapter divided software functions into two groups. One set of functions is common to all of the accounting software modules provided by the same publisher. Seven types of these so-called global functions were described together with a discussion of their applicability and usefulness.

Another set of software functions is unique to each module. The text presented a number of examples of functions provided by different software products in the most popular accounting modules: general ledger, accounts receivable, order entry, accounts payable, and inventory.

The purpose of presenting these function lists is to impress upon the reader the tremendous variety of functions that is available, and the need to search out the software that will perform the necessary operations.

8

Connectivity

INTRODUCTION

Up to this point accounting software has been viewed as groups of programs (modules) that process business operations. Chapter 5 described the operations performed by the most popular accounting software modules: general ledger, accounts receivable, order entry, accounts payable, purchasing, inventory, and payroll.

In this chapter, the discussion will be about software functions that tie modules and workstations together in order to:

☐ Transfer information between modules (module integration)

☐ Transfer information between workstations in a computer network (A network is sometimes referred to as a LAN which is an abbreviation for "local area network.")

These functions are very important in some applications but may not be significant in others. Potential users should find the following discussion helpful in determining which functions are meaningful.

INTEGRATION

How important is it for different modules of accounting software to be able to exchange information? In some instances the need is highly exaggerated.

In others it is vital. For example, the ability of accounts receivable to transfer summary accounting information to general ledger usually is of minor significance, because the summary entries created in receivables are short. Payables affect more accounts and therefore generate longer entries. General ledger postings from both accounts receivable and accounts payable usually are made once a month, so that the time required to enter and post may not be significant.

Integration is more important when detail information must be passed from one module to another, such as the transfer of sales and purchasing data to inventory records, the need to access inventory and accounts receivable information when entering sales orders, or the importance of charging payroll costs to jobs.

The most frequently found integration capability is among general ledger and the modules that feed into it—accounts receivable, accounts payable, and payroll. Indeed, a few software products require the installation of the general ledger module before other modules can be added. Accountants who use data from client records to prepare financial statements and tax returns will be interested in the integration among various modules and general ledger.

Users who wish to process sales orders and invoices require smooth integration among accounts receivable, order entry, and inventory—a complex process. The data files for all three modules must be properly designed and set up in order to produce optimum results. Careful planning and testing should be done, particularly in selecting the best options and codes. An operator should not expend the effort of keying in the data for setting up customer and inventory files, a task that can be very time consuming, until successful tests have been run using a few customer and inventory records. Such tests frequently disclose the need to make some changes in planned procedures before the installation is started. Operators must have a clear understanding of the nature and format of the information that must be keyed into the system. Problems can be avoided by preparing clear procedure manuals and arranging for adequate training.

Those who use job costing may require integration with a number of modules: accounts receivable, accounts payable, payroll, and inventory. This is one of the most complex processes that one finds with accounting software. Extensive tests usually are needed before the best method of operation is selected.

Virtually every publisher who offers many modules in its product line will state that its products are integrated. Readers are led to believe that all modules are fully integrated and that the transfer of information is simple and virtually automatic.

This is not always true.

Many software products do not provide integration among all of the modules in their product lines. Some job cost modules cannot access payroll or inventory. Some accounts payable modules cannot work with inventory. Users must compare their integration requirements with the capabilities of candidate software—module by module.

Some products provide the option of transferring either summary or detail information to the general ledger. This feature can save time when looking up information and analyzing general ledger accounts.

The fact that the software provides an integration capability does not mean that the transfer of information is automatic. Software products that require the general ledger module for the other modules to function, usually provide the smoothest integration with the general ledger. Some software utilizes a general ledger account file in each module in which the user must enter the codes of the general ledger accounts that will be referenced by that module. There may be a limit on the number of accounts that can be listed, thereby limiting the number of accounts that can be integrated with general ledger. (This is one of the capacity restrictions discussed in Chapter 6.)

Some packages request general ledger account numbers at the time of data entry but do not verify the validity of the number until the time of posting. This is a clumsy approach, because error correction at the time of posting can be time consuming and troublesome. The best method is found in those products that check with the general ledger chart of accounts at the time of data entry and immediately report nonexistent account numbers.

The treatment of transaction dates and accounting periods can be bothersome. The best treatment is offered by software that asks users to enter the accounting period for each transaction. But not all software does this. At the time of transfer, many programs look to a date in either the sending module or the general ledger module to determine the accounting period. This critical date in the sending module may be called the "system date," or a similar term. It rarely is clear that this date determines the accounting period. If the critical date is in the general ledger, the current accounting period usually is clearly displayed at the time of transfer, and all data transfers are assigned to that period. In some cases, the screen that initiates the transfer asks for entry of the accounting period.

The transfer of data may be made directly to the individual accounts or indirectly to a journal file in the target module. The journal file approach is useful for accumulating data for review and posting at a later time or at a remote source such as an accountant's office or a separate bookkeeping facility.

The distinction between posting within a module and posting to accounts in other modules is not always clear. Many users prefer to make certain postings more frequently than others. For example, the posting of sales invoices from order entry to accounts receivable may be done daily, while the posting of sales to the general ledger may be done monthly. With some software, all posting is performed at the same time. This usually applies to programs that provide only one active batch in each module. (For an explanation of batch processing, see Chapter 5.) In other cases, particularly those that transfer data to journal files, the two types of posting may be done at different times.

In summary, so-called integrated software may be subject to the following limitations:

☐ Not all modules may be integrated.

☐ A limited number of general ledger accounts may be accessed by the other modules.

☐ An invalid general ledger account may not be detected until the time of posting.

☐ Accounting periods may not be clear from transaction journals.

☐ Batch posting from a source module may have to be made to all target files at the same time.

NETWORKS

There a number of reasons for networking accounting software:

1. There is too much work for one person to process at a single station. An example would be a three-person office in which a chief bookkeeper handles general ledger and payroll, a second person deals with billing and accounts receivable, while a third is concerned with processing and paying vendor invoices. Another example is an order department office in which a work group enters and processes sales orders.

2. A number of people require access to the same information. This situation arises, for example, when personnel in a customer relations department need to share information in customer order files, or when executives need access to general ledger data.

3. Costs can be reduced by sharing devices such as printers or modems. For example, costs can be saved by using one printer for orders that are written by several people in a sales order department. Or an expensive

laser printer can service a number of accountants preparing financial statements.

4. The important responsibility of backing up computer files can be centralized. With stand-alone systems, each user must perform this function, and experience has proven that memories do not always respond! On a network, backup is one of the important responsibilities of the system manager.

Many discussions about networks bandy about a number of technical terms that can daunt the uninitiated. Some of the greatest confusion centers around different meanings for the terms "network," "LAN" (local area network), and "multiuser." In theory there are two types of networks. In one type, each workstation does virtually all of its own processing, and the network permits users to call up files produced at other stations. The characteristics of this type of network is that each station stores its programs and files. This is a "distributed processing" network and is most useful for a group of people who use the computer for word processing and spreadsheet applications.

The other network type, called "multiuser," requires the centralized storage of programs and files because many people require access to the same programs and data. In some multiuser systems, all processing is done at a central computer ("server") that is wired to a number of "dumb" terminals. In other systems, the central processor sends program and data files to workstations for processing. The processing is done at the workstation, which in turn sends the updated files back to the server for storage. Accounting software must run on a multiuser network.

There are many offsetting factors to be considered before a decision is reached about networking. Networking is still a new technology in the microcomputer world. Many installations take a considerable amount of time and technical support for successful completion. After successful installation, networks require more attention than do stand-alone systems.

Networks are much more than glorified intercom systems. They comprise a system of wires, electronic hardware, and software that performs a number of functions:

1. The network passes instructions and files between computers and related devices in such a way that the receiving unit understands what it is receiving and can properly react to it. In order to do this, the network software must verify the accuracy of transmission between units.

2. The network is an electronic switch that connects sending and receiving devices.

3. The network is a security officer. Passwords are used to make certain that only authorized personnel are allowed to look at or change specified programs and files. As part of its security work, a network program usually maintains logs of network activity.

4. The network must regulate the conflicting requests of several users who wish to work with the same files and records. The network must prevent different users from changing files without regard to what the others are doing. Otherwise one change would supercede an earlier one, and many changes and updates could be lost without a trace. The network software performs this function through "file locking" (preventing access to a file when another user is working with it) and "record locking" (preventing access to a record within a file when another user is working with it).

5. The network queues work that is sent to the printers. This function, technically called "print spooling," allows computers to continue functioning without being slowed down by the printer. Some spooling software programs permit users to give priority status to urgently needed reports.

The network must perform all of the aforementioned functions without causing an unacceptable amount of delay. This delay, also called "degradation," shows up as the time lapse between the moment that a user asks the program to do something and the time that a response is received. During the waiting period, the computer appears to do nothing. If the delay is very long, a user may assume that there is a malfunction, when in fact the problem is simply the speed of the network. Degradation increases as more workstations and other devices are added to the network. A system that works fine with three workstations may become intolerably slow when a fourth station is added. Tests run by *PC* magazine, as reported in its issue of January 26, 1988, show that the performance of one particular brand of network software ran from 432 seconds with one station to 868 seconds with five stations. A competing product ranged from 280 to 345 seconds.

There are limits to the number of units that can be networked together. Some of these limits are restrictions of the network hardware or software. Some are the practical restrictions of degradation (the time lost because more and more users are trying to access the same files). Vendors of network software usually provide theoretic maximum limits based on the number of stations that can be connected to the system without regard to degradation. The publishers of accounting software should be able to provide more practical limits based on user experience. For PC-based networks of accounting software, it is advisable to check performance carefully. In many situations, the practical limit will run between four and seven stations, depending on usage.

The network software should also provide some diagnostic help in case of trouble. With all of the wires, connections, and electronic devices that are part of a network, many things can go wrong—from the selection of the cabling material to misunderstanding the instructions required by the network software. Someone tripping over a wire, or the installation of a new piece of office equipment, can give rise to a network malfunction.

The fulfillment of each of these functions and requirements takes some doing. For that reason, networks are complex and must be carefully evaluated before a decision should be made as to their applicability.

Specifically, one must evaluate the following:

☐ Cost

☐ Limited choice of software

☐ Hardware compatability

☐ Degree of attention required.

Cost

A network consists of a number of components that must be added to single-station computers. These components consist of:

☐ Wire or cable that connects the components. Different types of connecting media are used depending on the network hardware, the distance between units, and operating conditions (such as electrical interference). Wiring costs (usually computed on a per foot basis) vary among the different types of connecting media—from twisted-pair, which is the cheapest, to fiber optic. Cable and its installation can account for 50 percent of installation costs.

☐ Special electronic hardware. Usually a special network board (called a network interface card) must be inserted in each workstation. A hub (called a port) on the board is used to receive the wire or cable. The attachment device at the end of the cable must be the proper one for the system and must be affixed to the cable in the correct manner. Some networks also require additional electronic components (separate "black boxes") that are wired into the network. Usually a separate computer is required to store all files and programs used on the network and to run the network software. This computer is called a server. With the exception of small networks of two or three workstations, most servers are "dedicated" and cannot be used for any purpose other than supporting the network. Some networks require a minicomputer as a server.

☐ Network software (the program that performs the functions just enumerated). Network software varies with respect to the number of components that the software can address, ease of installation and use, and the range of network functions that are provided.

☐ Accounting software. Network versions of accounting software cost more than single user versions.

All of these factors must be added to the cost of a single-station system. However, there are some significant cost trade-offs:

A network may reduce the number of devices that must be purchased. Perhaps one printer can serve five workstations, instead of one printer per station.

A network may reduce the cost of workstations. In general, workstations that include computer capability ("intelligent" workstations) cost more than workstations that consist of nothing more than a keyboard and monitor ("dumb" workstations). However, the use of a diskless "intelligent" station can also bring costs down. The selection of the proper workstation depends on the requirements of the network software and the type of work that one expects to perform at each station.

Therefore, as networks grow in size, the increased cost of the network components can be offset by savings in workstations and other devices.

Limited Choice of Software

In order to run successfully on a network, accounting software requires modifications that will permit it to integrate with the functions of the network software. The network software provided by each publisher is distinct from network software provided by others. Therefore, application programs such as accounting software require a separate modification in order to work with each type of network software. Thus accounting software designed to run on an IBM token ring network will not work on Novell or 3Com. One cannot assume that an accounting program will run on a specific network unless the publisher clearly states that it can do so.

Thus the decision to run accounting software on a network limits the choice of software:

1. The selection must be limited to software that will run on a network, or

2. If a network has already been installed, the software must be compatible with the existing network.

Hardware Compatability

Network software will not necessarily work with all microcomputers. There are a number of software programs designed to work with IBM PCs and related computers. Differences in design may result in a compatability problem. When planning a network, the user should make certain that the network will function properly with existing hardware. The vendors of network software should be able to provide this information.

Degree of Attention Required

Most single-users pay very little attention to computer hardware, often less than they should. However, one should not consider using a network, even a small one, without assigning maintenance responsibility to a person who is willing to learn something about network operations. This person is usually called the system manager. Remember that one misfunction on the system can affect every workstation and cause a widespread shutdown of operations.

Some of the functions of the system manager include

☐ Entering instructions to the network whenever a new device is added to the system—instructions such as the name, description, and other specifications required by the software

☐ Controlling passwords. For security reasons, every change in computer personnel, or change in their responsibilities, requires a change in password instructions. For added security, passwords should be changed periodically. (For further discussion, see Chapter 12.)

☐ Instructing new users in use of the system

☐ Performing backup procedures

☐ Reviewing disk usage and unused storage capacity

☐ Making simple diagnostic tests of the system

☐ Arranging for outside maintenance, when required

☐ Helping to track down malfunctions that indicate a conflict between the application and the network software.

Because of the added cost and complexity, there are many who believe that the importance of networking is frequently overrated, especially in those circumstances in which very little information must be passed back and forth between the various accounting modules. If separate stations are required for accounts receivable and accounts payable, month-end postings from these operations can be summarized at each workstation, printed, and passed to the general ledger bookkeeper for entry. An alternative is to write summary information onto a diskette and then bring that diskette to another workstation where the information can be read and posted to the general ledger. The small additional month-end work is scarcely enough to justify a network.

Some simple techniques are also available for connecting such devices as printers and modems to several workstations without using networks. These techniques use relatively inexpensive devices to switch between printers (switch boxes), and hold information until the device or devices are ready to process it (file buffers).

Even though the accounting software that is selected limits the choice of network software, a number of decisions must be made for choosing the correct network version. The following questions should be considered:

1. How large a system should be planned? Even if starting with a small system, plans to enlarge the system in the near future may affect many hardware decisions described below.

2. Should a dedicated server be used? A dedicated server means investing in a computer that cannot be used for running any program other than the network software. A nondedicated server may save money on a small system (up to four workstations) but can slow things down considerably when there is a lot of traffic on the system.

3. What kind of workstations should be used? Diskless stations and "dumb" terminals are cheaper but can only function with networked programs. "Smart" terminals with disks can function both on a stand-alone and network basis. Such a computer can run programs that are not suitable for the network (perhaps for reasons of privacy) and can also run some networked programs should the network go down. A mix of different types of workstations can be used, but the user must make certain that each station is compatible with the network.

4. What network hardware should be used? Network software and hardware do not necessarily have to be supplied by the same manufacturer.

5. What printers should be used, and where should they be located? Different printers may be required for different purposes. (More infor-

mation about this is found in Chapter 9.) Printers can be connected either to the server or to a workstation.

6. What cabling media should be used, and how should it be routed? Planning ahead for cabling can save long-run costs.

7. What is the best network scheme? A number of schemes (called "topologies") have been developed that provide different trade-offs between costs and performance. In most instances, the choice of topology is best left to an expert. However, users should inquire whether there is a choice and discuss the relative advantages and disadvantages of each.

The most important decision of all is the choice of the network vendor. A competent vendor should

☐ Provide advice on hardware and cable selection. People with installation experience know which devices are easy to install and which ones cause problems.

☐ Provide advice about running wires and cables, even if the actual work may be done by others.

☐ Review all network connections and deliver a tested system that is functioning properly.

☐ Set network parameters that are appropriate to the needs of the user. Good parameters will provide the best performance in terms of speed and hardware utilization. Someone skilled in installing the network software is required for this.

☐ Provide training. A good installer may not be the best person to do the training.

☐ Provide maintenance on a timely basis. The number of people qualified to do network trouble shooting is limited. Beware of vendors who have a limited staff and cannot respond to maintenance calls within a reasonable period of time.

☐ Obtain assurance that the vendor selected has a proven record of success with the network that has been selected.

SUMMARY

This chapter has discussed considerations related to the transfer of accounting information between modules (module integration) and computers (computer network).

Integration is the term given to data transfer between modules. Integration is most important when the different modules must interact on a daily basis. The most frequent interaction paths are among

- ☐ Order entry and accounts receivable
- ☐ Order entry, billing, and inventory
- ☐ Purchasing, accounts payable, and inventory
- ☐ Accounts payable, payroll, and job costing.

Integration capability and ease vary from product to product and cannot be taken for granted. There may be limits on the modules that are integrated and the number of accounts that can be accessed. The relationship between transaction date and accounting period may be restricted, and integration procedures may be clumsy.

Networking is important when two or more persons require access to the same information. Networks involve a number of costs that must be added to the costs of stand-alone systems. However, some of this additional cost can be offset by the use of less expensive workstations and device sharing.

Networks are complex. The network software that is used must be compatible with the accounting software. A network requires more planning and attention than do stand-alone systems in order to minimize malfunctions and degradation. The choice of a network vendor must be made with care. A potential buyer should make certain that the accounting software of choice has been run successfully on a network equal to or larger than the one that the buyer is contemplating.

SUPPLEMENTARY TECHNICAL INFORMATION

As of this writing, most network versions of PC accounting software are compatible with network software produced by Novell, 3Com, and IBM. An article in *Today's Office* magazine reports that Novell has "the largest market share in high-end PC networks" and that "Novell and 3Com products are the most widely installed and supported." A limited number of PC accounting software products are compatible with other network software such as Xenix. Apple®-based accounting software is limited to Appleshare® software.

Many industry watchers believe that networking capability will change as operating systems based on new microchip technology come on the market, such as new versions of OS/2.

The cost of network software can vary with the number of users on the network. For example, Novell Level I (four users) retails for $595, while Level II (eight users) carries a list price of $1,395. The cost of the network board that must be placed in each unit ranges from about $350 to $750.

Servers on small systems can range from about $4,000 to $10,000. Remember that time response can be very slow, on all but the smallest systems, without a properly selected server.

9

Acquisition Costs

INTRODUCTION

The preceding chapters have discussed three important attributes of accounting software that must be considered by a potential user before commencing the search for a specific solution:

Capacity. Chapter 6 explained why all software has capacity limitations. Every user must determine his or her capacity requirements in such terms as the number of records to be stored, the size of each field, and similar specifications. Software with capacities below user requirements probably will be useless or too cumbersome to manage. Software with excess capacity provides flexibility for growth and change but might be unwieldy or too expensive.

Functionality. Chapter 7 discussed the functional differences among accounting software products. With this wide variability from one package to another, users must look for software that will come closest to performing all of the functions that are required. Some functions must be considered an absolute requirement. Additional functions provided by the software might be considered useful but not necessary. Some software functions might be totally irrelevant or even confusing.

Multiple users and modules. Chapter 8 considered the need for the integration of software modules, workstations, and programs. Some software programs have some or all of this capability, some do not. Users must consider the importance of these functions, because their requirements will limit the software search and can add to the costs of installing and administering the system.

When prospective users have finished setting out "wish lists" of what they would like the software to do for them, it is time to begin the actual software search. Two important related factors should guide the quest; cost and control. Both of these factors are complex. Cost involves three major elements. Each element will be discussed in a separate chapter. This chapter discusses acquisition costs—that is, the cost of software and hardware. Chapter 10 discusses installation costs such as setting up master files, designing and applying codes, training users, and parallel operation. Chapter 11 discusses operating costs such as ease of entry and error recovery and speed of operation.

Cost considerations can be easily understated in the micro world, because acquisition costs generally are small compared to the costs involved in installing and using the system.

SOFTWARE COST

Comparison price shopping of accounting software can be very confusing. It is a challenge just to identify products and their related prices because of the confusion in names. Some products are known by the name of the publisher, others by a trade name. There are many publishers with similar names, and many products with similar names. For example, one publisher calls itself the Small Business System Group (Westford, Massachusetts). Another is called Small Business Systems, Inc. (La Grange, Illinois). At least three products use the name CPA: CPA, CPA+, and CPA11. The only clear method of identity is by name of both publisher and product.

Micro accounting software comes in a wide range of prices. Packages are being offered today for as little as $70 (for a set of many modules) and as much as several thousand dollars per module. The software price may or may not include installation services.

The various modules of accounting software were named and described in Chapter 7. That chapter indicated that the functional names are too general to provide a precise description of what each module can do. For example, some accounts receivable modules can be used to print sales invoices, while competitive products require the order entry module for this function. Similarly, one publisher might make sales analysis available in accounts receivable, while another requires the purchase of a separate module for this purpose. Pricing cannot be truly comparative without first listing all the modules that must be used for comparable functions.

Some accounting software requires the installation of a master module that coordinates the resources and facilities of each application module. Master modules may be given such names as Library Master, Resource Manager, or System Manager. Their costs must be added to the costs of the application software. In some instances, a special language program must be purchased and installed in order to use the accounting program.

As mentioned in the previous chapter, networks add additional software costs. The networking versions of accounting programs are more expensive than single user versions. And to this must be added the cost of the network software itself.

Accounting software is constantly being improved and modified by publishers. Vendors who stock accounting software may offer merchandise that has been superceded by later versions. Some publishers offer different versions of their products at different prices. Some publishers provide upgrade kits or permit their resellers to replace older versions of their products with more current ones. But not all publishers follow such a policy. Prospective buyers must make certain that product comparisons are based on comparable versions of each product. In most instances, this should be the latest version.

Another complication is the competitive pricing of the marketplace. Virtually all accounting software bears a listed retail price. However, this price is often honored in the breech. Computer magazines and newspaper ads frequently advertise accounting software at prices far below the listed price. Since these ads rarely show the version number, potential buyers should make inquiry before placing their orders. They should also consider very carefully the degree of support required for software installation (discussed in the next chapter), since such support may be difficult to obtain from a discount resource.

Up to this point, it has been shown that meaningful comparison of software prices must take into account

☐ The possibility that modules with the same name may actually perform different functions

☐ The possible need for special manager or language software

☐ The importance of determining the version numbers of the products that are being compared.

Another significant element of software cost is the support provided by the publisher to end users. Each publisher determines the policy; there is no industry standard.

Software support comprises many elements. To a first user, the most important aspect of support is the availability of technical personnel to answer questions about installing and using the software. Most problems can be addressed over the telephone. In complicated situations, the technician will guide the user step by step while both are sitting at their computers. Telephone support is provided both on toll-free and regular lines. Publishers usually provide a callback service. There may be a long delay before the callback is received.

Some publishers do not provide any telephone support to end users. These publishers expect their dealers to field all customer questions. In turn, the dealers usually are given technical assistance telephone numbers by the publisher. Frequently this arrangement is unsatisfactory, because dealer personnel rarely have a good understanding of accounting software and the details of customer requirements. The communication process can be fraught with misunderstanding, which can result in long delays in obtaining satisfactory answers.

Some publishers provide free telephone assistance for a limited period of time, usually 90 days from date of purchase. On a practical basis, one should wait until the software has been installed and ready for use before registering for this service. Frequently, software installation starts many days, even months, after purchase. Not all modules are installed at the same time. It often takes many months before a user can start using all of the features provided by the software. Different modules are introduced over a period of time. The modules may be operated separately before data is integrated between the modules. The year-end closing, a critical function in accounting operations, may occur long after the computer operation has begun. A user is frequently surprised to realize that the free technical support period has lapsed and the software has been used very little, or not at all.

A few publishers provide unlimited telephone support to end users. Such a policy eases the pressure to commence operations quickly and is also valuable in situations with high turnover and the probable need for ongoing training.

A second important element of support, often overlooked, is the publisher's policy with respect to software corrections and upgrades. Accounting software is complex. Software bugs may surface months, even years, after the product is introduced. Problems with new versions of general use software, such as a new version of a popular spreadsheet or word processor, are given quite a bit of publicity. Similar problems arise with accounting software but usually are known to a limited circle. Publishers react in different ways as these problems surface. Some publishers distribute diskettes with program corrections. The correction diskettes may be sent to end users or may be sent to retailers with the expectation that the retailers will send copies to their customers. Some publishers wait for users to call in with problems before providing correction routines.

There is no easy way to determine whether a particular software package is error-free and how responsible the publisher is about corrections. A helpful technique is to check with end users who have used the specific version for six months or more. If a brand-new untested product is very appealing, the buyer should inquire about the publisher's policy on corrections.

What is the difference between a correction and an upgrade? The distinction is not clear. Generally, an upgrade increases the capacity or functionality of the software. An enhancement might increase the number of departments handled by the software or change from a single state to a multistate payroll. It might add additional fields to the customer master file or change capability from a single warehouse to multiple warehouses.

Many publishers bring out upgrades every year. These upgrades are offered to users at special prices. In some cases, the price of the support service includes upgrades. Users who do not purchase upgrades may find in time that the publishers will no longer support outdated versions of their software.

Software changes can also be required by government regulations. Payroll deduction tables must be changed to comply with government regulations. Subroutines for printing government forms, such as tax and 1099 forms, must be changed whenever the government form is altered. The method for processing these changes varies. Some software requires the user to key in the tax tables, or to modify printing locations on forms. Since this work can be tedious, many users purchase update programs provided by the publisher.

Another publisher support service is the distribution of user bulletins containing operating tips and responses to user questions and problems. Some publishers even go further and have organized user groups that meet periodically for information exchange.

Many publishers maintain lists of installers who have been qualified by them to offer services on site. The qualification procedures generally are limited to a few days training on the software.

This array of support services—help on the telephone, software corrections and upgrades, user bulletins and meetings—is offered and priced in many different ways. Some publishers provide no direct support of any kind. Others provide unlimited telephone support including software corrections and minor enhancements. Some charge separately for each type of support service. The charge may begin at once, or after a stated period of time. It may be a fixed sum for a stated period of time or may be charged at an hourly rate.

The importance of these services depends on the sophistication and experience of the user. A novice must consider the value very carefully before selecting a software publisher, and in most cases should stay away from any product that is only supported through dealers, unless a qualified consultant is in the picture. More knowledgable users usually require very little telephone support and should concentrate on determining whether the software is well "seasoned" and will perform with little error.

Finally, one must consider the cost of any special program modifications, if required. Publishers vary in their approach to custom modifications. At one extreme are publishers who will not permit any modifications. Another group provides modifications at additional cost. Some publishers provide source code to programming groups that offer a modification service. These organizations even publish catalogues of the modifications that they offer for sale. Many publishers will not support products that have been modified by third parties.

Anyone considering a custom modification should determine what support will be provided if software upgrades are not compatible with the modification.

In sum, meaningful comparisons of software costs require an evaluation of many cost elements. These elements include

- [ ] The total cost of all modules that must be purchased to provide comparable functions
- [ ] The lower value of superceded versions of the same product
- [ ] The cost of modifications
- [ ] The cost of network software
- [ ] An evaluation of support services.

However, just to put everything in perspective, in the micro world, software costs are usually the lowest component of the cost picture.

HARDWARE COST

The selection of hardware depends upon

- [ ] The requirements of the software
- [ ] The work load, such as size of files and transaction volume
- [ ] User needs in terms of number of connected workstations and other devices.

The hardware buyer has many options to consider:

- [ ] How much internal memory (RAM) is required to run the software?
- [ ] What kind of computer is needed?
- [ ] Should a hard disk be purchased? If so, how large a disk is necessary?
- [ ] What kind of printer is needed? Should a narrow or a wide printer be used?
- [ ] What provision should be made for backup?
- [ ] If a network is planned, what kind of wires are needed to connect the workstations? How rigid or flexible should be the physical wiring?
- [ ] Where should all of this equipment be located? Are there any technical restrictions with respect to locating equipment because of the need for ventilation, the distance between units, or other factors?
- [ ] Are any other purchases required such as furniture, additional electrical connections, and so on?
- [ ] What is the best resource for obtaining all of this equipment?
- [ ] What arrangements should be made for installation and maintenance?

As mentioned in a previous chapter, the cost of computer memory, both internal (RAM) memory and file memory, has plummeted in the past few years. Years ago, when memory costs were high, programmers devoted a great deal of effort to making their programs as compact as possible in order to save memory space. Now that memory costs have dropped precipitously, a reverse trend is in effect. The newer micro programs, with enhanced functions, require more internal memory and file memory than ever before. Some network version accounting programs require internal memory of 640K, a number unheard of just a few years ago. In general, programs operating under the DOS operating system, require between 256K and 512K, depending on the software selected. (Keep in mind that the biggest RAM hogs are spreadsheets such as Lotus and Excel. A user planning to run spreadsheets on the same computer as accounting software will determine his or her RAM requirements from the spreadsheet software, not from accounting.) If the software selected requires more RAM than the installed amount, additional internal memory must be purchased. Operating System 2 (OS2) is too new to provide any meaningful indication of RAM requirements, although OS2 itself requires much more RAM than does DOS. Some accounting software can function with different microprocessors; others cannot.

There is some confusion in differentiating between computer types and computer brands. A computer type is defined by the processor chip (usually referred to as the central processing unit, or CPU) that is the heart of the computer. These chips have names such as 8088 and 80286 and are rated in clock speeds measured in megahertz (MHz). The higher the clock speed, the faster the operation of the microprocessor. Computers that are "PC compatible" use a different set of microprocessors than do Macintosh computers, and the programs are not interchangeable.

The first microcomputer to have a serious impact on small business used a computer processor chip that ran at a speed considered quite slow today. Since that time, newer chips have been introduced, each one faster than its predecessor. The newer chips offer expanded functions with greater computer power and functionality. However, there is a time lag between the introduction of a new computer chip and the availability of computers and programs that can take advantage of the enhanced processor capability.

Computers with faster processor chips cost more than the slower variety. In most situations, the additional cost can be justified by the increased operating speed and other features provided by the newer hardware. If the software provides a choice in the type of computer, the buyer should make certain to view a demonstration on the same hardware that he or she plans to purchase. When working with the same software, there usually is a noticeable difference in operating speed between slow and fast microprocessors. The slower operation shows up in sluggish responses to keyboard entries, annoying delays for screen changes, and long waits during a sorting process.

Unless transaction volumes are very small, one should avoid computers with slow cycle times, such as the IBM PC and the older version of the IBM XT that used the 8088 microprocessor. PC-based accounting applications should be run on computers that operate at 8 MHz or faster (they go as high as 33 MHz). As of this writing, Apple-based accounting programs are limited to two microprocessors that are used in Macintosh computers: the 7.83-MHz MC68000 (in the Macintosh Plus and the Macintosh SE) and the 15.7-MHz 68020 (available in the Macintosh II).

However, the tricky part is the fact that the speed of the processor chip does not necessarily provide a good indication of the operating speed of the system. The reason is that the processor must work with other components such as disk drives and printers. In many applications such as accounting programs, the processor must wait while information is being passed back and forth between these units. If budgets are tight it may be preferable to invest in a fast printer and disk drive than in a fast microprocessor.

New operating systems, such as OS/2, allow the processor to jump to another program instead of waiting to get back control and continue processing. This capability is called multiprocessing. Few accounting programs take advantage of this capability.

Disk drive speeds are rated in milliseconds (ms) of average access time. The higher the average access time, the slower the disk. Disk speeds available today range from about 80 ms to less than 20 ms.

There are some who still believe that one can operate accounting software for a small business on diskettes. However, even if the software can run on diskettes, most people find that the act of constant shuffling, filing, and labeling is more trouble than the cost of a hard disk. Additionally, the erroneous choice or labeling of a diskette can create unnecessary problems.

File sizes are also increasing. In 1983 virtually all micro accounting programs functioned with diskettes. Most of the programs and enhancements released since that time that offer greater capacity and increased functions require hard disks. As more functions are added, the hard disk sizes required by the software have also increased. The first micro hard disks boasted of 10 million bytes (megs) of storage. Today, one can purchase disks with more than ten times that capacity. Many accounting software packages, if installed with a number of modules, require more than ten megs of storage just for the program. (The sizing exercises discussed in Chapter 5 are important for determining the required disk capacity.)

Purchasing a hard disk that is too small for the job can result in a great deal of trouble, trouble that may not show up until many months after the software has been installed and data files have grown with use. With today's low prices for hard disks, very few accounting applications are run on floppies. The size of the hard disk depends on file requirements. Most PC accounting applications use 20–40-meg hard disks. Some accounting software handles files on multiple hard disks.

There always are exceptions. One that comes to mind is a bookkeeping service that keeps records for many small businesses. Such a service might find it easier to keep the data files for each business on a separate diskette so that updates can be performed at different workstations without the complexity of a network.

The choice of a printer will also affect acquisition costs. Three types of printers are in general use, each with unique capabilities and qualifications.

Dot matrix printers are the preferable choice for accounting software because they function faster than other printers, can create multiple copies, and can print on wider paper. While dot matrix printers cannot duplicate the quality of daisy wheel printers or lasers (to be discussed), the newer models provide a quality that is generally acceptable for business correspondence. Since accounting work requires a great deal of printed output, including the printing of business documents such as checks, invoices, and statements, as well as the printing of journals, reports, and financial statements, fast printing generally is preferable to the slightly improved quality of the other types of printers.

Dot matrix printers come in two sizes, narrow and wide. The narrow printers work with letter-size paper (paper that is 8.5 inches wide); wide printers work with 14-inch paper. An important feature of these printers is their ability to use a number of type sizes, ranging from 16.6 to 5 characters per inch. Many of the older accounting software packages confined printing to 80 characters per row, the same number of characters displayed by the computer monitor; 80 characters is also the maximum number of characters that can be printed by a narrow printer at standard pitch (10 characters per inch). Of course this limits the amount of information provided per line. Newer software prints some reports with 132 characters per row, the number of characters that can be printed by a wide printer at standard pitch. These reports can be printed on the narrow printer by choosing a smaller type size. Some accounting software provides an optional switch between small and large type depending upon the width of the report. The narrower paper width facilitates the filing and copying of material and is preferable, provided the smaller type does not provide any visual discomfort and one does not require reports with more than approximately 135 characters per line. Wide printers are more likely to be used for spreadsheet work than for accounting. One should view reports printed by a number of printers and inquire about ease of use (such as inserting new paper, using single sheets, and changing ribbons) before deciding which one to purchase.

Older dot matrix printers used nine wires to form each character, and were called 9-pin printers. A major improvement in the quality of dot matrix printing has been the introduction of 24-pin printers that create a better looking image without sacrificing speed. The 9-pin variety is still preferable for heavy-duty work and for printing multiple-ply forms. Few printers can print more than five clear copies.

Paper handling is still a bit clumsy on these printers. It usually takes a bit of doing to learn how to insert fanfold paper so that it will not jam in the printer. Changing forms can be clumsy and time consuming. Some operators prefer to use separate printers for handling routine forms such as sales invoices. The use of expensive forms such as letterheads can be made easier with printers allowing the feed of single sheets.

Until recently, **daisy wheel printers** were used for high-quality images, such as for the printing of correspondence and presentations. Their most significant limitation was their speed, since they ran much more slowly than dot matrix printers and were not suitable for volume printing. Daisy wheel printers are being replaced by **laser printers**, which offer much greater flexibility in graphic design as well as faster speed and quieter operation. Laser printers involve more complexity in setting up print controls. Accounting software publishers are slowly introducing these controls, but many accounting software products do not provide this capability. Easy use of laser printers is found most frequently with software programs for word processing and desktop publishing. Laser printers are limited to printing on narrow (8.5 inch) paper.

Printers come with varying speeds. The speed of dot matrix printers is rated in characters per second (cps). These printers vary their speed with the type of printing. Rated speeds for the fastest printing range from 100 to 800 cps. This slows down to a range of 16 to 96 cps for quality printing. Daisy wheel printers, by way of contrast, generally go no faster than 60 cps. The speeds of laser printers are rated in pages per minute (ppm). Laser printers for microcomputers range in speed from 5 to 18 ppm.

Some printers are better at creating copies in multiple plies than are others. If the user needs to print forms of more than four plies, test copies should be made before selecting an appropriate printer.

Thought must be given to the best method for backup. The first PCs offered little more than the DOS commands required to back up files on floppy disks. This type of backup proved to be very cumbersome because large files required a lot of disk handling. The procedure was slow and cumbersome, and many backups were done improperly or not at all. Today, users have a number of choices in the selection of the backup device, backup media, and backup software.

The need for file backup leads to additional hardware considerations. Many different backup devices are available with a wide range in cost, ease of use, and speed. Backups take time. A poorly conceived backup system can eat into production time, discourage backups, or both. Before deciding on backup hardware, the buyer should inquire about its reliability, capacity, speed, and ease of use.

The backup media can be diskettes, tape cartridges, and/or tapes. Diskette storage capacities range from 0.360 to 1.4 megabytes. Cartridges can store as much as 40 megabytes. Magnetic tape offers the greatest storage capacity.

At one end of the spectrum is a user with small files who spends less than a quarter of his or her time at the computer. Backup on floppy disks would probably be satisfactory for such a user. As the number and size of the files gets larger, the required number of floppy disks will increase until the work of juggling many disks on a daily basis becomes clumsy and time consuming. If diskette backup is feasible, programs are on the market that have been designed to simplify and speed the process.

Special backup devices are available that use cartridges or magnetic tape and come with their own backup software. Cartridge devices can be placed inside the computer and look something like a disk drive. Some backup devices come in boxes that sit outside the computer.

As discussed in the previous chapter, networking adds an entire new layer of hardware, software, and cabling costs. There are significant differences in installation cost between one type of network and another. Existing and planned future needs will affect the network choice and cost.

Finally there is a miscellaneous group of items to purchase: furniture, electrical items, and supplies. A great deal has been written about ergonomics, about the importance of workplace design for optimizing human productivity. Consideration should be given to using properly designed workstations. Desk heights should be about the same as the heights used for typing—about 26 inches (regular desks are 3–4 inches higher). Monitors should be placed so that they can be viewed without neck strain or glare. Properly designed printer stands facilitate printer use and reduce paper jams.

Some thought should be given to problems that can arise with respect to power supply. Frequently, devices are needed that monitor the power supply. Computers are very sensitive to changes in the power supply. A sudden burst of voltage, so short in duration that a human might not notice it, can burn out the system. *Varbusiness* magazine reported in December 1987 that power surges caused almost 250,000 PC losses in the prior year. A brief termination of power, even for an instant, also poses a threat because it can wipe out all data in RAM and cause program and file confusion. A number of electronic devices address these problems. The cheapest units, called surge protectors, guard against sudden voltage increases such as those caused by electrical storms. More expensive devices, using batteries, provide enough power for users to terminate operations in an orderly fashion when electrical service is interrupted.

Some optional devices facilitate the use of printers. People using a number of printers may find life easier with a switch box for directing work to a selected printer. Buffers allow printing work to be queued and free up computers for other work.

Users must not forget supplies that are critical to the operation, such as portable storage media (diskettes, cartridges, and magnetic tape), computer paper, and printer ribbons.

If all of this equipment will be used in business operations, what is to be done if something goes wrong after the end of the guaranty period? Some thought must be given to hardware maintenance services. Many companies offer such services. Some companies have associations with computer retailers. Others are independent. Services are sold on a "walk-in" or "on-site" basis.

A fractured marketplace exists for purchasing all of this material. Potential purchasers have a choice of

☐ mail-order houses
☐ discount retailers
☐ specialized sales and service organizations
☐ full service retailers.

Mail-order selling has become an accepted practice in the computer world, despite a few bad suppliers that show up now and again. A reputable mail-order company will offer good customer service including telephone technical help. Computer clubs are good resources for obtaining the names of such organizations. Mail order addresses the needs of people who are comfortable working with hardware and software. It is not a good resource for beginners who require assistance in getting started.

Discount retailers are available in large cities and are somewhat akin to mail-order houses in price and service. Generally they are not a good resource for help and advice.

Many companies offer specialized computer services. They may focus on one specialty, such as networking or vertical software designed for a particular industry. Their services may range through consulting, programming, and product sales all the way to a complete turnkey package of hardware and software. These types of organizations aim to provide the kind of in-depth service and specialized product that is not offered by retailers.

Full-service retailers are the most visible af all computer resources. Many such retailers test equipment before delivery and provide installation at the customer site. Good retailers recognize that the field of computers covers a body of knowledge and range of products that cannot be addressed by one organization. Many full-service retailers maintain a network of independent specialists who are called in for help when required. A major service provided by full-service retailers is the availability of financing for both hardware and software.

REPRESENTATIVE PRICES

Now, how much should all of this come to? The following takes a look at some typical numbers (as of June 1988).

Software Price Ranges

There is a wide spread in the prices of accounting software offered for general business applications. Low end products that incorporate a number of modules in one package range from $60 to $300. The prices of the most popular programs designed for the serious business user range from $600 to $1,000 per module, although some products go even higher. There may be an additional cost for a system manager that, for a single user, may add another $100 to $300. Assuming most single users require four accounting modules, accounting software acquisition costs will probably range from $2,500 to $4,000. This price difference is justified by higher performance in many attributes including capacity, functionality, networking, and control.

Modules for network management of the accounting software can add another $500 to $750. And the network software itself will add another $600 to $2,000, depending on the size of the network. The network accounting software acquisition costs will probably range from $4,000 to $5,500.

Higher prices will be encountered for many vertical packages that are designed for specific industries and applications.

Additional sums must be expended for the operating system software (about $300). Many users find it helpful to purchase utilities that facilitate backup and help in working with hard disk files. These utilities run about $100 each.

Many situations call for higher software costs. Users may require more than four modules, or may need specialized software that commands higher prices. Modification, if required, also add to software costs.

Hardware Price Ranges

In the PC world, the choice is between floppy disk computers (slow speed), 286 microchip computers (medium speed), and 386 microchip computers (high speed). Floppy disk computers with two diskette drives and 256K RAM are available for $700 to $1,200. These computers are really limited in use to running inexpensive accounting software for a very small business with low transaction volumes and small files. The 286-based machines with a 20–30 meg hard disk, one floppy disk drive, 256–512K RAM, and a monitor run from $1,700 to $3,000. The fast 386 machines start at about $3,500 and can run considerably higher.

In the Apple world, the choice is between the Macintosh SE (medium speed) and the Macintosh II (fast). The SE sells for about $2,000 (floppy disk) or $2,500 to $4,000, depending on the size of the hard disk. The Macintosh II ranges from $5,000 to $6,000.

Bear in mind that every computer comes with a number of options that affect price, such as choices of the microprocessor chip, size of random access memory, type of diskette drive, and the size and speed of the hard disk drive.

Network servers should be fast devices with large hard disk memories and tend to run about $6,000.

Backup devices run about $500.

Dot matrix printers range from about $400 to $1,200, depending upon width and speed. Laser printers start at about $1,800.

Networking adds about $1,000 per workstation for hardware and cabling.

Computer furniture (a computer desk and printer stand) can run from $300 to $500.

Overall Price Ranges

Because requirements vary from one user to the next, the total projected costs can be only a rough estimate.

For purposes of discussion, three typical situations will be considered here. Situation one is a small home operation with low transaction volumes and very simple requirements. Situation two represents a fairly substantial business that requires a single workstation. Situation three applies to an operation requiring a network of three workstations.

	SITUATION		
ACQUISITIONS	**One**	**Two**	**Three***
Software			
Programs	$300–450	$3,000–4,400	$3,500–5,000
Network			600–2,000
Hardware			
Computer(s)	1,000–1,400	1,700–4,000	5,100–12,000
Backup		0–500	500
Server (if required)			4,000–6,000
Network Interface Boards			600–1,000
Printer	350–500	350–1,800	350–1,800
Furniture	0	350–500	350–500
Other Costs			
Supplies	100	100	100–200
Cabling			500–1,500
Totals	$1,750–2,450	$5,500–11,300	$15,600–30,500

*Network requirements vary so much that cost estimates, at best, are subject to wide variation.

In sum, acquisition costs (as of June 1988) will probably vary from less than $2,000 for a very small application to about $30,000 for a three-station network that requires a server and fast components.

Users should keep in mind that leasing arrangements are offered by most vendors. Leasing, although costlier than outright purchase, can plug a big hole in cash flow and can cover both hardware and software.

Annual maintenance charges for software varies with the publisher and number of modules. Some publishers place a maximum fee of $750. Annual hardware maintenance runs about 15% of the purchase price.

SUMMARY

This chapter has discussed acquisition costs, one of three important cost factors that affect the economics of computerized accounting. A complete system requires the purchase of software and hardware. Comparative software pricing is a challenge. There is confusion in names and versions. Products vary in capacity and functionality, support, and other factors that will be discussed in subsequent chapters. While accounting software usually represents the bulk of software costs, other software for the operating system, utilities, and networking must also be acquired.

The choice of hardware, and its cost, depends upon the software, the work load, and network requirements. Most PC-oriented software will function with a wide range of computers. Users must make many decisions that affect cost, ease of operation, and speed. Apple-oriented software leaves a much more limited hardware choice to the user.

Networking adds both software and hardware costs.

Both hardware and software can be obtained from a variety of sources that vary in price and support.

A SUPPLEMENTARY HARDWARE REVIEW FOR BEGINNERS

The following discussion is designed to help readers who are new to computers and may have difficulty following the discussion about all the hardware choices that might come their way.

A microcomputer is a group of electronic components that are put together to form a computer system. Some of these components are put together at the factory. Others are assembled by the retailer or the user. End users can select, add, and change many of these components.

A minimum computer system requires a

- ☐ Motherboard
- ☐ Diskette drive and control board
- ☐ Monitor and control board
- ☐ Printer.

Most business applications also require a

- ☐ Hard disk and control board
- ☐ Backup device (e.g., cartridge drive).

Additional hardware that may be required includes

- ☐ Additional memory
- ☐ Modem
- ☐ Network interface card
- ☐ Print buffer
- ☐ Other hardware that facilitates the operation.

Each of these system elements is offered with a range of choices.

The **motherboard** is a metal box that contains the cpu chip, random access memory, expansion slots, and a power supply. The box also includes space for inserting drives for diskettes, disks, and cartridges.

The cpu chip determines the operating speed of the computer. Today they range in speed from 4.3 to 33 MHz. The cpu chip includes a data bus that determines the number of channels available for transferring information. More channels mean faster speed and programming capability. Today's microcomputers provide either 8, 16, or 32 channels.

The amount of random access memory (RAM) that comes with the motherboard varies. Most PCs come 640K, the maximum amount of RAM that can be addressed by the DOS operating system. PCs that come with smaller RAM can be upgraded by the addition of memory chips or a memory board.

Every device connected with the computer requires electronic circuitry in the computer and a hub for attaching wires. These circuits are provided on boards that fit into expansion slots on the motherboard. Circuit boards are available for other functions, such as increasing RAM and providing hard disk and other functions. The greater the number of slots, the larger the number of devices that can be incorporated into the system.

The power supply services the motherboard and the circuit boards, as well as the diskette and disk drives. The power supply includes a cooling fan and is the noisy component of the computer. On occasion, larger power supplies than the ones that come with the motherboard are required, particularly when many devices are added to the system.

Some motherboards are sold with helpful devices such as clock/calendars, additional hubs for connecting external hardware, and switchable processing speeds.

In sum, motherboards vary in the microprocessor chip, the amount of RAM, the number of expansion slots, and the size of the power supply.

Diskette drives have been getting smaller even though the diskettes they work with have increased their storage capacities. The first diskettes were 8 inches in diameter. Today, diskette drives for PCs come in two sizes, one for 5.25-inch diskettes, the other for 3.5-inch diskettes. At one time there were many varieties of 5.25-inch diskettes. This has narrowed down to the double density variety that has a storage capacity of about 360KB and the high density variety that stores about 1,200KB. The high density variety can read from and write on both double density and high density diskettes. However, the files they create on double density diskettes may not be readible by other drives. Older diskette drives took up twice the space of the current breed of half-height drives.

The 3.5-inch diskettes are the newest size. Drives come with either one or two read-write heads. The variety with one read-write head works with one side of the diskette and has a storage capacity of about 720KB. The two-head variety has double this capacity.

Monitors offer another range of choices. Most users of business software find that the monochrome monitor, which is the cheapest, is quite satisfactory. People who like to work with color have a choice of monitors running from the cheapest, the CGA (the earliest type with the smallest color palette and crude type), through the EGA to the VGA. Each type of monitor requires a different control board and different driver software. Those most interested in color should check to determine whether the software that they select can take advantage of the capability of the color monitor they would like to use. Many accounting software products are limited in their provision for color.

The different varieties of **printers** that are on the market, and their ranges of speed, have already been discussed. Most PC users find that a wide dot-matrix printer with a speed between 200 and 300 cps satisfies most of their requirements. The first such printers used nine pins to form the image. A later refinement uses more pins with a resulting finer image. Before selecting a printer, the user should determine whether the accounting software provides the instructions (drivers) for the printer.

Some of these printers are a nuisance when it comes to changing paper and forms. Users who require a lot of form printing, such as the printing of sales invoices or checks, often purchase a second narrow printer for this purpose.

Laser printers that can produce a finer print are used more for word processing applications than for accounting. Accounting software publishers are just beginning to include drivers for laser printers with their software.

Hard disks are made in a wide range of sizes and speeds and come in three varieties. The most popular is the fixed hard disk that occupies about the same space as a diskette drive. One alternative is the hardcard, a computer board that acts like a hard disk. Another variety is the removable hard disk, which can be used for backup as well as for regular storage purposes. Most accounting software requires a hard drive.

Backup devices are useful when data files are so large that backup on diskettes, even those with large capacity, becomes a nuisance. Cartridges are the most popular devices and go as high as 40 megabytes in capacity. Tape drives are also available. A new storage technology in the form of a WORM (write once, read many times) has come on the market; it combines compact size with very large storage capabilities. However, its use in the accounting software arena is limited because of current high prices and software limitations.

10

Installation Costs

INTRODUCTION

Chapter 9 presented a detailed discussion of the first of the three major elements of cost associated with accounting software: acquisition costs. It explained the difficulties involved in comparing costs among software products, even among different versions of the same product, and discussed hidden costs, particularly differences in product support. The chapter also explored the relationship between software requirements and hardware costs and described the various hardware devices that must be acquired for computer operations.

This chapter will cover the second and more complex cost element: installation costs. These costs are often buried in payroll and office overhead expenses, but they also include out-of-pocket disbursements for professional fees and temporary help. Many activities are brought into play during the installation process:

☐ Management decisions independent of software

☐ Management decisions based on software

☐ Hardware installation

☐ Software installation

☐ Form design and purchase

☐ Training

- ☐ Preparing master files
- ☐ Setting up master files
- ☐ Setting up reports
- ☐ Parallel operation
- ☐ Preparing written procedures

MANAGEMENT DECISIONS INDEPENDENT OF SOFTWARE

Some of the most elusive and yet vital elements in the successful installation of accounting software are the many decisions that should be made by management. Some of these decisions are independent of the specific software that will be installed. The very first one (discussed in Chapter 4) is the decision to install computer-based accounting software. Another (discussed in Chapters 6, 7, and 8) is the determination of minimum software requirements in terms of capacity, functionality, integration, and networking. During the software search, management must pay attention to other decisions:

1. How many people should be designated to learn and operate the system?

   At least two people should be able to work each phase of the software so that operations can continue with minimum disruption in case of absence or separation. The total number of people to be trained will depend upon the number of workstations and the manner in which the work is divided among employees.

   The introduction of computers may provide a good opportunity to restudy the organization structure. Perhaps existing lines of authority and responsibility should be changed. Perhaps the entire information management function requires the supervision of a top officer. Perhaps work assignments and responsibilities should be changed to provide better division of duties.

2. Can the preceding personnel requirements be fulfilled internally, or is it necessary to go outside the organization?

   The assignment of computer responsibilities is an important management function and involves a number of organization, personnel, and control considerations. Most managers assume that existing personnel will take over the computer functions associated with their present tasks. This assumption can be troublesome. Some office personnel look forward to learning computers; others fear it. If the fear is unrecognized it can express itself in slow or unsuccessful training. People with poor digital dexterity often have difficulty working computer keyboards.

Internal control considerations also affect personnel decisions. The operations manager must be someone who is trustworthy and responsible. Careless control of passwords can lead to unpleasant situations. Loss of passwords can bring operations to a halt. The presence of computer personnel who are related or are close personal friends might raise questions about the adequacy of internal control.

One person must be given the responsibility of operations manager. At a minimum, this person will control passwords, check unused capacity, and work with maintenance people whenever there are hardware problems.

The successful assignment of personnel to computer training and responsibility requires the concern and attention of top management.

3. How is the computer installation to be related to the perceptions and attitudes of the work force?

People often feel threatened when they learn that a computer installation is contemplated, particularly if they hear this first through the grapevine. Management must determine how computer plans are to be communicated to its organization and set policy with regards to the personnel changes and work pressures that will follow. A cooperative work force is an important asset during the stressful period of installation.

4. What work environment is required, and where should this environment be provided?

The proper placement of computer facilities depends upon both electronic and human considerations. Electronic considerations are easier to deal with. There are specific limits to the distance that wires can be run between computers, so the placement of hardware (computers, terminals, and printers) must conform to these limitations. Hardware problems can arise if electrical devices and wires are placed too close together to cause interference.

Humans are more flexible. They do not stop working right away if conditions are not right. Instead, they slow down, make errors, call in sick, or complain. Such problems can be minimized if attention is paid to three components of the work environment:

☐   Physical stress

☐   Glare

☐   Noise

Steady computer work involves different stress than does manual record keeping. Instead of bending over a desk, the computer operator sits facing a keyboard and monitor. This difference in posture requires a comfortable chair, a keyboard about the same height as a typewriter (usually 26 inches from the floor), a well-designed work space for laying out documents and reports, and storage for work and reference material. When space is limited, the computer can be placed on a floor stand under the desk.

The monitor should be placed so that continuous viewing does not place a strain on the back of the neck. The placement of windows, illumination, and monitor all affect the degree of glare and eyestrain. Special screens are available that can be placed over the monitor to cut down on glare.

Hardware can be noisy. Computer cooling fans whir, and printers, particularly the dot matrix variety, make a rather disturbing whiny sound. Sound absorption devices, running from a simple foam rubber pad under the printer to an acoustic enclosure, may be required to bring down the level of disturbing noise.

If resources, particularly printers, are to be shared, these devices should be located so that they are close to users. But there is more to the workplace; the need for privacy. Confidential work must be located so that the monitor screen and source materials are hidden from passersby. Access to confidential printers and files must be restricted.

Personnel and workstation planning require management attention as part of the basic set of management decisions.

5. What is the best installation timetable?

There are many timing factors to consider. A cyclical business might find it best to concentrate installation effort at a time of low activity because personnel have more time for training and file conversion. Voluminous files, such as receivable or inventory records, are installed most easily at a time when they contain the fewest transactions. There may be good reasons to start general ledgers at the beginning of a fiscal year or to start payroll at the beginning of the calendar year. Most users prefer to start with one module and introduce additional modules over a period of time. If many people require training, it may not be practical to assign all persons to training simultaneously. Training must be scheduled so that there is a minimum time gap between the completion of training and the opportunity to apply the skills that have been learned.

6. Are the skills necessary for directing the installation available in the organization, or should people outside the organization be engaged?

The task of searching for suitable software can be time consuming and frustrating. A consultant can be most helpful in reducing the search time and in pointing out the strengths and weaknesses of competitive products. The consultant can also guide management with respect to the decisions that will obtain the most benefit from the selected software.

The challenge for management is to find qualified outside personnel. Most organizations serving the accounting software industry are familiar with very few accounting software products. Consultants should have a broad business and software perspective and be able to provide an informed professional evaluation of different products that appear to provide a solution for management.

Unlike personnel productivity software, such as word processors and spreadsheets, very little formal classroom training is provided for accounting software. Instead, many accounting software publishers and computer retailers maintain lists of people who offer installation and training services. Some specialists provide training services on the software that they sell. Others offer a turnkey package that includes hardware, software, and training.

The basic installation considerations of defining personnel requirements, communicating management plans to employees, designing the physical workplace, timing the installation, and evaluating the possibility of engaging outside consultants demand a great deal of management time and attention. These considerations must not be treated lightly. Management must be prepared to spend sufficient time on these matters in order to insure success.

MANAGEMENT DECISIONS BASED ON SOFTWARE

Once accounting software has been selected, another set of decisions must be considered:

1. What should be the responses to performance options provided by the software?

    Many accounting software publishers include a number of options in their software. These options are designed to meet the varying requirements of different users. Unfortunately, very few manuals clearly explain the options and their effects on the functions of the software. The option screens usually appear early in the process of software installation. Choices must be made before the software installation can proceed. In some cases, the choices cannot be changed without a great deal of difficulty.

One possible choice relates to the organization. These queries ask whether records and reports should be kept by department, branch, or profit center. Unless an accountant is consulted, the user may not clearly understand the significance of this query. The fact that an organization functioned in the past without department or cost center reporting may not mean that such practice should continue. Decisions about reporting belong with management.

Another possible set of questions relates to record storage. These questions are designed to use disk space in an efficient manner. Responses require a balance between information needs and considerations of disk size. The choice usually is not as clear as this. Instead, the software might ask a question such as, "Should sales history be maintained?" A wrong answer might result in the loss of significant data.

Some questions affect the functions of the system. Does the user wish to compute sales commissions at the time of invoicing or when cash is received from the customer? Should accounts receivable aging be based on invoice date or due date? Responses to these questions should be provided by accounting or financial personnel.

Others questions relate to matters of control. Should the software or the user assign invoice or credit numbers? Are sequence numbers required on journals? Must journals be printed after posting? Should journals be printed at the time that postings are made to the general ledger? These questions are best answered in consultation with accountants and others concerned with internal control.

The user is usually not prepared for these questions. Installation of the software often is performed by personnel who are not well enough informed or are not in the position to provide proper responses. However, the software insists upon answers before the installation can proceed. In an effort to get started, answers may be provided without careful thought. Frequently, a lot of work must be repeated when it is discovered that poor choices were made.

This annoying and frequently wasteful condition can be avoided if management determines prior to installation exactly what options, if any, are provided by the software and what the proper responses should be. It is advisable to carefully review the screens that must be completed in order to set up each software module. These screens carry such names as "Setup" or "Customization" and usually ask a lot of the basic questions. The problem with these queries is that they often mix a number of concepts that can be confusing to the uneducated user.

2. What coding schemes should be used?

Give a lot of thought to coding structure. Codes must be provided for all accounts—general ledger, customer, vendor, and inventory. Codes are used by the computer to locate records and to sort and combine information into totals. The coding scheme should take into account other fields that might be provided for purposes of selecting and sorting, such as customer class or type.

The code that is selected will determine how easily records can be found when information is requested and also how information will be presented on reports. Codes permeate the entire organization because they are required for almost every paperwork operation. They affect operations in the warehouse, in manufacturing, and in the office. They must be chosen with care. General ledger account codes usually are assigned in a sequence that conforms to the presentation of financial statements. Customer and vendor account numbers are frequently assigned in alphabetical sequence. Developing a good coding scheme for inventory can be a challenge. The tendency is to try to develop a rational code—that is, a code that signifies the nature of the item, such as its composition, shape, dimension, and assembly level. An elaborate coding scheme can be troublesome. Long codes are hard to remember. Even though gaps are usually provided for new accounts, in time it may become impossible to keep all codes in the intended sequence, and the coding sequence then becomes distorted.

The organization might already be using a coding scheme, although this scheme might not conform to the requirements of the new software or might limit the reports that can be produced by the system. The question of whether to change from an existing code to a new one can be very troublesome.

Some software simplifies the search for code numbers by providing "pop-up windows" that permit the user to make a selection from the list shown in the window. Another device is the use of function keys to display information in code number sequence.

The art of devising a good coding scheme that balances the need for simplicity with functional usefulness takes time and thought. A lot of effort must be invested in the coding scheme once it has been selected. Code numbers must be assigned to every master record and then keyed into the computer. These codes will be used for reference purposes on labels, reports, and lists. In time, people become familiar with the codes and remember them without lookup. The correction of a poor coding scheme can be very vexing.

3. What manual functions and procedures should be adopted or changed in connection with computer operations?

The installation of accounting software usually involves much more than replacing manual operations with a computer. Source documents may require redesign so that information can be easily entered on the keyboard. Special procedures may be required to handle functions that cannot be processed by the software, such as exceptional situations that occur infrequently. Organization changes may require a change in work flow. Plans should be made regarding the printing, distribution, and filing of the voluminous reports that can be generated by computers.

Expect many revisions to be tried and tested before new procedures are working smoothly. Document procedures as much as possible and make certain that all involved personnel understand what they are expected to do. Major causes of installation problems are misunderstandings about the new procedures. There is an ongoing need for clear communication on this subject, a need that is rarely fulfilled.

4. What system of internal control should be used?

Management has the responsibility of understanding the internal control environment associated with computerized accounting. Controls provided by the software must be properly applied. Additional controls are required outside of the software. (This important matter is discussed further in Chapter 12.)

In summary, once specific software has been selected, management should provide guidance regarding (1) the options provided by the software, (2) coding schemes, (3) changes required in manual operations, and (4) internal control.

HARDWARE INSTALLATION

The physical installation of the hardware, which involves setting everything in place, wiring components, and testing performance, can run from a painless experience to extreme frustration. Hard disk installations require that the disk be partitioned and set up with the appropriate operating system. Some retailers will bench-test hardware before delivery, set up the hard disk, and provide site installation. (Extra charges might be made for these services.) Those who purchase from discounters or mail-order houses may face a more trying experience. Printers and disk drives are the most frequent sources of trouble. A rule of thumb is that most hardware requires a "burn in" period of about 90 days for equipment problems to show up.

Additional installation work is required when computers are to be wired together in a network. (The steps required for this were briefly discussed in

Chapter 7.) The work of running the cables, making the connections, installing the network software, and testing the system should be performed by qualified personnel.

Users, particularly those who are new to the computer world, require some time to learn how to work with the hardware, particularly when dealing with tricky printer requirements for setting up paper feeds amd changing ribbons.

SOFTWARE INSTALLATION

The physical software installation is usually a two-step operation:

- ☐ The transference of the software from the original diskettes to working copies or to a hard disk
- ☐ The setting up of the drivers for printers and monitors.

The software installation might be included in the purchase price or might be subject to an additional charge.

The time required just to copy the software depends upon the number of diskettes involved, the speed of the computer, and the nature of the software program. It can run from as little as 15 minutes to 3 hours or more. Most accounting software provides the drivers for popular brands of monitors and printers. (But watch out for offbeat devices.) Before purchasing such equipment, obtain assurance that it will run with your software. Otherwise the money saved in the equipment purchase can be more than offset by the cost of getting it to work with the software.

Accounting software usually includes an installation program that guides the user through the two steps just mentioned. Special screens are provided for setting up the drivers for unusual monitors and printers. These screens usually require the attention of someone with a technical background.

Some software publishers add to installation headaches by their copy protection schemes. One of these schemes requires that one of the original diskettes be placed in the diskette drive before the software will function. Another one limits the number of software copies to two. A third requires special unlocking codes. It is very easy for an unsophisticated user to have trouble with these schemes, due to errors and mistakes that occur during the installation process.

First attempts at software installation can be troublesome unless the user has some familiarity with the basic commands of the operating system.

The physical installation must be successfully completed before users can proceed to the other steps required to prepare the software for use. (These steps are described in Chapter 14.)

FORM DESIGN

Accounting software is used to print many business documents, such as sales order acknowledgments, sales invoices, customer statements, and checks. If the computer forms are different from existing forms, carefully monitor supplies of the old forms. One must balance the risk of running out of the old forms before the new system is ready, and the cost of scrapping a lot of stationery.

Remember that software programs are not as flexible as the typewriter and may not adjust for misplaced areas on the printed form. Software manuals usually include printing guides or the names of printers familiar with the requirements of the software.

The degree of form design flexibility provided by accounting software varies a great deal from one product to another. Some packages provide no flexibility at all without special program modification (at additional cost). Others provide a great deal of flexibility. Most instructions for designing forms are rather easy to learn, but the procedure requires some patience.

Computer printers cannot prepare as many simultaneous copies as can a typewriter. Laser printers prepare one copy at a time. Dot matrix printers produce from four to six acceptable copies, depending on the printer and form construction. Users may require more than one run to produce all of the required copies.

In any event, initial printing runs on business forms will probably cost more than the old forms because

☐ Some copies of the old forms have to be scrapped

☐ Short runs of new forms will be ordered until everything is running smoothly

☐ Time must be invested in learning how to align forms in the printer and get the software to print the form properly.

TRAINING

Training is often the most expensive component of the installation. Training can be a time-consuming and even frustrating process. A number of factors affect training time and costs. Some of these factors relate to the nature of the software. Other factors can be controlled by the user.

Training Costs Related to Software Design

Accounting software is complex and requires knowledge of two disciplines: office procedures and computer operations. Accounting software programs deal extensively with codes and are less flexible than manual systems. Moving around the software, jumping from screen to screen, going from setup to data entry, posting, and information retrieval require knowledge of the way that the program is designed to communicate with users and perform its functions. Unlike more popular software such as word processors and spreadsheets, it is not easy to find other users who can share advice and suggestions.

People have problems learning how to deal with all of this. In order to overcome their concerns, the advertising community coined the phrase "user friendly," a term that was soon viewed with skepticism because learning problems were still very much in evidence.

One of the easy ways that some publishers addressed training difficulties was to design simple software that was limited in function and therefore easier to learn. Many inexpensive products fit this category. They provide a much more limited set of reports and functions than can be found in more costly products. For example, the general ledger module may not provide for monthly budgets or comparative data. Accounts receivable may not compute sales commissions or limit sales taxes to one tax jurisdiction. Accounts payable may be limited in the way that invoices can be selected for payment. The publishers also realized that simple software often gets high ratings because it is easier to learn.

Other publishers are adopting more sophisticated techniques to simplify the learning process without sacrificing software capability. For starters, a more selective choice of key words will avoid the confusion caused by the terminology problems discussed in Chapter 1. The basic terms of bookkeeping, such as "journal," "post," "accounting period," and "consolidation," should be used wherever appropriate.

Much more attention is being paid to the clarity of the text. Chapter 1 suggested some of the reasons, perhaps better called excuses, for poorly written manuals. Competition and the passage of time has forced publishers to become more sensitive to the value of documentation that is written in clear English and uncluttered with technical jargon.

The path from one operation to another is becoming simpler and more straightforward. Many beginners waste a lot of time searching for different functions. They also have difficulty understanding how to exit from screens when they are finished and move to the next step in the process. They stumble when they try to jump to a more distant operation.

Functions are becoming standardized; the same method should be used throughout the software to do the same thing. Publishers have a number of programmers working on different parts of the program. They are coming to realize the importance of having each part work in the same fashion. The same keys should always be used to move the cursor, to go from one screen to another, to stop printing. Functions should be standardized throughout all of the program modules. Similar functions in accounts payable and accounts receivable should be invoked in the same way.

Coupled with the standardization of function is the greater attention being given to the design of prompts, the words and symbols that appear on the monitor to guide the user. Some prompts are frustrating by their absence, as in the case of a blinking cursor that refuses to budge. Some prompts are so general—such as a beep or a phrase such as "wrong choice"—that they are virtually useless. Some prompts are fine for the experienced user but present a challenge to the beginner. Examples are "OK?" or "K5—Next Screen." A good set of prompts will display and explain the acceptable responses. Good prompts help the beginner find the way and are important for rapid learning.

The help screen is another useful training device provided by many programs. This is a screen containing explanatory material that can be called up by pressing a function key (usually the F1 or F10 key) or by pressing the "?" key. A touch of a key (usually the escape key) brings back the original screen so that the user can enter a response and move on.

Of course, some programs provide better help text than do others. Well-designed help screens will display text related to the field position of the cursor—this is called context-sensitive help. For example, if the user is entering a new customer and does not understand the required response for the field called "Terms," the help screen will explain how sales terms must be entered. If the help text is too long for the screen, the user can scroll through the text in order to read all of it.

Some texts are vague and do not address the specific requirements of each field on the screen. Some even confuse the issue by labeling pop-up windows (discussed earlier in this chapter) as "help screens."

One of the most effective ways for the publisher to simplify learning is to coordinate software with the manual. Each screen displays a unique number, and the manual follows in the same numbering sequence. Each field on the screen is numbered so that the manual can cross reference by screen and field number. This cross reference scheme eases the task of searching for explanations in the manual.

Many manuals can use better design and organization. Each page should clearly describe the topic under discussion as well as the screen number. The table of contents should be easy to find and direct readers to the appropriate subsection of each chapter. Indexes frequently are woefully inadequate. Publishers often complain that users are too lazy to look things up, that they call with questions that are easily answered in the manuals. A good part of this problem lies in the organization, design, and text of the manual, as well as in the associated software and help screens. Some programs come with sample sets of data so that trainees can work with the software without fear of damaging live information. Frequently the data is accompanied by a tutorial that guides the the beginner. This material not only speeds initial training but is helpful when new people must learn the software.

However, despite all of the shortcomings that may be found in one product or another, it is not wise to fall into the trap of judging software solely by the clarity of software screens and manuals. As the preceding indicates, some software is deliberately designed to be easy to learn but can be too limited in function and clumsy to use. Greater functionality requires a longer training period. The additional investment in training is justified if the result will be software that does a better job.

Training Costs Affected by Management

This text has leaned quite heavily on the software publishers and the techniques they can apply to simplify the learning process. But there is also a great deal of training cost that lies within the control of management.

A basic management decision is the determination of how training is to be provided. Accounting software publishers and retailers rarely provide training facilities. Even if they did, a classroom of people with different applications and needs could be confusing and inefficient. In an effort to address a large customer base, many programs include functions and explanations that may never be needed by a particular user. People who sell specialized programs frequently offer training and support for these products. However, a purchaser of a more general software package must decide whether to engage a professional trainer or consultant or to expect personnel to train themselves. Most people with little experience in accounting software require some outside help to get started. A consultant who is familiar with the program and understands accounting and business operations can ease the strains of learning the program and help avoid misunderstandings that lead to error. In addition to training, such a person should be able to offer suggestions that overcome some of the apparent limitations of the software and simplify its operation.

Whether or not professional assistance is required, suitable arrangements must be made for trainees to study manuals and try things out at the computer. Training should not start until people can actually apply the skills that they are learning. Pressure of work may make it difficult to schedule training time. Worse yet, interruptions and a noisy environment during training can seriously impede the effort. Management must make an effort to provide uninterrupted training periods. Lengthy training sessions should be avoided; three hours is enough. Trainees need time to try things out at the keyboard before absorbing additional material.

PREPARATION OF MASTER FILES

Master files are computer records that store account data such as information about customers, vendors, and inventory items. Computer programs frequently are designed to store more information than can corresponding manual records. For example, a computer customer record might provide fields for storing such information as telephone and telex numbers, contact names, whether the customer will accept part shipments and substitutions, credit rating, salesperson and terms codes, and tax-exempt number. Some of this information must be entered for the program to function; some is optional. In order to get started, the user must enter all mandatory fields of information, such as those described in Chapter 6.

The task of assembling this information can be quite time consuming. If a new code scheme is to be used, individual code numbers must be assigned to each account. Text information such as names and addresses must be verified and abbreviated if they are longer than the field size provided by the software. Historic information (used in various reports) may have to be compiled.

Before the work begins of assembling all of this data, some thought should be given to timing. Information for optional fields (such as telephone numbers or the names of contact persons) can be introduced at a later time, after the stress of installation is over. Many choose not to enter historic information until, with the passage of time, the software generates the data.

The initial work of preparing master files falls into two time phases. One phase involves obtaining data that is not time sensitive, such as names, addresses, and codes. This work can be stretched out over a period of time prior to installation. The second phase involves time-sensitive information such as account balances and details of unpaid invoices. Time-sensitive information must be compiled so that it can be entered into the system in a very short period of time. This work frequently is performed after the close of an accounting period and before processing the subsequent period. Often this must be done under pressure, at night, and over weekends.

Spot checks should be made while this starting data is being accumulated to make certain that the information is being compiled correctly. A misunderstanding about requirements can result in wasted time and effort. For example, a clerk may enter wrong credit ratings because the person does not know how to read credit reports. Or an outdated list might be used erroneously to compile ship-to addresses.

Some thought must be given to the verification of this information prior to computer entry. In most situations it is better and easier to verify information after computer entry, because the printouts are easier to read and verification will include the accuracy of the entry clerk. Checking prior to computer entry is advisable if the source information will not be readily available at a later time.

Chapter 7 described the import function provided by some accounting programs. This function can save time and effort for users who have sizable master file data that has been compiled by other programs. With the proper technical advice it may be possible to convert the files to a format that can be imported into the new accounting program without the need to reenter all of the data.

After master file data has been compiled, it must be entered into the computer. If few records are involved, the task can be easy. Setting up thousands of records, a situation frequently encountered for inventories, can take a lot of time and requires careful scheduling.

The work of compiling, entering, and verifying master files can stretch over many months. In order to ease the burden, the work may be done in phases or segments. Data entry can be facilitated through the use of office temporaries skilled in this kind of work. College students and others with computer experience may also be available to assist with this effort.

SETTING UP REPORTS

The design of computer reports and documents is another important component of software installation. The task of formatting financial statements and documents can be quite challenging. (See the discussion in Chapter 7 for more information.) The number of options and choices distinguishes sophisticated software from the simpler variety.

The degree of flexibility provided by the general ledger module for designing financial statements varies from one product to another. Two approaches are used. Some software links financial statements directly to the chart of accounts. The user of this type of software must understand how the financials are formatted before setting up the chart of accounts. The alternative approach is to design the financial statements from report specifications that are independent of the chart of accounts. In this instance, the user can postpone learning these specifications to a future period.

Management reports and business documents generated by other modules (accounts receivable, order entry, accounts payable, inventory, etc.) may be rigid in format, or might permit user modification. Many publishers offer separate modules that enable users to design reports. If modification is permitted, the user must spend additional learning time similar to that required for financial statements.

An alternative to report modification within the accounting software is the device of exporting information from the accounting software to a word processor, spreadsheet, or database. This technique requires knowledge of the file structures used in both programs as well as an understanding of the software.

At the outset, the engagement of an outside consultant to set up the financial statements and management reports is preferable to undertaking this work in-house when so much else must be learned and applied. In time, personnel should acquire the necessary skills in order to process changes and modifications as they are required.

PARALLEL OPERATION

The final installation phase to consider is parallel operation. While a few foolhardy souls have successfully avoided the stress of a parallel operation, there are many more who avoided serious headaches by this highly recommended approach, as troublesome as it may be.

In most situations, the installation of accounting software impacts almost everyone in an organization, because of the changes in procedures and operations. Many questions arise during the installation period (and often for many months thereafter) because of misunderstandings or failure to plan for unusual situations or conditions. Parallel operation is designed to identify and correct these situations.

Accounting questions may arise with respect to the proper classification and treatment of certain types of transactions. For example, the software may not clearly indicate how the user should enter miscellaneous cash receipts because the accounts receivable module can only process cash received from customers. Perhaps the software is too limited in the number of general ledger accounts that can be credited for sales from the order entry module. Procedures must be devised for these conditions.

Other procedural questions must be answered. What is to be done if a sales commission is to be split and the software computes one sales commission per invoice? What if items must be substituted when shipping sales orders, but the software does not provide for substitutions?

No installation proceeds without some deviation from prior practice. The parallel operation provides assurance that the new procedures will work properly and provides the feedback for correcting procedural errors before they are serious.

PREPARATION OF WRITTEN PROCEDURES

In addition to other installation responsibilities, management should provide for committing the new procedures to writing. This task can be difficult during a period of change, but a reliable and clear set of procedures becomes vital when there are many troublesome errors or when turnover requires a great deal of training. A formidable software manual should be reduced to a few pages summarizing the routine functions required at each workstation. The use of redesigned forms and procedures should also be documented.

SUMMARY

This chapter has provided an overview of installation tasks so that they can be planned and the associated costs can be controlled. Many of these costs are difficult to budget and track because they are buried in the accounts, particularly payroll costs.

The specific costs discussed were

- ☐ Management time for making basic decisions about
  - —. installation
  - —. personnel
  - —. computer work environment
  - —. installation timetable
  - —. project leadership
- ☐ Management time for making decisions based on the selected software, such as consideration of
  - —. options provided by the software
  - —. adoption of coding schemes
  - —. design of manual procedures and controls
- ☐ Hardware installation

- ☐ Software installation
- ☐ Stationery
- ☐ Training
- ☐ Preparing master files
- ☐ Setting up reports
- ☐ Parallel operation
- ☐ Consultant fees.

A list like this seems formidable. The actual time and cost in each instance depends not only on the degree to which procedures are being computerized, but on matters that are within management control:

- ☐ The intelligent choice of software
- ☐ The intelligent choice of hardware
- ☐ The proper selection of computer managers and operators
- ☐ Good managerial direction, support, and supervision
- ☐ The documentation of decisions and procedures
- ☐ The proper degree of management concern about morale and training during the installation period
- ☐ The review of performance before serious errors occur.

11

Operating Costs

INTRODUCTION

The prior two chapters discussed two of the three cost elements that must be evaluated when computerized accounting is under consideration—namely, acquisition and installation costs. Those chapters discussed the difficulties in estimating and controlling such costs because of the interplay of many elements; how the choice of the software affects hardware, personnel, and other costs; how more sophisticated software with greater functionality can increase the time and cost of training; how network decisions impact on cost; and the difficulty of estimating and measuring payroll costs, from management down, that relate to the tasks associated with installation.

This chapter will cover costs that, in the long run, are the most significant of all—namely, operating costs. Generally, the most significant operating cost is payroll. Added to this is a miscellany of other cost factors including hardware maintenance, stationery, supplies, and support.

PAYROLL COSTS

There are significant differences in the time required to operate various software packages, differences that are independent of the hardware that is used. This disparity arises because of the different ways in which the programs are designed. Some programs run more slowly than others.

There are significant delays while screens are changing, when information is being sorted or searched.

Some programs take a lot more printing time than others. In some instances, printing is a serious bottleneck.

Some programs make data entry quite easy. Others are clumsy, resulting in lower productivity.

Some programs provide simple procedures for correcting errors. Others are cumbersome and error prone.

Some programs are more sensitive to file corruption than others. Data files may become unusable if the power supply suffers a momentary interruption, or if an operator presses the wrong key at a critical time. When this happens, the files are said to be "corrupted," and a message to this effect usually is displayed on the monitor screen. Computer operations must stop until data files are recovered from backups and lost data are rekeyed into the system. Frequently this is a time-consuming and troublesome process.

The following examines the ways program design affects operating costs.

Speed

Nearly everyone is aware of the fantastic numbers regarding computer speed. Some computer speeds are measured in mips (millions of instructions per second). Therefore, many computer neophytes are shocked when they discover that their operation runs too slowly and wonder what is wrong. They may have attended software demonstrations where the computer speed was impressive. They might have inquired about speed and been assured that they would have no problem. Yet, there it is, a crawling computer and an unhappy user. Why does this happen?

First of all, one must understand that a computer system involves the integration of many hardware and software elements. The speed of operation changes as different elements are called into play. At one moment, the system depends on the speed of the hard disk, then it must wait for the microprocessor. The design of the program will affect the number of instructions that must be executed. The size of RAM will influence the number of disk reads and writes necessary to perform a long sort. The printer may slow everything down to a crawl.

In some situations, the appropriate selection of hardware elements can improve the speed of the operation. (These choices are discussed in Chapter 9.) The choices include the selection of microprocessor, hard disk, RAM, and printer.

Networks add another speed factor. As indicated in Chapter 7, the impact of the network on operating speed depends upon the network software and hardware, as well as on the number of workstations using the network at any one time.

File sizes can have a significant effect on speed. An increase in the number of records in a file will be attended by longer transfers between disk and RAM, as well as longer sort and printing times. The result is a progressive slowdown as file sizes increase. Software that runs very quickly in a demonstration because files are small may be sluggish when files are expanded to a realistic size.

Why this difference in speed? Certain programming languages are more appropriate for business applications. Some programs have been converted from other systems and do not effectively address the capabilities of the microcomputer. Some programs are more concerned with speed problems than are others and are more selective in the choice of methods and subroutines that will provide maximum speed. Some programs use sort utilities that work faster than others.

Many of the newer high-end programs incorporate a number of functions designed to make life easier for the user, functions such as the use of pop-up windows (discussed later in this chapter), context-sensitive help screens (explained in Chapter 10), easier menu paths, and simpler operations. These functions were not practicable years ago when computer microprocessors were slower and RAM sizes were smaller. These additional functions can take their toll in processing time, unless the software is installed on the proper computers.

Some programs must quickly access many different files. For example, the function of entering a sales order involves moving data in and out of customer and inventory files. Job cost programs may have to work a number of files: accounts receivable, inventory, payroll, and accounts payable. Some programs are overwhelmed with all of this searching and slow down to a crawl.

Remember the simple but disconcerting fact that the prediction of computer system operating speeds is more an art than a science. There is no easy and reliable way to determine the speed of a computer system in advance of actual performance. How then can prospective users avoid the problem of purchasing and installing systems that prove too slow for their needs?

Here is some helpful advice:

1. Make a careful determination of the transaction volumes and file sizes that will be involved in computer data processing.

Obtain transaction volumes by counting the number of sales orders, invoices, cash receipts, vendor invoices, cash disbursements, journal entries, and other transactions that must be processed daily. Take into account seasonal variations and make provision for growth over the coming years.

Determine file sizes by counting the number of customers, vendors, ledger accounts, inventory items, and employees that must be addressed by the computer's existing data and project these numbers into the future. Also consider the rate of turnover in these master file records.

Activities with high transaction volumes and/or large files are the applications that are potential time eaters.

There are no strict rules, but time concerns should be raised by

☐ Files that will contain more than 1,000 records

☐ Documents such as sales invoices or order acknowledgments that run more than 50 per day and carry an average of 5 or more line items

☐ Seasonal businesses that have large swings in transaction volume

☐ Operations in which rapid service is critical and computer production must be fast.

2. Attend software demonstrations and observe the speed with which screens change, files are updated, and reports are printed.

Remember that performance speed depends upon both software and hardware. Get specifications about the hardware that the demonstration is running on for comparison with the speed of the hardware that you plan to purchase. With a little experience, one quickly senses whether computer responses are fast or sluggish.

Software demonstrations can be very misleading when it comes to operating speed for a number of reasons:

☐ The demonstration hardware is different from the hardware that will be in actual use.

☐ The demonstration files are much smaller than the application files.

☐ The demonstration hard disk might be well organized while the application hard disk might have many scattered files.

☐ The demonstration network, if any, might be smaller and have less traffic than the user network.

The specific information required for hardware comparison includes

☐ Speed of the microprocessor and printer

☐ Average access time of the hard disk

☐ Network or stand-alone

☐ Number of records in the files used for the demonstration.

Insist that the demonstration include the printing of forms and reports. Many demonstrations are held without printers, because
additional time is required for printer setup. However, no demonstration
is reliable without the production of some business forms and reports.

3. Speak to users who are working in situations comparable to yours.
Inquire about their experience with the software and the speed with
which it runs. Ask which operations are running slower than expected,
or are causing problems because of computer delay.

4. Consider a number of alternatives if the system is too slow.
Discuss the following remedies with a competent technician:

☐ Installing a faster microprocessor or hard disk

☐ Using a disk organizer utility program. Over a period of time, with
files added and erased, the files on a hard disk become fragmented
as the operating system scatters them over the disk wherever it finds
empty spaces. Scattered files take longer to retrieve and store than
do organized files. Disk organizer utilities reorganize the hard disk
by bringing together the scattered portions of files.

☐ Using a disk cache utility. Disk cache programs allocate a portion of
RAM for a disk cache, a technique that reduces the number of times
that the program must look to the hard disk for information.

☐ Reviewing the technical choices buried in the operating system that
can affect speed. The selection of interleave at the time the disk is
formatted, and the number of buffers and files opened at startup
time, will have an affect on speed.

☐ Making certain that network software has been "fine tuned" for
maximum speed

☐ Using a backup utility program to speed up backup operations

☐ Determining whether printer utilization can be improved. Use
printer buffers to free up computers during long print jobs. Consider using multiple printers to save time in changing paper and
forms. Explore the possibility of accumulating print jobs on disk so
that real printing can be deferred to off-hours.

Remember that all of these remedies suggest sources of improvement
but will not guarantee satisfactory results. No such guarantee is available.

Some reputable dealers will replace software if it proves unsuitable. However, it may take many months before all modules are fully installed and all files have grown to full size. The slowdown may be imperceptible. And changing software after many months of operation is expensive and difficult.

Data Entry

A program may run very fast, but results can be disappointing if keyboard operations are slow. In fact, after installation, the greatest ongoing cost is in the payroll of data input clerks. There are a number of program design factors that affect the productivity of the computer operator.

1. The design of input screens affects the speed of data entry. Some screens are linear, which means that each transaction is entered on one line of the monitor. Operators can see previous entries, which facilitates lookup for purposes of comparison or resuming work after interruption. A program that requires a separate screen for each transaction line is less desirable.

2. Special key strokes are required in every program for a number of purposes, such as changing screens, calling up help screens, and moving the cursor. Some programs require many keystrokes for a single function, such as entering the words EXIT or MORE. Other programs use one key for the same purpose, a faster process.

3. The display of totals provides helpful guides for the operator. The number of totals displayed varies from program to program. Some programs do not display any total. The operator must run a written report or exit from the input screen in order to read the totals. Some programs display one total, a net figure of both debits and credits. Others provide a running total of both debits and credits. A third batch total (provided by some programs) insures against the omission of a transaction. Some programs even provide a transaction total, which helps in distributing transaction amounts among a number of accounts.
   Accounting programs that do not display running totals during transaction entry invite error. Programs that provide two or more totals facilitate data entry even more.

4. Data entry involves a great deal of repetitive information such as the date or explanation. One transaction may require many entry lines in order to distribute amounts among a number of accounts. Some programs speed input by repeating dates, reference numbers, and explana-

tions until changed by the user. For cash disbursements, some programs will increment check numbers automatically.

5. Code numbers can be a problem. Good control requires transactions to be coded before computer entry. This may not always be practical, and even if done, coding errors and omissions are bound to occur. Until recently, one had to refer to printed code lists for purposes of account coding, a tedious and cumbersome job. Today, many accounting programs remove some of the coding burden by permitting the operator to look up codes during data entry. By pressing a function key or special key, such as the asterisk (*) or question mark (?), a pop-up window appears, displaying names and account numbers. The user can scroll through the list to look up the desired code; then, by moving the cursor to the selected item and pressing the enter key, the selected item is brought into the entry screen together with all associated information.

6. Prompts and help screens were discussed in the previous chapter in connection with training costs. They are also important in the production environment, particularly for routines that are used infrequently. Clearly worded prompts and help screens speed up entry and processing. Poor prompts are virtually incomprehensible. One example is the program that beeps when the operator makes an incorrect entry but makes no effort to explain the problem. The cursor just sits in place and continues to blink, while the operator tries desperately to determine what is wrong so that the entry process can continue. Petty errors such as the wrong selection of upper- or lower-case characters, or the wrong way of entering the date, can cause the program to stall. There is a difference between a prompt that says "ENTER CURRENT DATE" and one that says "ENTER CURRENT DATE MO/DY/YR." Good prompts should clearly display the choices available and the correct form of response as the cursor moves from field to field. Prompts and help screens can also be helpful in displaying and describing various codes used by the program, such as transaction and source codes.

Difficulties may arise when the user must differentiate between mandatory and optional fields. Some mandatory fields may be useless but must be filled in anyway. For example, the customer screen may require that a salesman code be assigned each customer, even though the user does not use salesmen. The program may lock until at least one salesman code is keyed into the system.

Delays can occur when the user attempts to enter information in the wrong sequence and the program locks without explanation. This might happen if certain initializing procedures are required to block out file space or to set up accounting periods and these procedures are not executed. Without clear prompts, the user may not understand the problem and stay "stuck" until the problem is solved via a telephone call on the help line or the assistance of a consultant.

The phrase "help screen" in itself can be confusing. Help screens are explanatory texts that appear on the screen when requested. Some software companies incorrectly use the term "help screen" to refer to the code lists that appear in the pop-up windows described in item five.

7. Some software requires that new account data must be keyed in prior to transaction entry. This means that the entry clerk must interrupt the work flow if the need to enter a new account is recognized during transaction entry. This problem has been identified by programs that permit the entry of new accounts at the time of data entry. This feature can be significant to a business that has a rapid turnover in its master files, such as customers, vendors, inventory items, or employees.

8. Decimal points and commas are handled in many ways. Some programs require that the decimals be entered by the user. Others insert decimals automatically. In some cases, the user is provided the option of entering or not entering decimals. The automatic insertion of decimals is significant in high-volume data entry. Some programs automatically insert commas into the dollar amounts that appear on screens; others do not. The insertion of commas makes it easier to read large amounts and therefore reduces entry error for applications dealing with large numbers.

9. The requirements for cursor movement affect input speed. Many users are surprised to discover that moving the cursor on a computer is quite different from moving the carriage on a typewriter. Indeed, different programs use different keystrokes for moving the cursor. In some software, one can go forward on the screen but cannot go backward. Some programs permit jumping around the screen; others require pacing from field to field in sequence, even though entries are not required in all fields.

Going back to a specific field may require pressing a special key to bring the cursor to the first field and then moving forward through the screen until the desired field is reached. Other programs assign a number to each field and let the user go directly to the field requiring editing by entering the field number. The user whose application requires high-volume production, should make certain that cursor movement is easy.

10. Up to now, the text has stressed the importance of selecting software

that will effectively perform all of the functions that the user requires. But what about software that will do all of this, and much more— software that offers functions that will never be used and provides fields of information that are meaningless? A screen that offers unnecessary functions can be confusing. A data entry screen that requires stepping through a number of useless data fields can slow down the entry process.

A program that is unnecessarily complex or provides more capability than required can impede training and slow down data entry.

Error Recovery

Well-designed error recovery routines can make life easier for the computer operator and save time as well. Many of the techniques that speed production also reduce the incidence of error. Linear input screens make it easier to scan previous entries and spot mistakes. Running totals indicate the entry of wrong amounts or the omission of items. The ability to process new accounts at the time of data entry minimizes the disturbance of work flow.

There are additional aspects to software design that affect error recovery:

1. Most software displays an account name when the corresponding account code is entered. A warning is displayed if the account cannot be found, and the user is required to enter a legitimate account code. However, some software does not verify general ledger accounts until one attempts to post from a separate module to the general ledger. This form of account verification is clumsy because the error is not detected until after data entry, and error correction becomes more time consuming.

2. Different methods are used by various accounting packages to accept and process input. Most software uses a batch method whereby all input is kept in temporary holding files and not posted until the operator activates the posting operation. These programs permit users to list the contents of these files and make corrections when necessary. For example, lists of entry journals, sales invoices, and vendor invoices selected for payment are helpful in the detection and correction of errors. The ease of correction varies with each program. Some programs permit changing or deleting every bit of information that has been entered. Some permit changing but do not permit deleting entries (resulting in some entries with zero amounts). Some programs permit deleting the entire batch; others do not.

   Some programs are much less flexible, if not downright difficult, when it comes to error correction. Programs that use the "real time" method give the user one chance to spot errors. A prompt appears after each entry, asking the user to accept the entry or begin the entry again. Once accepted, the entry is immediately posted. Thereafter, the only way to correct the error is to make an offsetting entry. In order to maintain an audit trail, such programs usually print each entry at the time of posting, which means that a printer must be committed at all times during data entry. Because of the limited ability to review work before posting, and to assure an accurate printout for purposes of audit trail, real-time programs are best used in environments that require current updating of files, such as an active order entry situation that must update inventory availability as orders are accepted. Even then, there is no need for the general ledger to be on a real-time basis.

Another error recovery technique to review is the way programs permit users to reenter data. Many programs will blank a field as soon as the user starts to reenter information. This prevents some of the old information from appearing if it used more characters than the new information. Otherwise, the user must be careful to blank the excess characters.

3. Some programs provide batch and entry numbers that facilitate finding and recalling the entries that require correction. These numbers are particularly useful when each line entry requires a separate screen.

4. The process of printing long reports can be quite time consuming. What happens if the operator starts the wrong printing job by mistake, or for some other reason wishes to terminate printing? Some programs let the user stop the printer; others do not. (If one cannot find a way in the program to stop the printer, the best way around this is to turn off the power to the printer. In some cases, even this does not work, and the program continues printing when the power is turned on again.)

5. Beginners press a lot of wrong keys, sometimes by accident, sometimes when the printer starts churning away on an unwanted long report, and sometimes when the user is stuck and cannot move the cursor or change screens. Some programs are pretty foolproof, which means that the operator cannot do much harm if wrong keys are pressed. In other programs, pressing the wrong keys can cause the loss of information and even damage data files. The user may suddenly exit from the program without warning and end up in the operating system or be dumped into a strange environment with odd characters appearing on the monitor. The only way to determine if the program is foolproof is to try out the software and to check with other users.

6. One major protection against damage caused by operator or computer

error is a well-enforced policy of preparing and maintaining backup files. Here again, there is a wide difference in the approach taken by different software products. Some software ignores the subject entirely and requires the user to have sufficient knowledge of the operating system to know how to perform file backup and restore procedures. Other software provides backup through one of its own utility menus. Some programs even record the date of the last backup and remind the user when backups should be made.

If diskette backup is slow (requiring 15 minutes or more per backup) or clumsy (because too many diskettes must be used), a separate backup device should be used. These devices usually provide their own software. In such instances, the backup capability of the accounting software is useless.

7. One function of accounting software is to print information on business forms such as disbursement checks and customer invoices. The insertion of these forms into the printer can be tricky. If the forms are not correctly aligned in the printer, information is not printed in the proper spaces. The software should permit the user to do a test printing to check the alignment. Some software provides for a rerun in case the misalignment is not detected in time (or if more copies are required than can be printed at one time).

System Management

All computer installations, however small, require some attention from a responsible person for the following functions:

- ☐ Reviewing available file and disk capacity
- ☐ Planning and allocating system resources
- ☐ Supervising system security
- ☐ Checking for system malfunctions
- ☐ Monitoring maintenance and backup.

Some software is more helpful than others in assisting with the administration of these functions.

Reviewing Available File and Disk Capacity

Even though computers can store a lot of information, as discussed in Chapter 6, there are finite limits to storage. Many accounting programs let the user control the amount of detail information that is stored. This amount will vary with user needs, the quantity of information, and the size of disk storage. Some users may be able to store all transactions for a year or longer. Others may choose to remove the detail periodically during the year, leaving only summary information in the computer for statistical and comparative purposes. Procedures for executing the function to compress information must be carefully controlled in order to avoid the possibility of erasing information by mistake. Well-designed software will provide some warning before erasing detail files. The responsibility for executing this function should be limited to the system administrator.

Storage limits place another important constraint on the program—that of providing a timely warning that the system is running out of space. There are different varieties of storage limits. Some accounting software requires the user to block out storage space for data files. Programs using dynamic sizing will automatically enlarge data files as needed. Programs that do not use dynamic sizing require more frequent review of files. Special utility routines are used to check on remaining file capacity and to enlarge files when required. Although accounting software usually provides a warning when files are getting full, operators may ignore these warnings. Serious problems can occur if file capacity is reached during data entry or processing. The system administrator should check file capacities quite frequently to avoid such problems.

Another serious problem arises if the entire hard disk is getting full. This situation must be recognized in ample time to take corrective action. In some situations, storage space can be recovered by compressing data files. If nonaccounting programs are stored on the same disk, one frequently finds many outdated files and programs that can be erased. There may be a situation in which there is no alternative but to transfer operations to a larger disk. Accounting software usually will not provide ample warning of this situation, particularly if programs, other than accounting programs, are stored on the same media. Careful planning is required if this transfer is to be effected without disruption of the work flow. The system administrator must periodically test available disk capacity and require users to remove outdated files.

Planning and Allocating System Resources

The best way to understand the concept of resource allocation is to contrast the requirements of a small and simple application with the needs of a larger business. A small business may involve one corporation, three or four accounting modules, and a low transaction volume. Contrast this with a larger business that involves a number of corporations or partnerships, five or more accounting modules, and a high transaction volume.

At times, even though a network may not be warranted, the need to process and store high-volume data or work with multiple corporations requires periodic attention to determine whether some change in resources would permit the system to function more effectively. The following matters might be considered:

☐ Has the hard disk been properly organized into directories and subdirectories? Are people losing time searching for files? Are files lost because of poor disk organization?

☐ Should a larger hard disk, or a second hard disk, be considered? The move to a larger disk or multiple disks should be made before a storage crisis occurs.

☐ Is it time to add or change printers because of time loss in changing forms or waiting for printed output?

☐ Is the system breaking down too often? Has repair been satisfactory?

☐ Has anything new in the way of hardware or software appeared on the market that would benefit operations?

Someone should have the responsibility of checking the computer operation periodically to make certain that its resources are being used effectively.

Supervising System Security

System control and security will be discussed in detail in another chapter. Some mention should be made at this point of the fact that two important areas of security—password control and backup—are treated in different ways that can either simplify or complicate the life of the system administrator.

As will be shown in the next chapter, accounting programs offer a variety of approaches to password control. Programs that offer greater levels and choices of password assignments require a greater degree of administration. Policies must be established and followed regarding the availability and assignment of passwords. Many organizations require password changes on a periodic basis. Changes may also be in order when employees leave or are given new responsibilities. Program routines for assigning and changing passwords should be easy to administer and yet be available only to authorized parties. Routines that are unduly complicated may not be followed, with the result that password control may lose its effectiveness.

Checking for System Malfunctions

Accounting software generally does not provide much help in this area for the system administrator. Some software does permit users to transfer to the operating system without leaving the accounting software (and losing information that might be still in RAM). This capability can be helpful at times when problems appear and the adminstrator wishes to run a few tests through the operating system before halting operations.

Monitoring Maintenance and Backup

Frequent backups are an important element in data security. Backups protect users against system malfunctions that destroy files and lose information. The enforcement of backup policies and procedures are important responsibilities for the system administrator.

OTHER OPERATING COSTS

Although payroll costs represent the lion's share of operating costs, one should not forget other cost elements.

System maintenance probably represents the second most significant operating cost. New hardware is guaranteed for a limited period of time. After that, some type of maintenance contract should be considered. One can choose between purchasing a service contract or paying for service when required. Service contracts can cover the entire system or be limited to the elements most subject to failure, such as printers and disk drives. On-site service nearly always costs more than service that requires the user to bring the faulty device to a service center. Service contracts are offered by computer retailers as well as by independent service companies.

Outside technical support may also represent significant ongoing costs. Some organizations are not in a position to provide system management and look to an outside organization for this service. Consultants and programmers may be called on from time to time to discuss changing needs or new applications.

The costs of stationery and supplies should not be overlooked. Computers can spin out a lot of paper. Multipart computer forms can be expensive. Wide reports are bulky and require the purchase and storage of large binders.

SUMMARY

This chapter has reviewed operating costs, costs that in the long run usually outweigh costs of acquisition and installation. Operating costs have been discussed as part of project planning because, like installation costs, they should be considered before the system is purchased, not later. Some operating costs do not become evident until months after operations have started, in which time, files have expanded and functions have been added to the system.

Most of the chapter discussed payroll costs because they are so significant. The factors affecting payroll cost are

- ☐ Program speed, including computer delays during transfers from screen to screen, sorting time, and printing time

- ☐ Ease (or difficulty) of data entry. After installation, the time and cost of data entry is usually the most significant element of operating costs

- ☐ Ease (or difficulty) of detecting and correcting errors. Clumsy error recovery procedures can waste a lot of time.

- ☐ Ease of system management. Complicated schemes for controlling passwords, checking available storage, and performing backup routines discourage use and lead to serious and costly problems.

Each of these elements are difficult to evaluate because different users avail themselves of different program features, have different file sizes and transaction volumes, and use different hardware. Suggestions were provided as to how to make inquiry about operating time and cost as part of the investigative survey.

However, an awareness of the relationship between software design and operating cost is important in planning for successful results.

The chapter concluded with a brief discussion of other cost elements:

- ☐ Maintenance
- ☐ Technical support
- ☐ Stationery and supplies

__ 12 _____

Control
_____

INTRODUCTION

Up to this point our discussion of accounting software has concentrated on the importance of (1) determining and evaluating user needs and resources; (2) compiling precise information regarding capacity and functional requirements, taking into account considerations of management style and the working environment, together with determinations about the significance of software integration, networks, and multi-user environments; and (3) considering the costs associated with computer acquisition (both software and hardware) installation, and operation.

There remains one final area that requires serious review, and that is the impact of differing hardware arrangements and accounting software products on internal control. The successful introduction and operation of computerized accounting procedures requires the development and application of an adequate system of control.

Accountants talk a great deal about control. Most people think of control as a tool for stopping people from stealing or spying. Stories about computer-based malfeasance are great sources of newspaper copy. An article appearing in *Office Systems* magazine estimated that 10% of business losses can be attributed to computer crime. Most of these crimes are committed by employees. The article estimated that less than 5% of business fraud is related to "penetration" by strangers. The *Small Business Guide to Computer Security* published by the U.S. Small Business Administration states that most computer crimes against small businesses are committed by current or former employees. Norman Jaspan, writing in the *CPA Journal*, estimates that trusted employees account for more than 60% of business theft. This theme is repeated by Robert Scheier, who states in *PC Week* that "the biggest computer security threat in most corporations isn't a virus, a hacker or a phone cleaning crew that comes at night and downloads company customer files. Rather, it's an employee who seems to be trustworthy, but who also is earning in the bottom 40 percent of the wage scale, agonizing over a divorce, nervous about a corporate takeover or angry about a missed promotion, for example." It is also interesting to note that Michael Kirkpatrick, an FBI agent writing in *Software* magazine, reported that computer criminals "take few vacations and generally work long hours."

However, don't make the mistake of assuming that controls are directed primarily at deterring or catching thieves. The greatest cost of poor controls are honest employee mistakes that go undetected. The article just quoted from *Office Systems* attributes between 50% and 80% of financial losses to innocent errors. Management rarely talks about this kind of problem.

Good control procedures are concerned with protection against loss through both dishonesty and error.

The control system must be considered from many perspectives.

Computerized accounting operations lie in a job stream that begins and ends outside of the computer environment. Transaction entry starts with source documents such as contracts, vendor invoices, sales orders, receiving tickets, payroll forms, and other business documents that originate with many people, some within and some outside the organization. In turn, accounting software generates important and often confidential management reports as well as business documents such as disbursement checks and sales invoices. The introduction of the computer usually mandates many changes in operating procedures, manual systems, and responsibilities. These changes require rethinking about controls.

Chapter 2 discussed significant differences between manual and computer operations. The computer introduces opportunities for dishonesty and error that are of much less significance in a manual system. These opportunities must be considered when computer procedures are introduced or modified.

Some programmers who develop accounting software are more alert to control considerations than are others. There are significant differences in control features among disparate accounting software products. Accounting software with poor controls should not be given serious consideration unless (1) the unusual features of the software far outweigh its weaknesses and (2) management installs routines that assure an adequate measure of control.

Anyone planning to introduce computerized accounting functions should consider the following aspects of control:

☐ Management plans and policies with respect to
—. Personnel (including training, assignment of responsibilities, performance review)
—. Control systems
—. Arrangements with accountants and auditors
—. Computer backups
—. Contingencies
—. Communicating and monitoring policies

☐ Controls provided by the accounting software,
—. Passwords
—. Logging procedures
—. Balanced journal entries
—. Assignment of transaction numbers
—. Forced printing of journals
—. Running totals
—. Verification of account codes
—. Logical controls
—. Master file controls

☐ Enhanced controls, provided by special hardware and software,
—. Logging procedures and reports
—. Sophisticated password controls
—. Encryption
—. Scrutiny of communications and callback devices
—. Magnetic card and biochemical readers
—. Virus protection software

☐ Computer protection,
—. Surge suppressors and line conditioners
—. Antistatic mats
—. Backup power supplies
—. Protection during a move

☐ Physical access,
—. Hardware locations
—. Keys
—. Storage facilities
—. Waste and discard facilities
—. Screen visibility

☐ Controls outside of the computer,
  —. Segregation of duties
  —. Dummy transactions
  —. Transaction review and audit

How do these controls work? What assurance do they provide? How important are they? Can a system be overcontrolled?

MANAGEMENT PLANS AND POLICIES

Good control really starts at the top. A management that is aware of the need for proper control will seek advice for making the best policy decisions, particularly when these decisions require an understanding of computer operations and a knowledge of the products designed to provide control.

The following discussion is designed to make readers aware of the availability and benefits of various control options In many instances a consultant may be required to develop a specific action plan.

Personnel

Control really starts with personnel, with people. Think for a minute about how quality of performance can be affected by a policy of hiring people without adequate screening, or running an organization with poor morale or excessive turnover.

People assigned to sensitive responsibilities should be given careful screening. They should be bonded and required to take vacations. A meaningful management response is required if personnel in sensitive positions are disgruntled for an extended period of time.

The introduction of a computer system must be handled with sensitivity. Most employees are concerned about change and worry about the ability to learn new ways. Some employees may be excited about acquiring new skills. Others may be fearful, even resentful, but may not display these negative feelings.

The training period is a good time to observe reactions to the new computer environment. Slow learning may indicate poor teaching, or it may signal resistance. A slow learner or grumbler may be a poor candidate for computer assignments. Such a person may work too slowly, make an excessive number of errors, or constantly ask others for help.

On the other hand, an overqualified computer "hacker" presents a different control challenge. So-called power users may use their computer skills to circumvent software controls. They may like to play games such as figuring out passwords assigned to others, or use utility software to look at and modify files that are out of bounds.

Good control starts with a management that makes informed decisions about personnel assignments, and then monitors results to determine whether changes in responsibilities and policies are warranted.

Control Systems

The second major responsibility of management is to make proper determinations with respect to the system of internal control and reduce these determinations to specific policies and activities. Control systems are forms of insurance. Overcontrolling results in wasted effort and expense. Undercontrolling exposes the organization to excessive risk. Management should understand the risks and evaluate the various control techniques and devices that are explained below to determine both the degree of protection provided by the control and the related cost. Administrators may have to spend a great deal of time dealing with control installation and maintenance. An extensive password system can be unwieldy. The segregation of duties can build up payroll costs. Management must make control decisions that strike the correct balance.

Arrangements with Accountants and Auditors

Accountants and auditors are important resources for assistance in evaluating risk and designing internal control procedures. Additionally, management should consider the use of outside accountants for period audits of computer operations.

Computer Backups

A computer is quite reliable, but there is always a time when the machine will not function properly. This may be due to a problem with the hardware, a momentary lapse in electrical service that disrupts the program, dusty conditions, an accident or operator error.

A business that relies on the computer for its daily operation can face a serious and expensive disruption of operations unless both the computer and its files can be brought back into action very quickly.

The best safeguard against this problem is a good policy for creating and storing backups of computer files.

Backups are created through the use of software and hardware that copies computer files onto storage media (such as floppy disks, cartridges, and tapes) that can easily be separated from the computer and filed.

Most practitioners advocate rotating three sets of backups. For example, if a daily backup is made, the three sets would consist of backups made on day one, day two, and day three. The backup from day one would be reused on day four, the backup from day two would be reused on day five, and so on. In this fashion there is protection against a faulty backup.

In order to guard against data loss due to catastrophes such as fire and water, some backups should be completely removed from the premises periodically and stored off site.

The amount of time required to perform the backup operation depends on the hardware and software that are used. The slowest backups occur on microcomputers when DOS backup commands are used and many floppy disks are required to store the material. The process becomes onerous as files get larger and backups take more and more time. This can become quite a nuisance and result in a failure to make backups on a timely basis.

Many techniques are available to speed up this process. The simplest is to replace the backup software provided by the operating system with software specifically designed to speed up the process. Storage devices such as cartridge and tape drives will cut down on the physical handling effort and work faster than floppies. Some of these devices are "internal"—that is, they can be placed inside the computer. Others come in their own metal containers and must be wired to the computer.

Management must set the policy for backing up computer files and select the software and hardware that are to be used for this purpose.

Contingencies

Of course, backups cannot solve all the problems that can arise from a computer failure or other serious contingencies that can affect computer operations. At a minimum, management should determine whether equipment at another site would be available for use if the computer breaks down or cannot be used because of fire or flood.

Computers must be turned off in an orderly way if they are to resume working properly. The program may not be able to restart if power is abruptly turned off in the middle of a critical operation. Operators must be instructed in the proper method for terminating operations and should avoid a sudden power cut unless absolutely necessary.

Communicating and Monitoring Policies

Internal control systems are fragile unless the control procedures are clear to all concerned, and these procedures are reviewed frequently to make certain that they are followed in the proper manner. Every accountant can tell stories of internal controls that looked good on paper until they checked and found that people got lazy or sloppy and just were not following them. Remember that a good internal control system is vital, but it can also be a nuisance.

Make certain that operating people understand the procedures that they should follow and that they review performance frequently.

CONTROLS PROVIDED BY ACCOUNTING SOFTWARE

The following discussion reviews most of the control techniques provided in one fashion or another by accounting software. Very few products, if any, provide all of these controls.

Many of these controls may not be significant in a specific installation. For example, the control needs of a small business, in which one of the owners operates the computer, is very different from the control environment required for a network in which many people have access to computer programs and data.

If a program is selected that does not provide sufficient control protection, additional controls must be installed to compensate for this weakness.

Passwords

The use of passwords is the most popular and most frequently abused technique for software access control. Passwords have been found written on computer tables, pasted to the sides of monitors, and bandied around the workplace like pieces of candy. Procedures for installing and using passwords usually arrive with software manuals that are open for all to see.

Passwords have also been lost or forgotten, thereby locking out all users and creating delays and other problems for the installation.

Password protection can be provided by

☐ Accounting software

☐ Network software

☐ Software specifically designed for access control.

The degree of password protection provided by accounting software varies considerably from one product to another. Some programs do not provide for any password protection at all and should be used only by a small business in which only the owner or trusted members of the owner's family keep the accounting records.

Generally, the password protection provided by accounting software is limited to preventing unauthorized users from having access to designated screens and the functions related to those screens. This access may function on one level or many levels. The single-level approach permits the assignment of passwords by module or company. The module approach permits all persons entering an acceptable password to work in payroll, accounts receivable, general ledger, or similar module. The company approach permits working in all modules of the designated company. However, one cannot limit access to some of the records and functions provided by these modules.

Multilevel passwords are more flexible, because they can control access to files and procedures within each module or company. Multilevel passwords allow users to permit some people to look at files but not make any entries or changes. For example, a salesperson might be permitted access to customer or inventory screens but not permitted to enter transactions. Or a bookkeeper might be permitted to enter journal entries but not have access to the procedures required for designing or printing financial statements.

Multilevel protection within accounting software is defined pretty much by the way screen menus are displayed. If the program uses the same screen for adding, deleting, and modifying employee information, there is no way to limit access to just one of these functions. If the program provides separate screens for adding, deleting, and modifying employee information, separate passwords can be used for each function.

Network and other software adds additional access controls. For instance, a user password can be used to permit access to a screen, but limit the functions that the user can perform. Novell network software, for example, can give the user the "right" to

☐ Read from open files

- ☐ Write to open files
- ☐ Open existing files
- ☐ Create new files
- ☐ Delete files
- ☐ Create, rename, and erase subdirectories
- ☐ Search directories
- ☐ Modify file attributes.

Files can be hidden from users. The network versions of accounting software provide a "record lock" that allows only one person at a time to work with a specific file record. Some programs provide a lock on individual fields in the record, allowing multiple simultaneous access to the same record. In some instances, "field locking" can be confusing.

Password protection is important in any business environment that relies on employees, not principals, for bookkeeping procedures. The required degree of password complexity and sophistication depends upon the hardware configuration and the manner in which computer procedures are performed. A small office with one workstation and a single bookkeeper will not require multilevel passwords. An office with multiple workstations, even if not connected on a network, should have multilevel protection. An office with a network and modem access needs to develop a more sophisticated system.

Management must carefully choose the person responsible for assigning passwords and must see that information about password procedures and the passwords themselves are properly controlled. It must not permit employees to use these passwords improperly, lest they lose their value. Management should also insist that passwords be changed when employees leave, as well as on a periodic basis. The passwords themselves should not be obvious choices. One computer security expert has been quoted as saying that with his list of commonly used passwords he can break almost any password code.

Logging Procedures

Logging procedures are software routines that keep track of the computer. Each user is required to enter his or her name (or code) when attempting to use the software. In turn, the logging software maintains a record of the time started and stopped, the name of the user, plus information about the files accessed and the programs used. This information is stored in a special log file and is available to persons who enter the required password.

Logging reports are helpful in determining who has used computer files and when they were used, and in providing some indication of what was done. Such reports disclose unusual activity, such as work performed after normal business hours or unauthorized access or work. Comparison with personnel records might indicate the unauthorized use of passwords assigned to others.

Logging routines are rarely included in accounting software. Most single users rely on simpler controls to prevent unauthorized access to files and records. Logging routines are usually provided by network software because the greater number of users and workstations require an enhanced degree of control.

Logging routines, like all controls, are only useful if properly administered through password protection and reviewed by management. If logs are available, don't wait to review the reports until after trouble starts. Insist on a periodic review and sign-off by a responsible officer.

Balanced Journal Entries

Most accounting software will not permit the posting of unbalanced journal entries. There are differing methods of dealing with this control. Some programs will not permit users to exit from journal entry screens unless the entries balance. Other programs will allow users to exit, but display an error message if users attempt to post from unbalanced entries. A third approach is to force the entry to balance by posting the amount of the difference to a special type of suspense account.

Most users favor the first method. Accountants who write up records for clients may find that one of the other two methods maintains a smoother production flow.

Assignment of Transaction Numbers

Virtually every accounting program on the market assures users that the program provides good audit trails. Beware! In many cases, the software provides little assurance that all journals are complete records of entries that have been made to the system.

The assignment of control numbers plus the forced printing of journals are the keys to good audit trails.

The designers of different accounting software products have used the assignment of sequence numbers in many interesting ways. One technique is to assign an access number every time a user enters the software. By keeping a daily record of access numbers, one can determine whether any person attempted unauthorized access.

Another technique is to assign a sequence number to each batch of journal entries. These batch numbers print at the top of each journal. Sequence numbers printed on the journals assure users that there have been no entries for which the journals have been destroyed. This important and highly desirable control is not available as frequently as it should be. If the software assigns batch numbers but does not reassign them if the batch is cancelled, the control has little value.

Forced Printing of Journals

Accounting software prints many reports that look like journals. The nature of these reports, and the titles given to them, depend on the method by which the software accepts and posts transactions.

In Chapter 1's discussion about terminology, it was stated that some software uses the word "register" instead of "journal." In some instances this is just poor terminology. In other cases, the term is used deliberately because the software cannot produce a true journal. Instead, transaction details are listed in the "register" in order of account or transaction number, but not in true chronologic order.

Accounting software works in either "real time" or "batch" mode.

Real-time software posts each transaction, line by line, as soon as it has been entered and accepted by the user. The usual requirement is an on-line printer, which prints each transaction line as it is being posted. This printout becomes the entry journal. Advocates of real-time software claim that this approach speeds the processing of information and produces faster results. In most situations, this is a spurious argument because

☐ Real-time posting does not allow for review and correction before processing. This results in a greater number of errors entering the system, errors that are harder to trace and correct because they have been processed.

☐ The computer process of batch posting adds very little time to the overall process.

☐ Useful financial statements require review and adjustment of trial balances. Raw data from the accounting system does not provide a reliable financial picture.

Most software functions in batch mode and permits the printing of entries so that they can be reviewed and corrected before posting. After transaction batches have been edited, a separate function is selected for posting. Good software controls should

□ Force a printing of the transactions at the time of posting. Some provide forced journal printing as an option, some do not require it at all.

□ Provide a clear distinction between the transaction lists that are printed for review and correction, and the record of transactions as they were actually processed and posted. Some programs use identical format for both reports so that the user is never certain if the correct list has been retained for the audit trail.

□ Permit users to print out journals at any time, not just at the time of posting. A single printout can easily be lost or discarded, thereby obscuring the trail, or even covering up error or dishonesty. The ability to print journals at any time provides the assurance that all journals truly present a list of all transactions that have entered the system. This important control function is provided by a limited number of accounting software products and generally is available only in the general ledger module. Audit trails in the other modules are weaker.

The situation is further complicated by the requirements of posting in the general ledger and posting in other modules such as accounts receivable and accounts payable. General ledger postings usually are done once a month. Postings are required more frequently in the other modules. If many batches are posted during an accounting period, the software will print a separate journal for each posting. Some products can combine all module postings made during the month into a true journal for posting to the general ledger.

Why all this interest in the way journals can be called up and printed? There are two important reasons for this. First, and most important, journals are an essential part of the audit trail. They provide important evidence of transactions that have entered the accounting stream. Second, journals provide a path for obtaining information. A system that prints only batch journals, and not period journals, obscures the path and adds to the task of looking up and verifying information.

Running Totals

Most accounting software displays one or more totals during journal entry. Totals are important for minimizing error and control. Watch out for software that does not show any totals during journal entry. These products display totals after data entry is completed, a very clumsy approach.

The number of totals, and manner of display, varies significantly from one product to another. Each user should determine how important these different methods are in their applications. An overview of the different varieties follows.

The simplest and poorest method is to display one running total, the net difference between debits and credits. The total informs the user whether entries balance but is no help in providing any protection against the failure to enter all of the items in the batch. If the entry clerk, through error, skips over a vendor invoice, a payment, or any other item, the one total display will not catch this error.

Next is the two-total method; the display of total debits and total credits. This method provides two safeguards. First, the user knows when entries balance because both totals must agree. (As an additional safeguard, most software will not post from journals that are out of balance.) Second, the user can compare the totals against a previously computed control total, thus proving that all items have been entered.

The three-total method asks the user to enter the control total in a separate field. The software then determines whether both debit and credit totals equal the control total. This method forces the user to pay attention to control totals. This safeguard can prove clumsy in situations requiring control totals of net amounts. An example is the entry of disbursement checks. The checks might be made out in net amounts—that is, invoice amount net of discount. Therefore, the batch total (control total) would be a number representing gross amounts less discounts. This number would not equal the total of the debits or of the credits required for journal entry. Because of this problem, the three-total method is rarely used.

Some software programs provide additional help when transactions have to be split among a number of accounts. The software provides a transaction total and then displays the undistributed amount. The user cannot complete entering the transaction until the undistributed amount is zero. This device is most useful for catching errors in entering payroll and disbursement checks.

Unfortunately, modules for order entry and inventory modules rarely display any running totals. This places an added burden on checkers and supervisors to determine that all transactions have been entered correctly.

Verification of Account Codes

Most software files are referenced by codes. The assignment and entry of codes is a major part of daily routine. Obviously, the entry of a wrong or invalid code creates errors. How does software provide assurance that this will not happen?

In most cases, the software will display the account name when the account code is entered. If one enters the code of a customer or vendor, the monitor will display the corresponding name. A similar display occurs when a general ledger account code is entered. Theoretically, the entry clerk should compare the displayed information with the name on the source document, and correct the code if required. If the clerk enters an invalid code—that is, a code not on file—the software usually will display a prompt indicating that an error was made.

Some partly integrated software does not verify general ledger account numbers at the time of data entry. The software will accept any account number until the user attempts to transfer transactions to the general ledger. At that point the software will display an error message and require the user to track down invalid account numbers.

Still, there is no assurance that all coding errors will be caught, particularly if the entry clerk is careless and fails to compare account names. Some software provides an additional safeguard by printing the account names on the journals. Unfortunately, other software prints the account code without the account name. This omission makes it more difficult to catch coding errors.

Hash totals of account numbers are another safeguard. This control, which applies only to numeric codes, requires computing a control total of all account codes. During data entry, the computer also adds up the codes. The proof of accurate code entry lies in the matching of the two totals. Software providing this feature usually permit users the option of using it or not. The task of totaling account numbers is time consuming and therefore the control is infrequently used.

Logical Controls

Most accounting software tries to prevent users from doing things that cause errors or permit dishonest activity. This is done by designing the software to refuse to accept or process information unless it complies with the following:

- ☐ The information is entered and processed in the proper sequence.
- ☐ The information carries an acceptable date.
- ☐ The information is valid.
- ☐ All required information is entered.

The need to enter information in the correct sequence often causes problems for beginners. Usually, one must set up a series of files and answer questions about software options before one can start using the software. For example, accounts receivable software might require the user to set up codes for billing terms, shipping method, and salesperson before allowing the user to set up customer files. Or a general ledger package might insist on the user designating the account code of the profit and loss account before allowing the user to set up other accounts. Frequently, the messages indicating that things are out of order are unclear. The software beeps or provides a very cryptic and unfathomable message.

Careful study of the correct sequence of steps required to get started can avoid a lot of frustration and wasted time.

Forced printing of journals is another example of software control over the sequence of operations. Some software will not execute the posting function until journals have been printed. As further control, some will not permit any changes to journals between printing and posting.

The manner in which the software determines that the information applies to an acceptable accounting period is another source of control that merits attention. All general ledger software requires that users define their accounting periods. Each period is given a number together with its starting and ending dates. The more limited varieties of software restrict users to making entries in one period at a time. In order to prevent entries into the wrong period, transaction dates must fall within the dates of the current accounting period. Otherwise, the software will not accept the information. This may be satisfactory for some, but most users wish to start entries in a new period, even if the old period cannot be closed, particularly at year end. The software limitation just described forces users to delay entering subsequent period transactions, thus developing a work backlog and postponing the processing of current information.

Better accounting software can handle a number of accounting periods. The total number of periods may be limited; the software will refuse to accept transactions that fall outside of these periods. There may be additional restrictions for assigning transactions to accounting periods that fall outside the acceptable range. These controls can be helpful or troublesome. The software cannot anticipate all conditions and may lock out entries that are required.

Some other examples of software verification of input include

☐ Refusal to accept duplicate check numbers

☐ A warning notice if two vendor invoices are entered with the same invoice numbers

□   A warning notice during order entry if customer exceeds the credit limit.

Most software checks to see that all required information is entered. Some examples are

□   Refusing to accept an order without the entry of an account code for payment terms

□   Refusing to complete a master payroll record without the entry of codes denoting payroll type, number of dependents, and similar information

□   Refusing to process a sales order without assignment of an order number or transaction date.

Information entry is effected with a series of screens. Each screen displays a number of fields. Usually entry is mandatory for some, but not all, of the fields. Manuals are often unclear in stating which fields are mandatory and which are optional. Users often try to skip fields that do not appear significant for their applications and find that the software locks on them. Watch out for software that insists upon the repetitive entry of information that serves no useful purpose.

Master File Controls

Master files are computer files similar to bookkeeping ledgers; they contain transaction records by account. Examples of master files are general ledger detail files and customer account files.

The task of setting up master files is required at the inception of a computer accounting system. Open transactions and balances are entered so that the files are current and can be used on an ongoing basis. This one-time effort usually gets a lot of attention because no one wants errors introduced right at the introduction of the system. When the initial entry is completed, file details should be printed and checked to confirm correctness.

Master files are the heart of the accounting system. And, just like the old-fashioned manual ledgers, they must be treated with respect and have very good controls. The software should not permit anyone to change the information in these files without going through routine entry and journal procedures. Nor should the system permit the deletion of any record as long as there are transactions in the record, even if the transactions net out to zero. Unfortunately, many accounting software products omit some of these controls.

Users frequently call up master file records in order to look at the information in the account. While the screen is displayed, some software permits entries to be made directly into various fields of the record, bypassing the routines of journal entry and printout. Sometimes, warnings are printed in the manuals about the danger of doing this, but the software still permits the changes to be made. The software may require a printout showing the details of the change. However, unless these printouts are given sequence numbers for control purposes, they provide no protection against unauthorized changes.

This is a serious lapse in accounting control. Be very cautious when choosing software that permits entries directly into master files.

If the software includes either or both of the aforementioned control deficiencies, access to the functions of changing or deleting master file records by password should be limited to a highly trusted individual. Insist on printouts of the records before change or deletion.

ENHANCED CONTROLS

There are situations in which it is advisable to enhance the controls provided by existing software with additional software that has been designed specifically for purposes of control.

If neither the accounting nor network software provides for logging, special software can be obtained to perform this function. This software is often combined with password functions that provide a greater element of security.

Encryption software will make computer records unintelligible unless the user has access to the encryption code. This technique guards against the unauthorized access by persons who could otherwise read and alter computer records.

Communication callback devices guard against unauthorized access to records via modems. These devices verify a seemingly authorized call by calling back to the authorized number and waiting for an acceptable response.

Magnetic card and biochemical readers are external devices that are used to verify the authenticity of users.

Dramatic stories about computer viruses have focused a great deal of attention to this new security danger. In fact, most of these attacks have occurred under one of the following circumstances:

☐ Very large networks that are accessed through telephone lines and modems have been breached by hackers.

☐ Smaller installations have been attacked through programs down-loaded from networks that are transferred from altered copies of programs. The best response to this threat is to avoid the temptation to copy free software unless the sources have been carefully checked.

Most accounting software applications are much more vulnerable to other problems than to software viruses, as indicated in the quote at the beginning of this chapter. For those who are concerned, it is strongly recommended that the article entitled "Virus Infection" in the April 25, 1989, issue of *PC* magazine be read. Eleven antivirus programs were reviewed and tested. Additionally, the article described ten virus protection techniques that do not require special software, only discipline. The article concluded with these words: "Our testing proved that no single program can deliver 100-percent protection from virus attacks . . . but many put up lines of defense that can do some good."

All of the add-on control programs and hardware devices add complexities and time constraints to the accounting process and are rarely warranted for use by the smaller business.

COMPUTER PROTECTION

The computer itself is an electronic device that is threatened by a number of conditions that are not significant in the world of pencil and paper. These conditions relate to the nature of the power supply, the fragility of read-write heads, and sensitivity to air pollution.

Computers are sensitive to changes in electricity. An increase in voltage, no matter how short in duration, can burn some of its components. Such increases can be caused by electrical storms and static electricity. A drop in voltage, or brief break in power, can result in malfunctions that corrupt data files and programs, making them unusable.

Many devices are offered that provide various kinds of protection against these electrical problems. Antistatic mats protect against the problems of static electricity. Inexpensive surge protectors guard against sudden spikes in voltage. Backup power supplies provide sufficient battery power to provide enough time to close down the computer in an orderly way.

Users should choose the protection that they need based on their experiences with the power supply.

Moving computers can be hazardous unless some thought is given to protecting the read-write heads in the disk drives. Diskette drives should be closed with diskettes in the drives. Hard disk read-write heads should be "parked." Some drives come with software that provides this function. Other drives always "park" the heads when the power is turned off.

The units themselves should be moved in their original container and padding.

Disk drives are very sensitive to dust and dirt and smoke. Computers should be located in a clean environment. Operators should not be permitted to smoke, eat, or drink near the computer.

PHYSICAL ACCESS

All of the preceding electronic protection schemes can be rendered useless if physical access to the computer and its products is not carefully controlled.

Computers should be located so unauthorized persons will have difficulty using them without being noticed. Monitor displays should be faced so that they cannot easily be viewed by any person other than the operator. A complicated password scheme to protect payroll information is not much good if passersby can look over the shoulder of the payroll clerk. Computer operators should be instructed to turn off their machines or log out of the network whenever they cannot be at their workstation.

Key controls should be used wherever practical. Key locking devices can be used for computer keyboards. Computers holding sensitive information and related files such as backup diskettes should be stored under lock and key.

Waste and discard techniques must provide for the destruction of old electronic files and reports. This material should never go out the door in the wastepaper basket. One of the largest computer scams was successful because of information gleaned from discarded manuals and other computer materials.

Some situations may warrant bolting computers to worktables in order to prevent theft of both the computer and the information contained on its hard disks.

Removable hard disk devices can also be used to limit access to data files. These devices look like diskette drives but can hold a lot of information.

CONTROLS OUTSIDE OF THE COMPUTER

The discussion of controls started with one important set of noncomputer controls, namely the plans and policies determined by management. Additionally, a good control system requires some activities that take place away from the computer. There are three fundamental reasons for this:

1. No software can insure the accuracy or reliability of the information entered into the system.
2. No software by itself can provide adequate safeguards against the dishonest activities of computer operators and managers.
3. No computer system can provide protection against catastrophes such as fire, water damage, and power failure.

Some manual procedures and documentation are required to complete the system of controls.

It would take many pages for a complete discussion of controls outside the computer. The successful application of these controls is best left in the hands of accountants who have the skills for evaluating risks and determining appropriate control responses. However, management should be aware of some basic requirements, including the need to

☐ Segregate duties as much as possible. For example, it is good practice to
   —. List cash receipts before handing them to the computer operator.
   —. Provide written approvals of vendor invoices before data entry; do not rely on the control provided by signing the check.
   —. Prevent the people who handle merchandise from also making computer entries.
   —. Prevent computer operators from handling incoming or outgoing mail.

☐ Test the computer system by slipping dummy transactions into the system and seeing how they are processed.

☐ Ask an accountant to review computer operations and make recommendations about internal control and audit procedures.

Above all, top management personnel should not short-cut some of these rules just because they are in higher positions.

SUMMARY

This chapter has reviewed the various categories of controls that must be considered in connection with the installation of accounting software. Six different categories were discussed:

- ☐ Management plans and policies
- ☐ Controls provided by accounting software
- ☐ Control enhancements provided by special software and hardware
- ☐ Computer protection
- ☐ Controls on physical access to the computer
- ☐ Controls outside the computer

Users should be aware of the type of control provided by each category. No single type of control can provide an adequate system. One must not count on the accounting software to provide all the answers. Each category has some function in the overall scheme, but the method of implementation varies in simplicity and cost.

Instead, after reviewing the risks inherent in the accounting software, the computer configuration, and the personnel who will work with the computer system, consider how each control category should be implemented. Evaluate the benefits of each control with the costs of installation and operation. A small single-user system operated by management requires a very different set of controls than does a large networked system that involves a great number of sensitive materials. A control system is an insurance policy: Underinsurance can be disastrous. Overinsurance can be costly.

13

The Search

INTRODUCTION

A lot of territory has been covered to prepare the reader for the software search. Many elements must come into play for a successful search and installation. One cannot overstress the importance of taking the time necessary to determine business needs, including reasonable projections of future requirements, and acquiring an understanding of the basics of accounting software including the arcane and often tortured vocabulary associated with it.

After reading the first chapter, the reader should not be surprised to discover that the marketplace for accounting software is somewhat chaotic. There is confusion in product and company names. Terminology is not standardized and often flies in the face of accepted accounting nomenclature. Products are offered by many small publishers located in many parts of the United States and Canada. The task of obtaining specific and meaningful information is difficult and challenging.

Chapter 2 explained the difference between manual and electronic accounting systems and stressed the importance of understanding the implications of this difference when considering the installation of accounting software.

Chapter 3 focused on the importance of considering the tone and style of an organization when selecting accounting software. Management attitudes toward risk and the perceived affect of change on status and power must be taken into account when considering whether to make simple or drastic changes in operations. The quality of the personnel environment, including the rate of employee turnover and the level of morale, affects the acceptable degree of complexity involved in a new system. Poor internal control presents an important danger signal.

Chapter 4 raised five basic questions that must be answered before starting the search for suitable accounting software, including the fundamental question of whether computerization is really an appropriate goal and, if so, making some determination about the timing and scope of the installation.

Chapter 5 presented an overview of the design and operation of accounting software programs. This background information should help novices find their way through the maze of operational detail presented in software manuals.

The first five chapters, therefore, provided the background necessary to condition the prospective user for the challenges and problems that usually arise in the search for suitable software. They also stress the importance of preparing a detailed list of software requirements and distinguishing between vital needs and those of lesser importance.

Chapters 6 through 12 provided detailed explanations of 12 significant attributes of accounting software. Most buyers tend to concentrate on function and purchase price. These chapters suggest that there are many other attributes that affect the ultimate success of the installation.

Prospective users who have taken all of this seriously will have prepared themselves by

☐ Determining which accounting applications should be considered and their relative importance, as outlined in Chapter 7

☐ Listing their capacity requirements, as discussed in Chapter 6

☐ Listing their functional requirements and distinguishing between those that are essential and nonessential, as discussed in Chapter 7

☐ Evaluating the capability of their organizations to accommodate to computerized accounting systems and setting reasonable software goals, as discussed in Chapters 3 and 4

☐ Preparing a budget and financing plan for all of the cost elements that will be incurred in connection with the installation, as discussed in Chapters 9 through 11

☐ Developing some idea of when installation events should occur, as discussed in Chapter 10.

With this information, prospective buyers should have a good idea of what they are looking for in terms of capacity, function, control, ease of learning, costs, multiple-user capability, and installation timing.

This task is not as overwhelming as it may sound. Much of the planning requires serious thought, but does not take a great deal of time. The failure to plan properly can be very costly and is not worth the risk.

So armed with all of this information, how does one find the best solution? There are many resources. Unfortunately, none are ideal. A person who has had some familiarity with accounting software and feels confident that he or she has a clear perception of the kind of product that will provide a good solution will probably start on a direct path by calling consultants, retailers, and others in order to determine which resource is most promising.

However, even when a conclusion is reached that an organization should computerize an accounting function, many concerns stand in the way of implementing a solution:

- ☐ A concern that one should wait for a better solution that seems imminent

- ☐ A concern about overpaying when a cheaper product might do just as well

- ☐ A concern about time, about the many hours that can be spent in tracking down and implementing a solution

- ☐ A concern about failure, about making the wrong selection of software and hardware

By now, most managers understand the folly of postponing computer installations because of the promise of better products that will soon be brought to market. Experience has demonstrated that many promised software innovations take much longer to perfect than anticipated. Additionally, new products require some seasoning in the field before they are relatively free from error. These conditions are particularly significant with respect to accounting software. Many computer innocents also realize that a learning period of six months to a year is usually required before they will have acquired the skills that will permit them to optimize their use of the computer. Delaying an installation in order to wait for better products also postpones the development of these skills, skills that are becoming more and more important in the competitive business environment.

Of course, if no suitable solution can be found with existing products, the solution is either contract programming or waiting for something better to surface.

The concern about overpaying usually is highly exaggerated, particularly when it comes to the software itself. The chapters on cost clearly indicated that software prices represent a small part of the total installation. A serious mistake can be made by opting for a cheaper product for which there is little support, one which proves clumsy and constrictive in application. The additional cost of a higher performance product is well justified if it results in appropriate savings in time and frustration.

The concern about time commitments must always be addressed, because every installation will create time stresses. Management must be prepared to commit the time required for administering planning and installation. Personnel must be available for performing these tasks plus training and parallel runs. Time resources must be made available, or the installation can founder because of lack of direction, poor morale arising from a stressed staff, and failure to recognize the early warning signs of problems because people are too busy to pay attention. Concern about time is best met by working out a practical time schedule that will provide the necessary hours for operating personnel, as well as a commitment by management to spend the supervisory time when needed.

The concern about failure can be significant. A manager who takes pride in results and feels ignorant about computers may have a strong concern about making uninformed decisions that result in failure. Everyone must recognize the fact that stories of computer failures and losses abound.

A fearful management should first search for a consultant who has the technical qualifications and the patience and temperament to work effectively with a cautious and nervous administration. The installation should be executed very slowly and be carefully controlled until confidence grows along with good computer knowledge and skill.

Another suggestion is for management to purchase one of the low-end integrated packages referred to previously, just for purposes of education. A few hours spent with the software will provide a great deal of insight into the functions and limitations of accounting programs. After this experience, the prospective user often will be in a much better position to understand and evaluate the software characteristics described in this book.

PREPARATION FOR THE SEARCH

A few simple but important decisions are still required before starting the search for appropriate software:

1. If the organization is already using a computer, should the search, at least initially, be confined to software that will function in the same

environment? Macintosh users may wish to confine their search to Macintosh programs. Organizations running on a Unix™ network may decide to look first for software that is compatible with Unix.

2. Software searches can take a lot of time. Should this be done by a person within the organization, or should an outside consultant be engaged for this purpose?

    A competent consultant can save a lot of time and provide essential guidance in planning the installation. Locating a consultant can be a challenge: Look in the telephone book. Obtain recommendations from retailers and professionals such as accountants and business advisors. Make inquiries at business shows and conferences. The prospective buyer can save a lot of the consultant's time and personnel cost by first preparing a list of specific accounting requirements.

3. Should prospective buyers start by looking at generalized programs, or confine their searches to products specifically designed for their industries?

    Usually it is best to begin with general business accounting software that is distributed in the buyer's area or familiar to the buyer's consultant or accountant. A number of software lists are available, setting forth the names of well-known accounting software publishers. Although these lists differ, there are approximately 15 publishers whose products are recognized and distributed nationally. Some publishers offer a number of product lines. There are advantages in working with nationally recognized products that are distributed in one's area:

    ☐ Products with wider distribution tend to have fewer problems because more people have used the product.

    ☐ Local people familiar with the product can assist with installation. Some publishers distribute through area representatives who will also provide training and support.

    The alternative is to concentrate on vertical software that offers programs specifically designed for a particular type of operation. Examples of vertical software, as described in Chapter 5, are

    ☐ Medical practice
    ☐ Dental practice
    ☐ Real estate management
    ☐ Construction
    ☐ Manufacturing
    ☐ Professional practice

Since these products are written for a limited market, they are usually marketed through ads in industry journals and through trade conferences. Vertical market software frequently provides some very good functions, records, and forms oriented to a specific industry coupled with relatively clumsy operations with respect to general bookkeeping and accounting. Prices can be considerably higher than general business software.

In some instances, potential users are faced with a difficult choice between general and industry-oriented software products.

Users cannot expect to find perfection. Despite all of the software on the market, it is almost impossible to find a perfect fit. No one product will provide all of the desired functions and characteristics, or will fall within a reasonable price range. A number of compromises must be considered as the search continues. Some desirable functions will have to be foregone. Some changes in operation might have to be considered in order to accommodate to the requirements of the software.

Some publishers will modify their programs to suit specific needs, for an additional programming fee. Others provide source code to qualified programmers for the same purpose. Some programmers publish catalogues of their modifications to well-known accounting software products. However, once modified, the original publisher may not provide technical support. Some publishers make no provision for custom modification. Minor modifications, such as changing the field titles or report column heads, are frequently made. Major modifications are risky because the effect of these modifications on overall performance is hard to anticipate. Modifications can also be troublesome when software updates are installed.

No matter what approach is used, whether through consultants or internal personnel, whether limited in scope to an existing hardware configuration or to a particular industry, users must be prepared to review and modify search guidelines as they gather and analyze software information. No user can expect to come across the ideal. The challenge is to find products with sufficient merit to offset their deficiencies and thereby justify their use.

The offset to the difficulty of finding an ideal solution is that the process of reviewing a number of software products frequently turns up useful ideas and functions that were not contemplated when the search began. As new solutions come to mind, existing requirements may not be as important as originally contemplated.

4. To what extent should the size and stability of the software publisher influence the buyer's purchase decision?

Software publishers are experiencing strong competitive pressures. Most of them are small businesses with relatively short histories. A number of publishers have gone out of business. Some have discontinued support on some product lines. Difficult decisions may have to be made between a strong product offered by a relatively unknown publisher, and a weaker product available from a company that appears to have greater viability.

THE SEARCH

Because the industry is so fragmented, software searches can be difficult. The following resources are suggested:

- [ ] Publisher presentations
- [ ] Magazine articles
- [ ] Trade journals
- [ ] Industry meetings and conferences
- [ ] Specialized resellers
- [ ] Software lists
- [ ] Computer stores
- [ ] Accountants
- [ ] "The Requirements Analyst," a software search program
- [ ] Word of mouth

Most software searches are conducted in two stages. Stage one consists of identifying products that merit serious study and review. One is fortunate if a number of qualified candidates can be found. There is also the possibility that nothing suitable can be located.

Stage two is an in-depth examination and analysis of the software. This examination should be done with a fully operational version, not a demonstration version with limited functionality.

If a specific product looks interesting, make certain to obtain the name of the publisher, the name of the product, and the version number. Determine how long the specific version has been on the market. As a rule, accounting software products are updated with new versions every one or two years. Some products, particularly those sold by mail order, are sold with a refund provision if returned within a specified number of days.

Publisher Presentations

Many software publishers periodically offer presentations of their products to interested viewers. These presentations are usually given in retail stores or meeting rooms. Invitations are distributed via targeted mailing lists. These presentations are most useful if

☐ Potential users do their homework and have a good idea of what they are looking for. The presentation will concentrate on the strength of the program. Viewers must ferret out weaknesses.

☐ Demonstrations are limited to groups of people with similar interests. Otherwise, topics may be covered that are not significant to many viewers.

☐ Demonstrations are located in areas without disturbance and background noise. Many store presentations are ineffective because the sound of outside conversations and machine noise interfere with concentration.

☐ A large monitor is used so that attendees can clearly see the demonstration material.

☐ Printed reports are prepared and distributed.

☐ Viewers are given to understand exactly what equipment is being used for the demonstration, so they can compare with alternative hardware.

Software presentations, if properly organized, are useful for beginning searchers in providing some insight into software operations and providing a meeting ground for sharing ideas. They are not detailed enough to provide definitive solutions.

Magazine Articles

Magazine racks are filled with journals about computers. However, very few magazines pay much attention to accounting software. When they do appear, accounting software reviews provide useful background information and highlight interesting features but rarely provide all of the information required for a product evaluation. Accounting software is complex. Many hours are required to install each module, put it through its paces, and write a useful critique. Most writers have little incentive to spend all of this time. They tend to go through the steps required to get a rough idea of a few modules (usually general ledger, accounts receivable, and accounts payable), scan the related manuals, and call the publisher when clarification is required. Functions and capacity are briefly explored. Many important characteristics such as speed of data entry and adequacy of control and audit trails are often ignored. A number of modules of great significance to the user, such as inventory and order entry, are rarely reviewed at all.

Magazine articles are useful for obtaining background information. The articles should be read carefully because weaknesses and criticisms, if discussed at all, are usually given a very light touch. The charts and lists of representative accounting software that frequently accompany the texts can be as informative as the articles themselves. Every list contains different names, although some nationally distributed products appear on almost every such list. It may be helpful to call some of these publishers and determine whether their products are distributed locally. This in turn can lead to the names of retailers and consultants who can be helpful in the software search.

Although magazines try to present current information, they frequently lag behind the market because of the time required to review, write, edit, and schedule their articles.

Trade Journals

Trade journals are useful for determining what software, if any, has been written for a specific industry. Industry specific software (also called vertical software) attempts to fill needs not addressed by general software, such as maintaining special industry information (such as patient or service records), filling out industry specific forms, and performing special functions.

Much of this software addresses a very limited market. Therefore, advertising and promotion is targeted through trade journals, meetings, and conventions. In many cases, the product itself is distributed by the publisher direct to the end user. In other cases the product might be handled by specialty consultants. Such software is rarely available through regular retail channels.

Because of its limited distribution, prospective users should check carefully into the reliability of the publisher and the quality of the software performance. Ask the publishers for the names of users and follow up on the references that are provided.

In some situations it may be feasible to transfer the output of a specific industry module into more general software. For example, industry software with special billing or inventory capability might be transferred to a more widely used general ledger module with better performance capability. In the technical jargon of the industry, this requires a general ledger package with an "import" capability.

Industry Meetings and Conferences

Industry meetings and conferences often provide an excellent way to learn about accounting software. Computers are hot topics today, and many conference programs provide a number of talks and discussions on computer subjects pertinent to the host industry. Many discussion leaders are either industry managers who are willing to share their experiences with others, or consultant/vendors who are looking for business. A lot of information and comment provided informally at these sessions are invaluable. Most conferences provide an exhibition hall where vendors display and discuss their products and services.

A prospective user who has done his of her homework and comes prepared with a good profile of desired software characteristics will often find that an industry conference provides valuable leads.

Specialized Resellers

The need to combine special industry knowledge with technical background in computers and accounting has led to the formation of a number of companies that offer complete computer solutions for specific industries. These products may include their own proprietary software plus an assortment of hardware configurations ranging from stand alone to extensive networks.

These specialized resellers are known in the industry as VARs (value added resellers). VARs usually work with specific software publishers and hardware manufacturers. Prospective customers frequently encounter them at booths in trade shows and at software presentations.

Software Lists

Software lists are also prepared and sold commercially by independent publishers. Some hardware manufacturers, particularly IBM and Apple, publish lists of software compatible with their hardware. The lists can be found in many libraries.

Information is grouped into broad general classifications that vary from one text to another. Data on accounting software may be listed by application, such as accounts receivable or general ledger, or by industry. Product descriptions are brief and usually are condensations of information provided by the software publisher. The lists make no distinction between small local publishers and those with large national distribution. Since the work of compiling and printing these lists takes many months, they often contain outdated information. Lists more than two years old are useless.

Because of their sketchy and untested information, software guides are most useful as a last resort when all other attempts to find a suitable solution have failed. At best, they open up inquiry into unknown products.

Computer Stores

Very few retailers carry more than one or two accounting software products. Even fewer carry a complete line of the latest version of the products that they carry. A few years ago, one major computer-store chain was reported to have placed an interactive program in every store that asked potential customers a single question and, depending on the answer, recommended one of the three products that they stocked. Not one of these products are on the market today! Many sales clerks avoid discussions of accounting software because of their unfamiliarity with these products and the large amounts of time required to explain and demonstrate them.

Some retailers recognize these limitations and channel special software requests to outside vendors and consultants. The salesperson will interview a customer to determine the customer's requirements (a needs analysis) and then arrange an appointment in the store with a consultant or software vendor for a deeper discussion or a software demonstration. This second meeting is most productive if the customer thoroughly communicates his or her requirements in advance.

Accountants

There are a diminishing number of accountants who do not encourage computer oriented questions from their clients. Many provide computer advisory services. The scope of these services varies with the nature and size of the practice. Smaller practices do not have the resources to cover many different accounting software products. They prefer to become familiar with one product and introduce this product wherever feasible. By concentrating on one package, they may offer the ability of working directly on data files prepared by client software, thereby reducing costs and speeding production. Accountants with specialized practices often become familiar with software packages designed specifically for the industry they serve. This knowledge can be invaluable for those in the industry. However, clients who cannot be satisfied with the software supported by their accountants frequently must look elsewhere for help.

Accountants tend to stress the value of software operations that are closely linked with their services, namely general ledger, followed by accounts receivable and accounts payable, and they tend to be biased in favor of software that is strong in these areas. They are less likely to be able to evaluate modules that are more closely linked to the daily operations of the business, such as sales order entry, inventory, and job cost.

Even if accountants are not proficient in accounting software, their knowledge of their clients can be very helpful in defining needs and setting up adequate controls.

The Requirements Analyst

One publisher provides software to assist in the search for an appropriate accounting program. The program is designed to be used by consultants and, among other problems, may be more trouble than it is worth for a single search.

The Requirements Analyst is published by Computer Training Services of Rockville, Maryland. The product comprises a manual and diskettes. The program itself is a set of Lotus worksheets. The manual includes a brief description of accounting modules and of the consultation/implementation process. Most of the chapters are devoted to descriptions of the accounting products covered by the software.

The Requirements Analyst covers a limited but growing number of products. Information about each product is scattered in a number of sections. In addition to separate chapters describing each product, there are comparison charts covering features, elements, system capacities, pricing, and operating systems. Information is scattered in a confusing fashion. The distinction among features, elements, and capacities is not clear. Features and elements are listed in cryptic language without explanations. Each item is presented with a yes or no response. In most cases, quantified responses, such as the maximum quantity or number of characters, would be much more useful. For example, it would be better to show the number of source journals or the number of open periods permitted by the general ledger function. Instead, *The Requirements Analyst* merely shows whether multiple source journals and multiple open periods are permitted.

The list of features and elements is useful but far from clear and complete. Very little attempt is made to discuss formats of sales invoices and management reports, two characteristics that are very important to users. Many software products provide reports with similar names that present very different kinds of information. The fact that a particular product provides sales analyses by customer is not very meaningful unless one knows what periods are covered, the type of detail information presented, and how information is grouped into subtotals.

A specific needs analysis is performed by scrolling through Lotus templates listing features or elements. Each item is rated as "needed" or "liked." *The Requirements Analyst* then computes the percentages of "needs" and "likes" for each software product. Users can add additional software products to the database. A nice feature of this package is the software evaluation provided in a section entitled "Executive Summary" that precedes each chapter of the manual. This evaluation is coupled with a comparative ratings chart and a list of strengths and weaknesses for each product.

The Requirements Analyst provides a limited but useful reference guide for people who deal with many accounting software questions. The current version covers twenty micro accounting products. Companion products cover vertical software for construction, property management, professional time and billing, and client write-up. Its greatest usefulness lies in the lists of questions presented, because these lists can remind potential users about overlooked qualifications that are significant.

Word of Mouth

Conversations with business acquaintances, industry representatives, software users, and others are most helpful. Check to find out what others are doing and get the benefit of their experience. Try to locate users whose requirements closely match your own, preferably those who have had many months of experience with the software. If the desired application involves large files or heavy transaction volumes, the only way to determine whether operating speeds will be satisfactory is to discuss performance with users who have similar requirements. (Refer to the section in Chapter 11 on speed.)

Communicate with a number of the references supplied by software vendors. The responses can be enlightening and surprising.

Word of mouth usually is most helpful in providing names of reliable resources, from equipment suppliers to consultants and software products.

MAKING THE DECISION

The search for suitable accounting software will probably result in identifying a few products that merit serious evaluation. The next step requires a closer study of the software in order to obtain a deeper understanding of its strengths and weaknesses. This can be a time-consuming task.

The process of comparing different products can be difficult and confusing. The task can be simplified through the use of a four-column rating sheet. In one column, list the 12 attributes presented in Chapter 6. In the second column, rate each product on a scale of one to ten. Use the third column to weigh each attribute. For example, one might assign a higher weight to functionality than to installation cost. Score each product by multiplying column two by column three for each attribute and then adding up the total.

It is not always easy to locate the resources necessary to make in-depth studies. One must be able to obtain working copies of the software, together with manuals and hardware. The job is compounded if modifications or add-on software products are part of the contemplated installation. If all necessary materials can be found, one must still go through the process of installing the software and entering test data (unless test data are provided by the publisher). Manuals rarely provide clear instructions, and calls for technical support may be required to complete the process.

The easiest approach, if at all possible, is to find a knowledgable person who can spend the time required to demonstrate the software in detail. This person might be a local representative of the publisher, a consultant, or a user. Do not expect to obtain this service from a salesperson in a retail store.

If a single product cannot be found that provides a satisfactory solution, a number of alternatives might be considered. At one extreme is the decision to forgo computerization until suitable software reaches the market. A compromise solution may be satisfactory. Such a solution might involve computerizing a limited set of functions, perhaps coupled with the use of a spreadsheet or database for other functions. A complete custom job may be much too expensive and risky. A software company executive was quoted in *Varbusiness* magazine as saying "with the advent of the microcomputer and the comprehensive vertical packages that were being brought out, the custom market was drying up." Limited program modifications might make sense. The same executive goes on to state that 25% of the programs offered by his company are modified for customers.

If any programming is required, whether a complete custom job or a program modification, the time, cost, and stress level will vary inversely with the time and attention given to spelling out precisely what is expected. Even with the best effort, expect some specifications to be misunderstood. If reports are included, have a sample page drawn up, including headers and footers, column formats, and sorting and totaling details. Obtain a copy of the source code so later modifications can be made, if required.

SUMMARY

This chapter first stressed the importance of preparing a needs analysis and referred to the chapters of the book that discussed the elements of such an analysis. The text addressed some of the concerns that stand in the way of making the decisions that will start the computerization process.

Next, four search criteria were discussed that affect the nature and scope of the search:

☐ Should the search be confined to software that is compatible with existing computer systems?

☐ Should the search be carried out by internal personnel or consultants?

☐ Should the search be directed to generalized software or software written for a specific industry?

☐ Should the search be limited to publishers with a proven record of performance?

This was followed by a presentation on search resources. A list of the various types of resources was presented along with a discussion of their relative merits. The reader was cautioned not to expect a perfect fit and that some compromise was to be expected in finding a suitable program.

The chapter concluded with suggestions about evaluating candidate products and arriving at optimum solutions.

__14__

Installation

INTRODUCTION

There is no easy method for predicting the time required to find suitable accounting software. Some make a determination in weeks; others may look for months, even years. The chance of finding an ideal solution is very small, so some degree of compromise is to be expected. The degree of compromise often is influenced by considerations related to installation planning. In some instances it may be better to forgo the possibility of finding better software in order to start the process of installation at an appropriate time. In other instances, the relative ease of installation is one of the primary considerations in the choice of software, since installation can be time consuming and expensive.

This chapter assumes that the reader has completed software and hardware selection and is ready to commence installation. Plans must be transformed into specific policies and activities.

People who are new at working with accounting software often find that their first attempts to install and use the software are fraught with stress and frustration. The tasks that must be performed at inception involve applying many different concepts. Some of these concepts relate to computer hardware, some to the operating system, some to the accounting software, and some others to accounting theory. For the neophyte this can be a tall order.

The experienced user can perform most of these tasks in a few minutes. However, if they are performed incorrectly, or in the wrong sequence, all kinds of problems arise. The monitor may remain blank or display odd-looking images or cryptic error messages. The printer may not respond. Reports may be garbled or contain wrong information. The software may act in a peculiar way or tell the user that an important function is no longer available.

Accounting software manuals attempt to address this problem by explaining the sequence of steps required for successful installation. Some even go as far as to provide a brief text in bookkeeping. Unfortunately, most of this material fails to provide a clear explanation.

This chapter should clear up the mystery!

The installation of accounting software involves three distinct phases:

- ☐ Preinstallation planning
- ☐ Installation and file conversion
- ☐ Inception of operations

PREINSTALLATION PLANNING

The activities that fall into this phase are

- ☐ Establishing the installation timetable
- ☐ Establishing personnel policies
- ☐ Assigning responsibilities
- ☐ Determining the placement of equipment
- ☐ Selecting auxiliary equipment
- ☐ Designing and purchasing forms
- ☐ Establishing noncomputer controls
- ☐ Establishing software controls
- ☐ Deciding on software options
- ☐ Selecting coding schemes
- ☐ Designing operating procedures
- ☐ Establishing a training plan.

The relative importance of the aforementioned activities will vary from one installation to another. A very small office may spend very little time on installation planning. A large installation involving a number of people and many workstations is quite a different story.

Establishing the Installation Timetable

The preparation of a written installation schedule helps to enforce discipline and create an appropriate sense of urgency. Be wary of the tendency to delay installation because of business pressures. Many an accounting package sits unopened on the shelf, and many a computer sits idle because the time is never found to get started. On the other hand, there is no sense in starting an installation when an organization is truly overburdened. Excessive time pressures can lead to serious errors and other problems.

Each of the three phases involved in software installation comprise a number of activities. Some of these activities are required only once, during the first installation of the software. Others require repetition as new modules are installed.

Installation can be staged in a number of different ways. One method of staging is to introduce modules at different times. One might start with general ledger, followed at later dates by accounts receivable, order entry, inventory, and accounts payable. Startup dates should be planned to coincide with slack periods in order to ease the burden on the organization.

Many computer master records provide for the entry of information that may be scattered in many different files. Some of this information must be entered in order to run the new system. Other data may be optional. A great deal of effort is required to compile and enter all of this information, particularly for large files such as a distributor with thousands of inventory items or a service company with a large customer base. In order to get started, one might organize and enter the records in groups and be prepared for manual processing of the missing groups until the entire file can be completed. The mandatory information can be entered first, followed by the entry of optional data over a period of time.

Staging can also relate to the number of workstations assigned to the accounting process. The system might start with a limited number of workstations and then expand as additional modules are introduced. Starting small makes it easier to distinguish between network and accounting software problems.

The installation timetable may require periodic revision if work falls behind schedule, or if a hold is placed on the installation because the initial effort exposes planning errors. Timetables should be set after the requirements of each phase of installation are understood. The installation process should be checked as the work proceeds.

Establishing Personnel Policies

Computer installations can be traumatic and troublesome unless management is sensitive to personnel concerns. Full cooperation is important for success. The introduction of a computer often brings on fear and stress. Staffing for the computer involves changes in work assignments and rhythms. New skills must be acquired while the existing work load is maintained. People are afraid of change, not measuring up, pressure, and layoff.

In order to obtain maximum results, management must consider the staffing required by the new system as well as the personnel demands that arise during installation, a time period which may last for many months. Management should minimize changes in responsibility. It is easier to teach computer skills to people with business knowledge than to train computer personnel in business skills. Hiring new people should be handled very judiciously since new faces will be viewed as a threat by the old-timers.

Overtime and weekend work may be required during the installation period. In addition to following a fair policy for overtime compensation, consider fringes to encourage cooperation such as paying for employee meals and providing free transportation related to late work hours. If possible, minimize overtime by using temporary personnel for routine functions such as copying data onto input forms and keying in master file information.

Assigning Responsibilities

The person responsible for supervising the computer installation must be chosen with great care. Frequently, an officer will be given the nominal responsibility. However, unless that person has the requisite time and interest, this task will be delegated to a subordinate, the system manager. This person becomes crucial to success and must be both technically proficient and trustworthy. The system manager must make many decisions affecting costs, decisions about hardware maintenance, the purchasing of supplies and accessories, and the need to upgrade or change hardware. Second, and equally as important, the system manager must have the master password in order to assign passwords to others on the system. The system manager holds a vital key to internal control.

The new system may require the assignment of new responsibilities and the reassignment of old ones. Prepare a list of job specifications and the names of people who will be assigned to each job. Next prepare a list of the assignments during the period of training and parallel operation. Avoid as much dislocation as possible.

Determining the Placement of Equipment

Equipment placement involves a number of concerns arising from both mechanical and human needs.

The computer may impose some physical restrictions. There are limitations to the distance between terminals on a network. Cabling can be expensive if not properly planned. Some equipment may require dedicated power lines. Spotting terminals in new locations may be more expensive than locating them near existing power and data lines. A dusty location can seriously impair performance.

Provide an efficient workplace. Design a well-illuminated but glare-free working environment. Don't be stingy with work and storage space. Room is needed for placing documents and reference binders so that they can be read without blocking out other work. Provide adequate and convenient storage space for work binders, documents, supplies, diskettes, and reference materials. Avoid placing workstations near aisles where noise can be troublesome. A crowded, noisy workplace results in time loss, slows down the work flow, and contributes to errors.

The importance of privacy is a third consideration. Confidential work must be placed where the monitor, work documents and printer reports cannot be viewed by others. Additionally, adequate storage space with suitable key controls must be provided for personnel who work with confidential material.

Physical controls should be considered for all computer equipment and files. Many computers are provided with locks to prevent unauthorized use of the equipment. This control becomes even more important if there is no provision for maintaining logs of computer users (see Chapter 11). Without good key controls and/or access logs, there is no assurance that unauthorized people have not gained access to computer files and programs.

Selecting Auxiliary Equipment

An investment in well-designed furniture and other equipment can result in considerable savings and improve job satisfaction. The cost of most of this equipment is usually very small compared with the investment in the accounting system.

In regard to furniture, for most users the computer keyboard should be placed on a desk or table that is 26 inches off the floor, which is lower than normal desk height. The monitor should be placed so that the user does not have to bend the neck for viewing. A number of devices are available for reducing monitor glare. Tilt stands are helpful in adjusting the angle of the monitor to suit the viewer, and no-glare screens are available that can be easily placed over the monitor.

Printers should be placed so that they can be readily observed and serviced. Beginners spend a lot of time with the printer. Learning time is shorter when trainees have quick access to printed results. Printer jams and out-of-paper conditions are easier to anticipate and correct when the printer is accessible. Printer tables with slots that facilitate paper feed are very useful.

Generally an "L"-shaped arrangement provides a very satisfactory layout for a workstation.

Filing also requires some thought. Manuals are important reference materials. All too frequently they are never taken out of their shrink wrap, or they lie unused in a remote cabinet. Insist that manuals be set up and placed where users can easily work with them. Working diskettes (other than those with confidential information) should also be placed in convenient trays at each workstation.

Review the material in Chapter 9 about the advantages of selecting condensed print for accounting reports. Narrow (8.5-inch wide) reports fit readily into ring binders, are easy to copy and file, and require less desktop space for viewing. Wide (14-inch wide) reports are easier to read but are a nuisance in every other respect. Many copy machines cannot handle the larger size. The paper must be folded for storage in file cabinets. Storage binders are bulky and clumsy to handle.

Whatever the choice, remember to set up binders for reference material that must be accessed frequently. This material usually consists of printed code lists of such information as general ledger accounts, customers, vendors, billing terms, and other information that is required for data entry.

Chapter 9 also provides advice about the use of equipment for maintaining the power supply and facilitating backup operations. Study this carefully.

Designing and Purchasing Forms

Most accounting software applications require the use of preprinted business forms such as order acknowledgements, sales invoices, and checks.

Some software is very rigid about the design of such forms. Any deviation from the standard requires a program change. Users have very little design choice except to determine whether they would like their business logos to be printed on the form. New forms must be purchased before the software can be used. Brochures from printers offering software-compatible forms frequently are enclosed with the manuals.

Other software provides user control over form layout. One can select the information to be printed and its print location. This feature permits continued use of the existing supply of forms resulting in a saving of stationery costs. Customers do not have to familiarize themselves with new invoice and statement formats. Users who are not interested in the form design feature can function with the default formats provided by the program.

Study format options carefully before placing the printing order. Test the printing of multiple-copy forms on the printer you select. Most printers can produce four copies, but it may be difficult to obtain more clear copies without using very thin paper. Some printers provide a stronger thrust than others and are more suitable for printing multi-ply forms.

Preprinted forms are a nuisance because they require a printer setup. Some accounting software can work with laser printers. Preprinted forms are still necessary because the software prints the variable data, not the form itself. However, paper handling is simpler on a laser than on other printers. Remember that lasers can only print one ply at a time.

In addition to considering new stationery required by the software, one should also review internal forms. The new accounting system may involve changes in internal procedures that require the redesign of existing forms or the introduction of new ones. Word processing software can make the job of preparing and revising internal forms much easier.

Establishing Noncomputer Controls

Chapter 11 described the various types of controls available to computer users and explained that some software provides a greater degree of control than others. The design of controls around the computer should take into account the controls that come with the application software. For example, if the software provides for logging controls, there is a lesser need for physical controls over computer access. A sophisticated password system provides better control against unauthorized access to private files. A program that assigns sequence numbers to all printed journals reduces the need to place the printer in a protected area.

The challenge is to design meaningful controls without incurring excessive costs and unnecessary effort. A balance must be found between control costs and risk.

The basic concerns of accuracy and honesty require that administrative control procedures be performed by noncomputer personnel, even under the best of conditions.

Control procedures are best discussed with an accountant who is familiar with the operation. The risk areas generally are cash, accounts receivable, accounts payable, and inventory. If at all practical, some person should total all input documents before they are given to computer entry personnel. In many instances, it is advisable to use these independent totals to maintain manual controls as a check against computer results. Other important control procedures include the proper segregation of duties, the marking of paid invoices and independent verification of account balances and inventory counts, and the review of transaction journals.

Arrangements should also be made for written transaction authorization where appropriate. Such authorization is frequently advisable for customer credits, payroll registers, and adjusting journal entries.

Computer applications are critical with respect to the accurate assignment of codes. The software may catch invalid codes, but will not catch valid codes that have been incorrectly assigned. People who assign codes should understand the coding system. Codes that involve judgment, such as general ledger account codes, should be listed and fully described in a reference manual. In some instances, a second person should review code assignments before data entry, particularly when the system is new and people are unfamiliar with it.

Catastrophe safeguards require both hardware and software considerations. A number of hardware devices are available to protect against problems with electrical service. These devices run from inexpensive surge protectors to more expensive backup power systems. (They were discussed more fully in Chapter 9, as acquisition costs.) The price of these various devices must be balanced against the risk of power interruption and damage to hardware components.

Generally, computer hardware is very reliable. Responsible dealers usually "burn in" the hardware before delivery. This means that they will operate the equipment before delivery to make certain that it is functioning properly. Most equipment failures occur within the first three months of service. Failures thereafter should occur infrequently if proper procedures are maintained. Management should insist upon the following policies:

☐ No food or beverages permitted near the equipment

- ☐ No smoking near the equipment
- ☐ Good housekeeping and cleaning procedures
- ☐ Parking disk drives before the equipment is moved, as discussed in Chapter 12
- ☐ Proper handling of diskettes. (Always keep 5.25-inch diskettes in protective sleeves. Handle diskettes only on the label side. Store diskettes away from heat sources.)

Hardware failure is usually covered by maintenance agreements. Some service companies provide guaranteed response times in their service contracts. They may also provide for loaners while hardware is down for service.

The most important safeguard of all is a well-designed and executed plan of file backup and storage. Program diskettes should be copied and the originals removed from the premises. Data files should be backed up frequently. Active applications require a daily backup, some more frequently than that. (The recommended procedure for rotating backups is described in Chapter 12.)

Although everyone recognizes the importance of a strong backup policy, many users fail to follow procedures until they are in trouble. Management must find an appropriate method of enforcing backup policies. Failure to make scheduled backups may be an indication that files are growing and backups are becoming time consuming and clumsy. This may be the time to look into more sophisticated techniques, such as the use of backup tape or cartridge devices.

Most backup software locks the computer from performing any other task during the backup operation. The loss of production time can be minimized by scheduling backups during a lunch period or after working hours.

Establishing Software Controls

Software controls provided by accounting software were discussed in Chapter 12. Now is the time to review the specific controls provided by the software that has been selected and determine how it will affect operations. Who will review and authorize input journals for posting? Who will account for sequence numbers on computer printouts? If entry logs are provided, management must determine who will have access to these logs and who will have the responsibility of reviewing them.

Some accounting software provides audit trails on changes to the master files such as general ledger and customer accounts; others do not. If the software selected does not provide such trails, insist on the use of written authorization forms for all master file changes.

Some software presents a number of control options. The software may allow the user to decide whether order and/or invoice numbers are to be assigned automatically or by the operator. One might have a choice of printing or not printing journals automatically after posting. Control options, if available, are usually lumped together with other options that require a response when the software is installed.

Accounting software is not the only software that can provide controls. A good part of network software deals with passwords and access controls because of the increased file accessibility in a network. Passwords can provide or limit many different functions from the right to view and modify all files in the entire system, to the right to view just one file without the ability to make any changes. Passwords can limit access by company and by function.

Management should set the policy for the administration of passwords. Rules are required for the assignment of passwords, for periodic reassignments, and for changing passwords when employees are terminated. Password lists must be highly restricted, but accessible to top management when necessary. The abuse of passwords requires a strong form of censure.

Special control software and hardware also is discussed in Chapter 12. If management has decided on the need for some of this software, it must now decide on the policies for its proper use.

Deciding on Software Options

Many accounting software programs offer user flexibility through the use of special option screens. Some of the terms used for these screens are "Setup", "System Control", and "Options". These options may cover a wide range of functions, from internal control to the amount of data to be stored. (Many of these options are discussed in Chapter 10.)

Unfortunately, the screens and related pages in the manuals frequently do not clearly explain what the choices are all about. This is compounded by the fact that some choices cannot easily be changed if a wrong decision is made, such as options about coding structure and the choice of accounting periods.

Locate and scrutinize the option section of the manual prior to installation. Unfortunately, this section is not always clearly marked. Call up the publisher and discuss the options if their significance is not clear. Be certain as to which decisions can be easily changed at a later date and which ones can lock in the user.

Selecting Coding Schemes

Chapter 10 discussed some of the considerations that affect coding schemes. Now that the software is ready for installation, management should review its coding plans to determine

☐ Whether existing coding schemes should continue or be changed

☐ If new codes are required, and if so, what coding schemes will be relatively easy to use and will facilitate the generation of computer records and reports. Some schemes make it easier than others to divide reports into logical reporting groups.

☐ The length of the codes

☐ Whether codes should be numeric, alphabetic, or a mix

☐ What separators, such as dashes or slash marks, should be used between code sections

☐ What plan should be used in assigning codes. Most people try to keep customer and vendor codes as close to alphabetic order as possible. General ledger account codes run in the sequence of the financial statements. Inventory and job cost code schemes vary among users.

☐ Whether gaps should be used to leave a place for new accounts.

Designing Operating Procedures

If it has not been done already, this is the time to put into writing all of the operating procedures that will be affected by the computer installation. The task of studying business requirements, searching for suitable software, and making detailed decisions about the installation leads to many conclusions and decisions about organizational functions and relationships. Unless put into writing, many of these decisions will be forgotten, misunderstood, or ignored. The result can be poor control, time waste, errors, and misleading results.

Additionally, one must expect to change some of these decisions once the system commences operation and revisions are found to be necessary. Many questions will arise during the break-in period. Written procedures insure that consistent and logical responses are provided. They are also an important tool for avoiding the repetition of error.

Despite all of this persuasive logic, many organizations function without a good set of written procedures. Many people find writing very difficult, let alone writing something requiring precision and clarity, such as the description of business operations. The difficulty is magnified by the many changes and insertions that will be required during the first months of operation.

It is important for managers to commit the planned procedures to writing with the understanding that polished English is not expected. One of the first benefits will almost certainly be better comprehension of the new system and the clarification of many matters that otherwise could lead to confusion. Another benefit is greater ease in training new personnel. One person, perhaps the controller or chief financial officer, should be assigned the responsibility of supervising this effort.

Establishing a Training Plan

There are a number of training considerations. The scope of training material will depend on the computer sophistication of the organization. If new to computers, some personnel will require training in basic computer concepts and the operating system commands required for day-to-day operation. (Chapter 2 discussed some of the computer functions that should be understood by computer personnel.)

Most training time will be devoted to learning how to use the accounting software. Personnel with limited responsibility may have training concentrated to their areas of responsibility. Other workers may require more extensive coverage. In any event, do not limit training to computer functions but also cover all aspects of each job that relates to the computer installation.

Make certain that a minimum of two persons are trained in each function. This will prevent the possible loss of the investment in training, as well as work disruption, when an employee leaves or must take time off.

There are many sources of training assistance. Computer fundamentals are taught by many organizations, including high schools, colleges, and retail stores. Good training in accounting software is more difficult to find. A few software publishers provide training: most will recommend retailers or installers. Many consultants provide this service.

Do not start training until the computer and software are in place.

Computer skills are best acquired and remembered when people can push keys and learn from their mistakes. The time required to learn the first modules of an accounting package usually is not representative of overall training time. Most people begin to grasp the software functions and start to learn on their own. An important key to successful training is holding sessions when people can concentrate on the new material and are not disturbed by interruptions or work stress.

Determine whether manuals provided by the publisher are adequate, or whether other materials should be used. Most manuals cover more conditions than are required for any one application. The extraneous material can be very confusing to the beginner. Many manuals use too many technical words, apply accounting terms improperly, and are just poorly written. A rewrite tailored for a specific application may be an effective training resource.

Preinstallation planning is important. Depending on the circumstances, some of the preinstallation activities just discussed will call for serious study. Others may require little time and attention. None of the activities should be ignored.

INSTALLATION AND FILE CONVERSION

Installation procedures generally must be performed in the same sequence regardless of the software selected. The following list applies to a hard disk installation and covers the mechanical sequence of steps required to get the software to function:

- ☐ Setting up and preparing the hardware
- ☐ Making backup copies of existing computer data files
- ☐ Making working copies of the distribution diskettes
- ☐ Copying the software onto the hard disk
- ☐ Starting the accounting software and configuring it to the hardware
- ☐ Responding to setup requirements and options
- ☐ Entering master file information
- ☐ Entering and proving start up data
- ☐ Designing and entering output specifications
- ☐ Making backup copies of the new data files

Setting Up and Preparing the Hardware

Neophytes can avoid problems of hardware setup by arranging for this service from their vendors. (Hardware purchased mail order must be installed by users, but this is not recommended for beginners.) The basic computers (motherboards) must be opened for the insertion of boards and other components. All units (computers, printers, modems, etc.) must be wired together. New hard disks must be formatted and the operating system such as DOS transferred from a floppy disk to the hard disk.

Additional steps are required for setting up a network, including cabling, copying the network software onto the server, and entering the network setup parameters, passwords, and logon scripts.

Finally, the operation of all units must be tested. Any problems that show up must be corrected before proceeding. Hard disks are getting larger, resulting in an increase in storage capacity. Attention must be given to the system used for organizing disk files. This requires an understanding of the concepts of disk partitions, directories, and subdirectories. Poor planning results in slow computer performance during file searches and the waste of storage capacity.

Many accounting software programs permit users to distribute program and data files among a number of disk partitions and subdirectories. These distributions must be made when the programs are copied onto the hard disk.

Users who are unfamiliar with these concepts should discuss them with their vendors before any software is placed on the hard disk. Generally, it is best to place a minimum amount of software in root directories and make generous use of subdirectories.

Making Backup Copies of Existing Computer Data Files

Make backup copies of any existing computer data files before installing new software or making hardware changes. The added insurance costs very little and can avoid a serious setback if the installation somehow damages these important files.

Making Working Copies of the Distribution Diskettes

The program diskettes received from the publisher are called distribution diskettes. Blank diskettes are inexpensive. Diskettes containing programs are expensive. An untutored neophyte, a careless error, or physical damage can easily render the distribution diskette worthless. The solution is to copy the programs onto working diskettes and store the distribution diskettes off site.

In order to make copies, users must learn how to perform a few simple tasks at their computers. These tasks are usually explained in the manuals that come with the hardware and operating system software:

- ☐ How to start the computer
- ☐ How to handle diskettes
- ☐ The significance of write-protect tabs on diskettes
- ☐ How to format diskettes
- ☐ How to copy computer files and verify the accuracy of the copy. (In DOS, these are DISKCOPY, DISKCOMP, and COPY.)

Copying the Software onto the Hard Disk

Accounting software generally comes with instructions about transferring the software to the user's hard disk. The language of these instructions is improving but is not always crystal clear. Some of the confusion is avoided by software vendors who place the software on the user's hard disk as part of the sale. Easy transfer is provided by vendors who include install routines with their software. The user places the first program diskette in the diskette drive, enters the install instruction (in the format shown in the software manual), and the install program guides the user through instructions that appear on the monitor.

Software that comes without an install routine requires the use of operating system commands to set up directories and copy programs. The manuals usually provide step-by-step instructions, but the entry of one wrong character can prevent a successful conclusion. One gets a sense of what is happening by the lights that go on and off on the diskette and hard disk drives, and by the file names that appear on the monitor as the transfer is taking place. Error messages, a blank monitor, or the absence of lights on the disk drives indicate that something is wrong.

Whether or not the publisher has provided an install routine, the transfer process must be repeated for each module that is to be installed.

Starting the Accounting Software and Configuring it to the Hardware

The aforementioned steps are frequently performed by vendors. If so, the user will first confront the computer and the software after the hardware has been set up and the accounting software has been placed on the hard disk.

How does one start the program? First steps can present a formidable challenge, because these simple procedures can be buried in the obscurity of the manual. Some programs are started by entering an abbreviation or name. In some cases, the programs are started from the root directory. Others require a change to the correct subdirectory before starting.

The start of the program may result in unexpected surprises. Most of these surprises come in the form of questions that must be answered before the program will continue. The software may begin by asking for a password, even though at this point passwords are the least important matter on the mind of the user. If a dummy company is provided for training and practice, the program may ask for the company code. Answers to both of these questions can be found in the software manuals, but this usually requires several minutes of frustrated search through the text.

The software may ask the user to verify the system date, without providing any explanation. (In some instances, the system date is the date that prints on all reports. In other software, the system date determines the current accounting period.) If a dummy company is used, the training manual may specify the dates to be used for practice purposes. Otherwise, one usually enters the current date until one has a better understanding of the software. The task of entering the date can be troublesome. Some screens show the user the correct format; others do not. If the wrong format is used, the program may beep or show other vague error responses. The user is left to figure out what is going wrong.

Once past the hurdles of password, company code, and system date, the user probably will arrive at the master menu. But he or she is far from ready to start using the software. The next step is to provide the accounting software with information about the hardware so that the program will be properly coordinated with the monitor and printer. These steps usually are called configuring the monitor and printer. The steps involved vary from simple to painful. The screens that are used for this purpose usually can be found under one of the menu captions on the master menu that will be entitled "setup," "utilities," or "configuration."

Many of the better programs make the configuration process quite simple, provided a popular model monitor and printer have been chosen. Once in the pertinent screen, the user can call up a list of popular names for monitors or printers, scroll through the list, and select the appropriate name. The selection does not have to be made again unless the hardware is changed. Programs that work with color monitors even let the user pick colors for various portions of the screens.

The configuration process can be troublesome, particularly with printers, if the list of hardware does not include the equipment that is to be used, or if the software does not provide the simple selection feature just described. Dealers and hardware manufacturers may have to be called in order to obtain the necessary information which is often expressed in a series of codes. The problem can be avoided by selecting hardware that is tested on the configuration screens, or by working with a dealer who will undertake this responsibility.

If configuration is successful, both the monitor and the printer should work properly. Wrong monitor configuration is easy to spot. Printer problems may not show up until a number of reports are printed.

Responding to Setup Requirements and Options

Most accounting software programs provide some flexibility by offering a number of options for using the software. Users must tell the program how they plan to use the options before they can use the program. These choices are made by answering questions that appear on one or more setup screens.

The documentation supplied to guide the user in making these choices is often very poor. The screens themselves can be confusing, because unrelated questions may appear on the same screen. Some programs display "default" answers to the questions; they show the answers that will guide the program unless the user enters other responses. Other programs leave blank spaces for the user to fill. Default answers are better, because they provide the user with some idea of the type and form of response that is required.

Unanswered (blank) responses can be troublesome because the program may not function until all of the questions have been answered.

The text that follows presents some examples of user options.

Account Codes

One startup task that is unduly troublesome is the need for entering general ledger account code numbers before one can use the software. The importance of the responses depends on the intended use of general ledger information. The choice of account codes is most important if the system will maintain a general ledger and print financial statements. In this situation, the coding scheme may affect the design of the financial statements. Still important, but less critical, is the choice of codes if accountants will use data produced by the system to maintain the general ledger. Codes should be used that will facilitate the work of the accountant. Account code selection is least important when little link is planned between the accounting software and the general ledger.

Each module usually requires the entry of codes for such basic accounts as cash, accounts receivable control, accounts payable control, and retained earnings. The code numbers are used by the software to accumulate accounting data. If the modules are not integrated with the general ledger, any number can be assigned.

The setup screen may ask other questions about general ledger codes such as

☐ Will the chart of accounts include subaccounts for departments or divisions?

☐ How many positions are to be used for account codes?

☐ How many for sub accounts?

☐ What character or symbol should be used to separate codes and subcodes?

Controls

Control options are frequently misunderstood by users. They should be discussed with accountants before responses are entered. Some examples include the following questions:

☐ Will invoice numbers be generated by the software or entered by the user? (If generated by the software, enter the starting number.)

☐ Should a transaction journal be printed at the time of posting?

Processing

Accountants are usually the people most concerned with general ledger account codes. Operating personnel are more interested in processing options such as

☐ Will commissions be computed on the basis of invoicing or cash receipts?

☐ Will a lot or serial number inventory be used?

☐ Will a billing table be used?

- ☐ Should accounts payable detail transactions be posted to the general ledger?
- ☐ How are finance charges to be computed?
- ☐ What time periods should be used for aging receivables?
- ☐ Should receivables be aged by invoice date or due date?

Data Files

- ☐ Should detail transaction files be maintained?
- ☐ For how long should such files be maintained?

Field Defaults

These options allow the user to indicate what information is to be displayed on transaction entry screens, subject to change by the operator. The use of defaults that cover the majority of situations (such as the use of current date as the transaction date, or "net 30 days" as invoice terms) can speed up data entry.

Integration

Users may be required to decide whether the various modules are to be integrated. Some may wish to integrate inventory with general ledger, while others may decide not to do this. The integration among modules requires careful timing. Some modules may be placed in service before others because of convenience or relative ease of startup. For example, accounts receivable, order entry, and inventory may start at different accounting periods. The task of entering the starting information usually should be done independent of other modules, in order to avoid duplicating the data. The switch to integrate with other modules should be made after the initial data files have been set up and their accuracy has been verified.

Do not respond to any setup questions or options until you fully understand their significance. In most cases, wrong responses (such as entering incorrect account numbers or the wrong dates for aging accounts receivable) can be easily corrected. However, the correction of some responses can be time consuming. And, in some situations, a wrong response can be virtually impossible to correct without starting from scratch. For example, the general ledger manual for one popular program advises, "Note that once the ledger is set up, you cannot change the number of fiscal periods the ledger uses."

Entering Code Schemes

After completing setup screens, the new user usually faces a number of screens asking for the codes to be used when setting up master files. Here are some examples:

Code	Where Used
Salesman	Sales analysis, commission computations
Sales Tax	Sales analysis
Sales Terms	Printing on invoice, computing cash flow
Price Code	Selecting price for invoicing
Discount Code	Computing discount for invoicing
Territory	Sales analysis
Warehouse	Inventory and order processing

Most manuals indicate the sequence in which the codes must be entered, some with more clarity than others. If codes are not established in the correct order, the software may stall when the user attempts to work with screens that ask for these codes. For example, the screens used for setting up customer files may ask for salesman, sales tax, and terms codes. If these codes are missing in the computer files, the user may be jolted with a beep, a question mark, or just a blinking and unmoving cursor.

The number of codes that can be used and the size of the related text is usually limited by the program. What is one to do if the user employs 15 salesmen and the program is limited to 10 salesmen codes? In some cases, a miscellaneous code will be satisfactory. In other circumstances, special procedures are needed to get around this capacity restriction.

The limitation on text size may also cause a problem if the codes are required to call up information for printing. For example, a sales terms code may be required to print the conditions of sale on the sales invoice. Careful editing may be necessary when entering the code text in order to fall within the number of characters permitted by the program. Special procedures may also be required to circumvent this restriction.

Entering Start-up Data

Up to this point, the installation process has required some knowledge of the routine commands of the operating system, plus an understanding of user options and other information that must be supplied to the program before one can set up master files. When properly planned and executed, very little time is required to perform these steps. Many programs require less than one-half hour per module. Long and difficult installations are usually the result of one or more of the aforementioned problems, such as misunderstanding the correct entry sequence or making entries in the wrong format or with the wrong data.

Having arrived at this point, the user is now ready to set up master and transaction files—that is, the files that contain account information and current accounting data. The amount of time and effort required to set up these files can be quite extensive.

Chapter 10 mentioned the importance of the master files required by computer accounting: general ledger accounts, customers, vendors, inventory, and cost files. It also discussed the fact that the information required for these files need not be accumulated all at one time. Data that is not time sensitive can be gathered over a period of time. Fields of information that are not critical can be keyed into the system after the installation has started.

Master files contain account information similar to the pages in a ledger. A master file record in the accounting software corresponds to a page in a manual ledger.

Module	Master File
General Ledger	Accounts
Accounts Receivable	Customers
Accounts Payable	Vendors
Payroll	Employees
Inventory	Inventory Items
Job Cost	Jobs

The information contained in computer master files, in some respects, is more extensive than the information found in manual systems and includes both general and statistical information. Study the sample screens and compare them with the information that iscurrently maintained in the ledgers.

Assign a qualified person to supervise data compilation, since this effort is often done after hours or by temporary personnel. Work must be checked periodically, particularly at inception and when new personnel are assigned. Make certain that the people doing this work clearly understand what information is to be compiled, so that time and expense are not wasted in compiling wrong or outdated information or in the need to repeat searches from the same files because necessary information was overlooked.

Master file information is usually compiled manually on forms, coded, and then keyed into the system. Since errors in coding can be very troublesome, this source material should be reviewed to see that the correct coding system is applied. Key the information into the system as soon as possible so that it can be printed and checked.

Pay serious attention to the date that will be used for entering time-sensitive information into the system. (Time-sensitive information is data that must be entered as of a specific date in order to coordinate with accounting requirements. Examples are account balances in the general ledger, open accounts receivable and accounts payable invoices, and inventory quantities and costs.) Each module that is brought into the system requires entering opening balances that will agree with information already in the system. All of this entry work must be completed and verified before new information can be entered. This work should be scheduled at a time that will minimize the delay in routine operations. General ledgers are usually introduced at the beginning of the fiscal year. Receivables and payables might best be started at a low point in the business cycle. Payrolls are usually started at the beginning of a calendar quarter. Because inventories frequently require a very large number of records, quantity balances might be phased in over a period of time.

There are many variations to the procedures recommended by different software publishers for entering time-sensitive information. Some of these procedures are quite complex. One publisher provides a chart showing five options for setting up accounts receivable! Carefully study the section in the manual about setting up these files before proceeding.

Some of the required information may already exist in electronic form, even though not in the format that can be used by the accounting software. This happens when one is converting from one accounting software to another, or when records have been kept by a computer service bureau. In some cases, the new software will provide the capability of bringing in data files that have been created by other software. This so-called import function, if available, can save many hours in entering data that already exist on the computer. Import procedures usually involve a number of steps. The entire procedure should be tested before a full-scale transfer is attempted.

If file import is not available, the software vendor may be able to make suggestions about easing the conversion, or provide the name of a programmer who can write a special conversion program. The cost may be justified when it comes to converting large files containing 1,000 or more records.

Entering Output Specifications

Many inexpensive programs are rigid with respect to the format of all output. Users of such programs have very little to say about what printed forms and reports will look like. This makes life simple at the start, but can be stifling as one gets used to accounting software and wishes to make it more responsive to the needs and practices of the user.

More sophisticated programs provide standard reports and forms plus the option to create new formats. In order to do this, the user must learn how to set up report specifications, a technique that requires some study. Most beginners start out using the standard forms and defer learning the techniques for report formatting to a later time. These forms and reports fall into three categories:

- ☐ Financial statements
- ☐ Business forms
- ☐ Reports

Financial Statements

The rigidity of some general ledger programs with respect to the relationship between the chart of accounts and the format of financial statements can create a problem. This rigidity appears in two forms. Some programs use the chart of accounts to control the format of the financial statements. Users must plan their charts of accounts at inception, including the special accounts that are used solely for printing the financial statements. The need to learn about these "pseudoaccounts" at the very beginning of the installation process can be a little unnerving.

Other programs use special screens for entering the specifications for printing financial statements, screens that are independent of the chart of accounts. This method provides a number of advantages:

- ☐ Users do not have to worry about formatting financial statements until they are more familiar with other aspects of the program.

- ☐ A number of different formats can be used for different purposes. For example, a detailed profit and loss statement can be prepared for management, and a summary statement for investors.

- ☐ Special financial reports can be designed, such as the preparation of financial data for entry into income tax returns.

The tradeoff is that every change in the chart of accounts also requires a change in the financial report specifications. Additionally, the task of learning how to write report specifications may not be an easy one.

The general ledger may also restrict the extent to which account balances can be combined and reported in the financials. These restrictions may force the user to assign account code numbers in a specified number range in order to effect the required account combinations. A decision to change the method of reporting a specific account may require a change in the account code.

Business Forms

A number of accounting programs permit users to modify the format for printing such forms as sales invoices, customer statements, and disbursement checks. In general, users can select the information to be printed together with its location on the form. The user can also decide whether or not to print captions. The number of print positions may be restricted by the size of the data field in the program. The design process can take some time until the results are satisfactory.

Most programs will store one specification for each form. A few provide the capability of storing a variety of formats.

Reports

Many accounting programs provide report generators that permit users to design their own reports. These report generators offer different capabilities. Some limit reports to information stored in a single module. Others permit the reports to access information from different modules. Some allow for adding new data fields to the report; others are restricted to the data fields in the accounting modules. Arithmetic and totaling functions also vary from one report generator to another.

One must not assume that report generators give the user full license to create any type of form so long as the information is available in the data files. All such programs are limited in one way or another.

Making Backup Copies of the Data Files

As the installation process nears completion, the user will have created a number of data files at a considerable cost in time and money. All of these files should be backed up as insurance against the need to construct them all over again. Beginners make many mistakes and may inadvertently erase or corrupt the files. Taking chances is a bad practice.

INCEPTION OF OPERATIONS

This brings the discussion to the end of the installation process.

Once time-sensitive information has been entered and verified, it is time to start operations. Do not be disappointed if first steps are slow and painful, despite all of the planning and training. During the first few weeks, many questions will arise when personnel start to use the new procedures. Some of their questions will be easily answered; others may be difficult. Be on the alert for changes that must be made in the original plan because of unanticipated conditions. Insist that such changes be noted in the written set of procedures and that all affected personnel are notified of the changes.

Feedback, evaluation, and change are important features of the inception period.

Parallel Operation

How vital is parallel operation? Operating the old system while people are trying to learn and apply the new system requires almost a doubling of effort. It adds to time stress and causes confusion, because people must remember two different ways of accomplishing the same result.

However, in most situations, parallel operation provides inexpensive insurance against the loss of or delay in producing vital information. If a month of parallel operation produces satisfactory results, the additional cost and stress is minimal. If the month comes up with unsatisfactory results, the additional cost and stress will have been well justified.

There are certain points to watch during parallel operation:

1. Make certain that detail master files agree with control totals at the beginning of the first period under the new software. For example, make certain that the total of the opening balances in the accounts receivable software agrees with the control total in the general ledger.

2. At the end of the first accounting period, compare the control amounts under the new system with the same amounts determined under the old system. For example, make certain that closing balances of cash, accounts receivable, and accounts payable are the same in both systems. A difference between these two amounts may indicate a procedure error in the new system.

3. At the end of the first accounting period, prepare supporting schedules and compare with controls as soon as possible. Delays may postpone

the detection of problems that require changes in procedures and affect the quality of results. Do not let work continue into the second period until the first one has been checked.

4. Usually, a new computer-based accounting system will provide a new and expanded set of management reports. Nothing can be more devastating than learning, after the first set of reports have been distributed, that the reports contain serious errors. Make certain that such reports are carefully reviewed by competent personnel before distribution.

5. If it is expected that portions of the new system will be used by outside accountants and others, ask them to review and comment on the first results. This can avoid problems (and extra costs) if at a later date the accountants feel that the system output is inadequate for their needs.

SUMMARY

This chapter has concentrated on a variety of matters that require attention during software installation. Many of these matters require little more than a small amount of management time and thought. Others, particularly the effort involved in training, setting up master files, and running a parallel operation, can be time consuming and costly. The purpose here is to provide the reader with a useful guide for avoiding pitfalls and achieving a successful installation.

Good selections of software and hardware are only part of the process. Intelligent decisions about personnel are equally important. The wisdom of these decisions often becomes evident during the installation period. Watch for signs of sagging morale, excess complaints, and poor compliance with new procedures. These may be signals that changes must be made— perhaps in personnel assignments, perhaps in policies and procedures.

The installation period is a critical time. Make certain that supervision and review are maintained at a high level and that first results are scrutinized promptly.

15

The Crystal Ball

INTRODUCTION

We have now concluded our discussion on the fine art of selecting and installing accounting software successfully on microcomputers. We began with the admonition that this process is not an easy one as demonstrated by the poor success rate reported in the press. We also noted throughout the previous chapters that software selection at best involves compromises, and that the ideal product is rarely found.

What are the prospects that these conditions will improve, that software selection will become easier and that the probability of finding effective software that is easy to install and use will be greater in the future?

There is probably no aspect of the business world changing faster than computer technology. Accounting software is party to this whirlwind change. Even during the writing of this book, a number of products have been brought to market with new features and capabilities.

This final chapter will try to take a look into the future and anticipate the coming world of accounting software.

First it will look at current trends in accounting software design, for which a peek into the near future does not require too much vision. The trends to be discussed include

☐ Improved documentation and training materials

☐ Easier installation

☐ Dynamic file sizing

- ☐ Increased flexibility in report and document design
- ☐ Easier use of graphics
- ☐ Increased use of laser printers
- ☐ Increased visibility of vertical software
- ☐ New operating systems
- ☐ Windows
- ☐ Easier and cheaper facilities for backup

Next the text will be a little more courageous and make longer-range predictions. These will cover

- ☐ Tailoring the software to user needs
- ☐ New methods of software distribution
- ☐ Improved support systems
- ☐ Better documentation of specifications
- ☐ Enhanced functions
- ☐ Mass information storage and retrieval
- ☐ Improved software controls
- ☐ Fail-safe routines
- ☐ Easier installation of networks
- ☐ Increased overlap between micro and minicomputers
- ☐ Standardization

CURRENT TRENDS

There has been a noticeable improvement in accounting software in the past two years. The publishers who have survived the competition of earlier years have made valuable enhancements and improvements in their products. Some of the earlier clumsiness has been corrected. Prompts are clearer. Enhancements provide greater functionality. The correlation between manuals and the related software has been improved. A more detailed discussion follows.

Improved Documentation and Training Materials

A few years ago software publishers tried to make their products more appealing by coining the term "user friendly." They were attempting to persuade would-be purchasers that their products were easy to learn and use. Unfortunately, the industry could not support this claim. Many users learned, with a great deal of vexation and frustration, that most of the so-called user-friendly programs were difficult to master. An industry grew up providing training in the most popular software applications—word processing and spreadsheets. But little training was available for the user of accounting software, because applications and requirements varied so much from user to user.

Accounting software publishers added to training difficulties by not paying enough attention to the design and quality of their manuals. Many of these manuals were written by people with insufficient knowledge of office operations and an insensitivity to the nontechnical background of users. The result was a series of efforts that used incorrect accounting terms and were peppered with technical and arcane terminology. Many users gave up trying to decipher the manuals and preferred to learn through personal training and telephone support. Others, learning of these difficulties, chose to defer computerizing until the entire learning process and related time commitment became more manageable.

Early accounting software was designed to function with small files and the Spartan use of RAM. Every year since then has seen a drop in the cost of computer memory and an increase in speed. One of the most dramatic improvements in hardware design has been the introduction of new and more powerful chips that are the heart of the computer: the central processing unit, or CPU. The first IBM PC used an Intel 8088 chip with a rated speed of 4.3 MHz. Later, the 8086 chip was introduced that could run two to three times as fast. Now, an 80386 has been designed that not only runs faster, but includes functional capability far beyond the design of most software that is on the market today. And a faster chip, the 80486, lies just over the horizon.

During this time, hard disks have increased in capacity and access speed. The original XT was rated at 10 megabytes. Today, microcomputer hard disks are available with capacities over ten times greater. At the same time, average seek times have been more than cut in half.

Newer accounting software is designed to take advantage of these hardware improvements by providing more functions and easier use. Among these functions are the tighter integration of modules and the better use of help screens and report design capabilities. The first microcomputer accounting software was designed to run on floppy disks and required 128K of RAM. Most current offerings require installation on hard disks and much greater RAM.

The drop in memory costs, increase in computer speed, and the experience gleaned over the past years have suggested many enhancements to make the software easier to use. The first, and continuing order of business, is the preparation of well-organized and well-written manuals that are comprehensible, easy to use, and effectively coordinated with software screens. Along with this trend is the greater use of help screens that are available to the user at the press of a key. Already, one publisher provides the entire manual on screen. Others are providing ever-increasing screen support with newer versions of their products.

The passage of time will see much better use of help screens. Explanations will become clearer. Text will be more closely related to each field (context sensitive). Error messages will become clearer along with suggestions for correction. Users will be permitted to write their own help text if they so desire.

Better screen design is another key to simplifying the learning process. Most screens require responses from the user. Beginners frequently have difficulty learning how to do this correctly. There are many such traps.

Some fields will not accept input unless information has been entered previously in another part of the program. For example, one cannot enter a sales tax code for a customer if sales tax codes have not been set up in another screen. Many programs have difficulty telling the user what is wrong. Some programs just "freeze" without any explanation. Others provide a message that is incomprehensible. A properly designed error message should explain why the user cannot proceed.

Certain fields may require the entry of a code such as a transaction code. What if the user does not know what is required? Some software provides no clue and expects the user to look up the information in the manual. The software should provide the information in a help screen or display the alternatives at the bottom of the screen.

Another source of frustration lies in the precise format of the required response. For example, some software is case sensitive—it finds a difference between "YES" and "yes." Other software is very fussy about the format used for entering dates and will not accept the wrong format. Such software can completely stymie a clerk trying to enter "5/12/90" when the software will recognize only "05-12-90." Case-sensitive software is a sign of antiquated programming. Software that requires a format that can be misunderstood should display a sample of the correct format.

Then there are fields that must be completed and other fields that are optional. How is one to know the difference? Suppose the software requires the entry of a salesperson code even if the business does not use any salespeople? One publisher uses little diamonds to indicate the mandatory fields.

In time, all of these sources of confusion and trouble will be corrected. Users will be told on the screen when they are trying to make entries in the wrong sequence. Operator choices will be clearly explained in help screens or with clearly written prompts. Special format requirements will be displayed and optional fields will be distinguished from required fields.

Easier Installation

The steps involved in installing accounting software have been described in Chapter 10. Older software products assumed that the user understood the commands of the operating system required to perform such tasks as making directories, copying files, and modifying the software configuration.

This task has become a lot easier through the use of install programs that perform most of these tasks automatically. The install program creates the necessary directories and sets up the required software configuration.

Unfortunately, even these new install programs offer a challenge to the uninitiated. The programs may ask questions that are obscure to beginners. How is a new user to respond to questions about which drive will be used to store the data, or whether test data should be copied to the hard disk? If an error is made during installation, such as inserting the distribution diskettes in the wrong order, the install program may bomb out without explanation.

In addition, the art of matching computer printers with the accounting software remains one of the most irritating challenges of the electronic world. Since there are no industry standards, each printer comes with its own command set that must be used by the application program in order for the printer to work properly. Most accounting programs include the command sets (called printer drivers) for many printers and provide screens that can be used to invoke the correct drivers. A user with a printer not included among the drivers provided by the accounting software must be able to obtain this technical material from the printer manual and enter it in the appropriate setup screens. Since printer manuals are no clearer than accounting software manuals, this task can be quite formidable.

Hopefully, the day will come when the software installation is virtually automatic. Written instructions will explain every prompt and question that appear on the screen during the installation process. Each question will be presented with an explanatory discussion. Wrong entries and other errors will be clearly explained on the screen. Printers will come with driver sets that can be inserted into the program.

Already many nonnetwork users find that one printer cannot satisfy all of their printing requirements. One printer is used for the printing of internal lists and reports, another for documents. While some accounting software recognizes this need by providing for a number of printers, switching between printers still requires some manual intervention. Users must remember to key in the alternate printer line or reset a switch. In time, accounting software will let users preset the assignment of printers and eliminate this extra step.

Dynamic File Sizing

Chapter 6 discussed the fact that many accounting programs require users to tell the computer, as part of the installation process, the number of transactions that are expected to be processed and stored. This information is used by the program to set up the data files that are used by the program. Problems arise if the user guesses wrong. The problem is not too serious if more space is allocated than necessary; the result is some unused disk space. The problem could be much more serious if the allocated space was too small. Unless the files are resized in time, the data files could become unusable. System managers are required periodically to use a special screen to check the file sizes and make necessary changes. Most programs flash warnings when the files are getting crowded, but there have been many instances when these warnings were ignored.

The program technique of dynamic file sizing overcomes this danger. Software using this technique automatically increases the sizes of the data files whenever needed. Dynamic file sizing should be available in all accounting software programs.

Increased Flexibility in Report and Document Design

Chapter 2 discussed the fact that computer accounting systems lack the flexibility of manual systems. One of the major causes of this rigidity is the fact that restrictions exist in document and report design. Most of the information accumulated by these programs are accessible in a very limited fashion. Frequently, there is very little choice about the information that can be printed on management reports. The entire format—report headings, columnar information, and totals—are preset by the program. The user is forced to accept the formats predetermined by the programmer.

A similar rigidity applies to the documents printed by the program, such as sales invoices, customer statements, and disbursement checks. Frequently, users must adopt formats designed by programmers, which entails a change from the forms that people are accustomed to and understand. Some programs limit form dimensions to one size, so that simple one-line invoices require 8.5-by-11-inch pages. At times, the computer forms, which have been designed for general use, print data that are unnecessary or even confusing. For example, the program might print a caption for sales discounts whether or not a business uses discount pricing.

A number of programs attempt to overcome this rigidity in a number of ways. Some provide the capability of transferring information accumulated by the accounting program into more flexible programs such as worksheets and databases. The transferred information can then be manipulated in order to print more functional management reports. This capability requires the user to learn two different programs and usually cannot be assigned to an unsophisticated operator. Additional difficulties arise if the user wishes to store information not provided for in the accounting program such as statistical or narrative information. Under these circumstances, some information must be entered into the accounting program, and other information directly into the spreadsheet or database. This can be a fairly clumsy arrangement.

Some programs offer choices in the design of output documents. These choices include decisions about what information will print on the forms, the location of the printed information and the size of the form. This flexibility can vary from one module to another. For example, the user might have some choice over invoice formats, but have no control over the form of disbursement vouchers.

A recent and welcome trend is the availability of report writer modules that give the user much greater latitude in the design of printed output. In some cases, these modules must be purchased separately; in others they are part of the basic software. The degree of flexibility varies from one publisher to another, but with time this capability will expand. Some programs limit the data they can access in one report to information residing in the master files of a single module. Some permit bringing information together from different modules. Others go further and permit users to store information not provided in the accounting module at all. In effect, these report writers are database programs designed to work with information from their related accounting modules and to work in a consistent fashion in order to simplify training and facilitate their use.

Report writers significantly enhance the flexibility and usefulness of accounting software, and it is reasonable to expect that they will increase in popularity and simplicity in the near future.

A third technique in providing greater flexibility in report design is to provide the user with a number of choices before printing a report. These choices may involve the selection of

☐ The range of items to be printed (such as all customers in a specified area)

☐ The range of transaction dates to be included in the report

☐ The way in which the data is to be sorted and totaled.

The inclusion of range and sort selections should also become a popular feature in software enhancements.

Easier Use of Graphics

Until recently, business graphics had been confined pretty much to presentations designed to influence decisions made by others. Information presentations, particularly presentations of accounting information such as financial statements and management reports, have been largely numeric in content, consisting of rows and columns of data. This method of presentation works well with some managers but loses the attention of many who do not have the temperament to sift through a lot of numbers.

A few software publishers have made timid attempts at providing graph capabilities with their software. However, in order to accommodate a wide range of monitors and printers, these initial efforts are not very effective.

There has been a steady improvement in hardware graphic capability, particularly with new monitors and laser printers. It will not be long before accounting software publishers will seize the opportunity to enhance their products with better graphics. These graphics, in turn, will permit busy non–number-oriented executives to quickly grasp important trends in their businesses, rather than postpone the review of numeric presentations because the task is unpleasant.

In time, users will be able to design and print a number of charts and graphs using data stored in accounting modules that will greatly enhance management capability to recognize significant trends and react more quickly to changing conditions. Sales management will improve through the timely charting of sales trends by company, region, and product line. Inventory management will be facilitated by charts of inventory turns and easier distinction between fast- and slow-moving products. Cash management will be assisted with graphs showing trends in collections and operating ratios. In fact, detailed financial statements and reports will become secondary to well-designed graphic presentations.

Increased Use of Laser Printers

The task of changing forms in the printer can be troublesome and time consuming. Each printer has its own paper mechanism, and it often takes trial and error, as well as a good dose of patience, to learn how to insert and align paper so that the printed material will register correctly, the paper will not jam, and pages can be removed without tears and wrinkles.

Users with applications that require fast printing speed, many form changes, and quality lettering often work with more than one printer, even if the volume of printing could be handled by one dot-matrix printer alone.

A newcomer on the computer scene—the laser printer—may soon be able to address these problems. These printers still cost more than most other microcomputer printers and, in some cases, run too slowly for commercial applications. The programs necessary to produce a completed form from blank paper have not yet been devised. However, improvements that lower costs and improve speed and performance are on their way. In time, accounting software will be able to print completed forms from blank paper, including multiple copies, logos, rules, and variable data. Multiple-ply forms will have each copy appropriately labeled. Form feeders will insert paper of different colors. The laser printer will supersede the daisy wheel and even the dot-matrix printer. At first, all commercial printing will be done in one color, but the day will come when multicolor printing will also be available at reasonable cost.

Increased Visibility of Vertical Software

Many potential users of accounting software find that off-the-shelf products designed for general business use are too far from the mark to be useful. Some users have had software written to their own specifications. Programmers who have completed such assignments have sought to increase their income by using their newly acquired industry knowledge to package and distribute specialized accounting software. Many of these vertical software products have had very limited distribution and have not been well supported because of the limited resources of the publisher. Frequently, their accounting functions, such as accounts receivable and general ledger, were much weaker than their special industry functions.

Publishers of general accounting software are becoming more interested in tapping the special industry market. In this manner, they can capitalize on some of their accumulated software investment and knowledge and compete in new markets. Already, a number of publishers distribute lists of vertical products that have been designed to work with their programs.

The accumulation of programming experience, together with the increasing speed and power of microcomputers, undoubtedly will result in an increase in both the number and quality of vertical software products. Potential end users will face the difficult choice between using general business software, which is becoming more flexible and easier to use, and software that has been designed for particular industries. Such software should be easier to install because information and reporting has already been tailored for a specific need. The choice may be difficult.

New Operating Systems

A number of operating systems were developed during the early days of microcomputers. CPM (control process manager) and an updated version called CPM-86 were fairly popular. Some hardware vendors offered proprietary operating systems that were the only ones to work on their machines. These different systems created serious problems for software publishers who had to write different versions of their products that would work with each operating system. The success of the IBM PC provided the impetus for almost general acceptance of one operating system for microcomputer business software—the DOS (disk operating system) developed by Microsoft. This, in turn, made life easier for software publishers who could now spend more time improving their products rather than creating different versions for different operating systems. This also was better for end users because more people became familiar with DOS and could help them with problems.

Now, just a few years after it was introduced, limitations in DOS are causing a serious search for improved operating systems, limitations probably never anticipated at the time of its design. DOS has limits on the amount of RAM and hard disk memory that it can access. The increased functionality of accounting software rarely uses all components of the computer system at the same time, with the result that hardware segments are idle until the task is completed. For example, the CPU can be idle while the hard disk is being searched for data.

Another problem arises because DOS was written for single-use applications, and networking has become a serious need. Networking software has been written for DOS, but its inherent design weakness has resulted in complex requirements and installation difficulties. One of the strengths of minicomputer software is the greater ease of use in a network.

Of course, the designers of DOS could not have anticipated the tremendous technological changes in microcomputers that make DOS limitations troublesome. But now that computer memory has become so inexpensive, computer speeds have increased, and computer chips have greater power, there is need to look for operating systems that can deal more easily with this enhanced hardware.

One answer to this search for a better operating system is the IBM OS/

2®, software that is the subject of much discussion in trade literature. The new software is expected to provide much greater facility for networks and a greater amount of addressable RAM. Its multiprocessing capability will permit more than one job to be done at the same time, resulting in greater operating speed. For example, an operator can enter data while the computer is performing a sort prior to printing a report. Hopefully, the new system will spur programmers to develop accounting software that is easier to learn and use and has fewer restrictions than the software on the market today. Current predictions are that it may take a year or more from this writing before any significantly new accounting software products using this capability will reach the market. How much time will be required after that to eliminate serious bugs remains to be seen.

A number of accounting software programs have been introduced for the Apple Macintosh. These programs appeal to users who prefer the more graphic style of the Apple operating system. While the number of such programs is far less than the number available under DOS, the choice will undoubtedly increase in the future.

Other operating systems are also contending for attention. One of the major strengths of Unix and it cousin Xenix is its superiority over DOS in dealing with networks. While success has been limited, Unix-based operating systems may become more significant as the interest in networks increases. The Pick operating system, originally developed for minicomputers, has not found much of a home with micros. However, the new 80386 microchip may provide the capability for Pick to perform effectively on micros. The Pick system provides a file flexibility unmatched by DOS or Unix that can be very useful in accounting applications.

New operating systems, together with cheaper and faster forms of computer storage, will bring about a major change in accounting software by permitting greater storage of records, together with faster and easier access to these records.

Windows

The life of the user will also be made easier through the growing use of an interruption capability that permits rapid movement among accounting functions. Normally, many keystrokes and screen changes are required to leave one accounting task and start another. The procedures for moving from module to module take time and may result in error and the loss of information if not performed correctly. The interrupt facility, often called "windowing," provides a much easier way to do this.

Windowing is the capability of having more than one menu or program accessible at the same time. Multiple screens are concurrently visible on the monitor. In order to accommodate to the limited size of the monitor, the screens may be overlapped or only partially displayed. A keystroke permits the user to switch from one program to the other. For example, one could leave off entering cash in accounts receivable in order to look something up in the general ledger, and then, at the stroke of a key, return to the original place in accounts receivable. This interrupt capability reduces the stress and time loss caused by interruptions in the work flow.

Easier and Cheaper Facilities for Backup

Another problem in computer operations still looking for a better solution is the backup process. Many devices are available including diskettes, removable hard disks, tape, and tape cartridges. One of the negative effects of cheaper electronic storage has been the increase in the amount of data requiring backup. Discipline is necessary to go through backup procedures, discipline that takes time and requires attention. The process itself involves a number of steps, keying in computer instructions, inserting and removing storage media, and labeling the results. Any error, from a wrong computer instruction to the entry of the wrong date on a label can be troublesome. Oversight and carelessness can result in the loss of important information. The backup operation itself is time consuming.

Additionally, backup will not provide protection against physical site damage unless the backup media is stored at a separate site. This means that backup materials must be physically taken and stored far away from the computer.

New backup systems are being developed that require less human attention. Already, a few programs have appeared that create backups automatically. In time, these programs will come into more general use and will, through modems, create off-site files for better protection. The backup storage media will handle large quantities of data without the need for human intervention, and the computer will perform backup whenever not occupied with other work. Today, many users learn the importance of backup after their first significant loss of information. Tomorrow, this lesson will not have to be learned at all.

How important are these trends for the person interested in computerizing business operations? The computer industry is famous for a constant stream of rumors and promises about better, faster, easier, and cheaper products. People who wait for the better machine or the better software often find that they have fallen far behind others who take the plunge, knowing that in a few years the products that they purchase may become outdated. Those who choose the best system currently available will obtain the benefits of a computer system much sooner and will have acquired the skills to augment those benefits as technological improvements become available.

However, one must be aware of industry trends and look to the future when planning current purchases. Whenever cost differences are not significant it may be prudent to purchase hardware with greater capacity and speed even if the software currently available does not take full advantage of these capabilities.

LONG-RANGE PREDICTIONS

Now, for those who are interested, here are some predictions of what will happen to accounting software in the years to come:

Tailoring the Software to User Needs

The previous section of this chapter discussed the current trend in accounting software of providing greater capability for the user to design forms and reports. In time, this flexibility will be extended to include (1) modifying and deleting fields and (2) easier movement of data between programs and locations.

Many potential users find that some screens are overloaded with meaningless detail. The unused fields cause confusion and error. These users would prefer to remove the unnecessary fields altogether, resulting in faster data entry and a reduction in storage space. Other users may wish to relabel the fields rather than delete them. For example, some accounts receivable software provides customer fields to indicate whether the customer will accept back orders and substitutions. This feature is very useful in some applications, and is ignored in others. Similarly a field for entering an inventory bin location might serve another application better if it could be used to record the date of the first order.

Some applications require links between accounting and other software. The steps for moving data among different software programs are generally somewhat clumsy and require some technical proficiency. In time, the steps required to transfer data to such commonly used programs as word processors, spreadsheets, and databases will be simplified and incorporated directly into the accounting software. The ability to import data from external locations via modem directly into the software will also be enhanced.

New Methods of Software Distribution

Present methods for distributing accounting software comprise one of the reasons why the microaccounting software industry is so fragmented and poorly understood. Generally, accounting software is distributed through retail stores and other organizations that specialize in a limited set of products. End users must spend a great deal of time in their search for software to obtain useful information. Frequently, software presentations and manuals fail to disclose all of the details required for potential purchasers to make intelligent decisions. Often it is difficult to determine whether the product that is offered is the latest version of the software. Dealers who stock accounting software may not be able to exchange easily for newer versions. Software corrections and enhancements follow a tortuous path. Some publishers send correction materials to retailers, who in turn must contact end users. Other publishers mail correction diskettes directly to registered end users with printed explanations or explanations on the software diskettes.

In time, software products will be distributed through modems and telephone lines. Prospective purchasers will be able to download and try demonstration versions. These versions may be restricted in the number of transactions that can be processed, or in the period of time that they can be used. Prospects that do not have the necessary hardware will be able to try the software at software demonstration centers that will be designed to provide the necessary facilities and assistance.

Once purchased, the software, including corrections and enhancements will be downloaded in a similar fashion. This assures that the end user will always receive the latest software and will get corrections as soon as they are issued. It also provides much more flexibility for retailers who will not have to stock software and attempt to answer technical questions. The movement of diskettes through the mail will be minimal. Manuals will be sent directly from a central warehouse.

Improved Support Systems

Presently, software vendors provide voice telephone support which can be time consuming. Heavy support traffic often follows the release of a software update; many of these calls can be attributable to undisclosed bugs. If the reported problem requires some sort of program correction, diskettes must be mailed to the user along with instructions for loading the corrections.

In the future, startup and other support will be provided via modems and communications software that will permit technicians to duplicate the screens of the user, and therefore be in a better position to advise when errors are made. Program corrections will be downloaded almost instantly, permitting the user to get on with the work.

The modem will also be used to advise users when program corrections and enhancements become available.

Better Documentation of Specifications

In order to be successful, a system of software distribution by modem requires publishers to prepare complete lists of product specifications. The present method of stressing a few highlights and skipping many important details results in tremendous time waste and frustration.

Rare indeed is the software manual that lists field sizes in one place. Just as rare is a clear presentation of the functions performed by the software. Statements that the software provides sales analysis or computes sales commissions are useless without details. Clear explanations are required for such basic functions as correcting mistakes, providing batch controls, and maintaining accounting periods.

In time, market pressure will force the industry to be more forthright in explaining the capability of its products.

Enhanced Functions

Today, many programs, even the better ones, are limited in the extent to which users can modify accounting programs to meet their specific needs and readily extract information. Exception information cannot be easily derived from voluminous reports. Business operations that carry common information for accounts receivable and accounts payable, such as drop ship importing, must enter the same information twice.

A new generation of accounting software should make it easier for users to tailor the software to their needs. Many more options will be available to select the software functions required by the business, such as choices relating to the computation of commissions and discounts, or the pricing of merchandise.

The design of forms and reports will be easier and require less need to export data in order to produce the required results. The need to print voluminous reports will be reduced by the ability to produce a greater variety of exception reports. Preprinted forms will be replaced by the capability of printing, via laser printers, both the form and variable information at the same time.

Mass Information Storage and Retrieval

Today, all accounting software suffers from limited storage capacity. Many programs were written when the software had to operate solely on diskettes. Others were written when 10 meg hard disks were the limit. As a result, some software is programmed so that it cannot store more than one month's detail. Other software extends this period to a year or perhaps two. The specific data that can be stored varies from one program to another. No program stores all of the information that it processes. Few programs maintain customer records in detail, an important requirement of many businesses.

Exciting new forms of large-scale storage, such as the WORM (write-once, read mostly) will soon change this situation. These laser devices, while no larger than an ordinary floppy disk, can store vast amounts of data. This storage capability could be used, for example, to store detailed customer service records and sales invoices, information that is vital to many service-related industries. Sales and other accounting data could be stored over many years of time, permitting improved trend analysis for management guidance. The use of these devices will take some time. As of this writing, they range in price from $4,000 upward and are not truly integrated with any application software. Prices must come down, and retrieval time speeded up. Software must be written to permit easy information storage and access. But there is a crying need for information storage, and these devices promise to provide the answer.

Improved Software Controls

One of the significant differences between one accounting software product and another lies in the degree of accounting control provided by the programs. Differences in these controls, as discussed in Chapter 12, are as follows:

1. Few programs provide for access logs. The logs provide a list of persons who worked with the program, together with the date and time of usage. Such a list discloses unusual use of the program, such as access

by unauthorized persons or off-hour work that was not scheduled. Most network software provides this control, but it is just as significant for single users.

2. The amount of password protection varies from one program to another. Some provide no password protection at all. Some provide one level of protection, by company or by accounting module. Some go further and permit passwords to be assigned for specific functions. Such programs, for example, will permit entry clerks to enter payroll hours but not allow them to change payroll rates. The procedures for assigning and changing passwords frequently are included in procedure manuals without any indication that this information should not be publicly available. Warnings are rarely found about the need to change passwords periodically, or after the separation of employees.

3. Many accounting programs provide little assurance that the journals are complete. They do not automatically assign sequence numbers to each journal. Some do not even require the printing of a journal at the time that transactions are posted to ledgers. Some erase the journal detail after posting, so that failure to print the journal before posting creates a major gap in the audit trail.

4. Master file controls frequently are poor. Well-designed software should not permit master file changes without the forced printing of a numerically controlled change report. One should not be able to delete a master file record, such as a receivable or general ledger account, if there have been any transactions in the account within the current fiscal year.

Unfortunately, many people who work with accounting software, including users and their accountants, are not aware of these deficiencies. Sooner or later, the resulting problems of theft and data manipulation will force the industry to build better controls into its products. The cost and effort of using these controls is insignificant compared with the risk of unauthorized access and use.

Fail-Safe Routines

One of the monitor error messages that can frighten a user is the one that indicates that files have been "corrupted" or are otherwise unusable. At this point, the accounting software cannot be used until a successful backup has been completed, a process that can take some time.

Frequently, the cause of this problem lies in the inability of the software to recover from a momentary glitch in the power supply that occurs during a sensitive operation, such as posting.

This situation occurs frequently enough for the accounting software industry to pay some attention to providing better protection from file corruption and easier ways to bring files back into a useful condition. Already, some programs store keystrokes for this purpose. However, this condition will improve as more attention is given to the problem.

Easier Installation of Networks

Today, the successful installation of a microcomputer network is truly an art. A successful network must integrate many hardware and software elements. Hardware components must be properly assembled; computers, network hardware, wires, connectors, printers, and modems. Software must also be coordinated; operating systems, network software, and application programs. The difficulty of matching these elements is compounded by the large number of hardware manufacturers, each producing hardware that is slightly different from its competitors. Proper coordination alone will not guarantee success. A well-integrated system can still produce poor results if the wrong network is selected, or if the system is not properly managed.

Despite all of these difficulties, interest continues to grow in networking microcomputers. This in turn is spurring the industry to find easier and cheaper methods to do this. Additionally, computers that can communicate with each other are beginning to take over many of the functions of telephone systems.

In time, virtually all computer components will include the electronic devices and connectors for network integration. At the same time, network and telephone wiring systems will be planned together so that system connections will be more easily available. This will lower both installation and maintenance costs and make networking within the reach of modest applications. Increased networking facility will further erode the distinctions that separate microcomputers from the minis.

Increased Overlap between Micro and Minicomputers

All of the aforementioned improvements in the micro world—larger RAM, faster microchips, easier networks, and the introduction of large-scale memory devices—are breaking down the walls between micro and minicomputers. In time, the distinction will disappear. Software will be recognized by the operating and network systems that it can work with, and not be designated as micro-based or mini-based. There will be a continuum in terms of cost, speed, and storage from the smallest computer through high-performance units. Even the main frames, with even greater and faster performance characteristics, will be part of this continuum. Accounting software, with greater capacity and flexibility, will reach to a much larger market and find greater success.

Standardization

The one important area that faces a stormy future is that of standardization. Unfortunately, the lack of standards in hardware and software creates many unnecessary and frustrating problems for the user. Training is more troublesome because different language is used to describe the same thing, and different keystrokes must be learned to perform the same tasks. Networking is troublesome because of different hardware characteristics.

Microcomputers are still the products of an infant industry. One evidence of the struggle for survival is the manner in which so many manufacturers and publishers go their own ways without serious efforts to standardize commonly used procedures.

Once the rate of innovation and the number of players in the field settles down, the adoption of standards will make life a little easier for everyone.

SUMMARY

In summary, the consumer can look forward to many changes in accounting software, changes brought about by user demand and technological innovation. These changes will result in software that is easier to evaluate, install, and use, with better controls, greater flexibility, and easier methods for capturing and retrieving information.

— A —

List of Representative Software

PRELIMINARY NOTE

The following list, compiled from numerous sources, presents data that was current at the time of writing. Obviously, in a volatile industry, the information may not be completely accurate as of any future time. Companies are bought and sold. Some leave the marketplace, while new ones appear. Product lines are changed, and new ones are introduced.

Chapter 1 indicated that there is confusion caused by similar company names. Some product names also are similar. Additionally, some publishers distribute a number of product lines. In order to minimize this confusion, both publisher and product names have been provided.

The list covers general-application accounting software. Publishers whose products are limited to special application software and vertical software (such as professional time and billing software or software written for specific industries) are not included.

ACCOUNTING SOFTWARE

Publisher Name and Address	Product Names	PC	MAC
ABS (American Business Systems, Inc.) 3 Littleton Road Westford, MA 01886	ABS ACCOUNTING	X	

Publisher Name and Address	Product Names	PC	MAC
Accountants Microsystems, Inc. 3633 136th Place SE Bellevue, WA 98006	AMI	X	
ADS Software, Inc. PO Box 13686 Roanoke, VA 24036	ADS	X	
Advanced Business Microsystems 15615 Alton Parkway Irvine, CA 92718	PLATINUM™	X	
Armor Systems, Inc. 324 N Orlando Avenue Maitland, FL 32751	EXCALIBUR™	X	
Bristol Information Systems 84 N Main Street Fall River, MA 02721	BRISTOL	X	
Business Tools, Inc. 4038-B 128th Avenue SE Bellevue, WA 98006	TAS BOOKS	X	
Certiflex Systems 2290 Springlake Dallas, TX 75234	CERTIFLEX™	X	
Champion Business Systems, Inc. 17301 W Colfax Avenue Golden, CO 80401	CHAMPION III	X	
Chang Laboratories, Inc. 5300 Stevens Creek Boulevard San Jose, CA 95129	RAGS TO RICHES	X	X
Charterhouse Software Corp. 31324 Via Colinas Westlake Village, CA 91362	CHARTERHOUSE	X	
Checkmark Software, Inc. PO Box 860 Fort Collins, CO 80522	MULTILEDGER		X
Circo Business Solutions 1729-A Little Orchard Street San Jose, CA 95125	QUICK CHECK		X

Publisher Name and Address	Product Names	PC	MAC
Computer Associates International, Inc. 1240 McKay Drive San Jose, CA 95131	ACCPAC PLUS® BPI ACCPAC EASY BEDFORD	X X X X	X X
Cougar Mountain Software, Inc. PO Box 6886 Boise, ID 83707	ACCTG1 SERIES	X	
Crossways Technology Corp. 200 Crossways Park Drive Woodbury, NY 11797	THE PROFIT SERIES	X	
Cyma/McGraw-Hill 2160 E Brown Road Mesa, AZ 85282	THE SHOEBOX ACCOUNTANT® PROFESSIONAL ACCOUNTING	X X	
Dac Software, Inc. 4801 Spring Valley Road Dallas, TX 75244	DAC-EASY ACCOUNTING™	X	
Decision Support Software, Inc. 1300 Vincent Place McLean, VA 22101	BUSINESS ACCOUNTANT	X	
FrontRunner Development Corp. 14656 Oxnard Street Van Nuys, CA 91411	CPA+	X	
Great American Software, Inc. 9 Columbia Drive Amherst, NH 03031	ONE-WRITE PLUS	X	
Great Plains Software 1701 SW 38th Street Fargo, ND 58103	GREAT PLAINS PLAINS & SIMPLE™	X	X X
H & E Computronics, Inc. 50 N Pascack Road Spring Valley, NY 10977	VERSABUSINESS	X	
IBM PO Box 28331 Atlanta, GA 28331	ACCOUNTING ASSISTANT	X	
Indian Ridge Enterprises, Inc. 508 Second Street Oakland, CA 94607	INDIAN RIDGE	X	

Publisher Name and Address	Product Names	PC	MAC
International Micro Systems, Inc. 6445 Metcalf Avenue Shawnee Mission, KS 66202	FOCUS ON BUSINESS	X	
James River Group 125 N First Street Minneapolis, MN 55401	ACCOUNTING FOR MICROS	X	
Lake Avenue Software 650 Sierra Madre Villa Pasadena, CA 91107	THE ASSISTANT CONTROLLER™	X	
Layered, Inc. 85 Merrimac Street Boston, MA 02114	INSIGHT EXPERT INSIGHT ONEWRITE		X X
Libra Programming, Inc. 1954 E 7000 South Salt Lake City, UT 84121	LIBRA	X	
M & D Systems, Inc. 3885 N Buffalo Road Orchard Park, NY 14127	MYTE MYKE™	X	
Macola, Inc. 181 S Main Street Marion, OH 43302	MACOLA™	X	
MC Software PO Box 1377 Davis, CA 95617	INCOME II	X	
MCBA, Inc. 425 W Broadway Glendale, CA 91204	MCBA	X	
Micro Associates, Inc. 2349 Memorial Boulevard Port Arthur, TX 77640	MICA	X	
Micro Business Applications, Inc. 12223 Wood Lake Drive Burnsville, MN 55337	MBA	X	
Micro Computer Business Services 12703 Veterans Memorial Drive Houston, TX 77014	MCBS	X	

Publisher Name and Address	Product Names	PC	MAC
Microfinancial Flexware 15404 E Valley Boulevard City of Industry, CA 91746	FLEXWARE®		X
Convergent Business Systems, Inc. 6477 City West Parkway Eden Prairie, MN 55344	OPEN SYSTEMS™ HARMONY®	X X	
Q. W. Page Associates, Inc. One St. Clair Avenue W Toronto, Ont M4V2Z5 Canada	NEWVIEWS®	X	
Peachtree Software 4355 Shackleford Road Norcross, GA 30093	PEACHTREE COMPLETE II™	X	
RealWorld Corp. 282 Loudon Road Concord, NH 03302	4-IN-1™ BASIC ACCOUNTING REALWORD®	X X	
SBT Corp. Three Harbor Drive Sausalito, CA 94965	SBT DATABASE	X	
Softsync, Inc. 162 Madison Avenue New York, NY 10016	ACCOUNTANT INC.		X
SourceMate Information Systems, Inc. 20 Sunnyside Avenue Mill Valley, CA 94941	ACCOUNTMATE™	X	
Star Software Systems, Inc. 367 Van Ness Way Torrance, CA 90501	THE ACCOUNTING PARTNER™ THE ACCOUNTING PARTNER PLUS	X X	
State of the Art, Inc. 3545 Howard Way Costa Mesa, CA 92626	MAS 90™	X	
Systems Plus, Inc. 500 Clyde Avenue Mountain View, CA 94043	BOOKS DOUBLE ENTRY	X X	
TCS Software, Inc. 6100 Hillcroft Houston, TX 77081	TCS®	X	

Publisher Name and Address	Product Names	PC	MAC
Timberline Software Corp. 9405 SW Gemini Beaverton, OR 97005	MEDALLION BUSINESS SERIES	X	
TLB, Inc. PO Box 414 Findlay, OH 45839	SOLOMON III® PROFITWISE™	X X	

Backup Software

Core International, Inc. 7171 N Federal Highway Boca Raton, FL 33421	COREFAST™	X	
Fifth Generation Systems, Inc. 11200 Industriplex Boulevard Baton Rouge, LA 70809	FASTBACK PLUS	X	
Gazelle Systems 42 N University Avenue Provo, UT 84601	BACK-IT	X	
Westlake Data PO Box 1711 Austin, TX 78767	PC-FULLBACK	X	

Virus Software

FoundationWare 2135 Renrock Road Cleveland, OH 44118	CERTUS	X	
Software Concepts 594 Third Avenue New York, NY 10016	FLUSHOT PLUS	X	
Paul Mace Software 400 Williamson Way Ashland, OR 97520	MACE VACCINE	X	
Worldwide Software, Inc. 40 Exchange Place New York, NY 10005	VACCINE	X	

B

Resource Information

PRINTED SOFTWARE LISTS

Software Encyclopedia, R. R. Bowker Co., 245 W Seventeen Street, New York, NY 10011. A two-volume publication issued annually. The text is divided into sections by hardware platform, then application heading. Software is listed by product title. There are more than 2,100 pages in the 1989 volume on applications. Most descriptions range from 100 to 200 words.

ICP Software Directory, International Computer Programs, 9100 Keystone Crossing, Indianapolis, IN 46240. In this ten-volume publication, Vol. 2 is devoted to general accounting and Vol. 10 is industry specific.

Software Handbook for DOS for IBM PC, XT, AT, PS2 & Compatibles, H. W. Parker, 1601 Woodrock Drive, Round Rock, TX 78681; 1989.

The Software Catalogue: Microcomputers, Elsevier Science Publishing Co., 52 Vanderbilt Place, New York, NY 10017; Fall 1988.

Computers in Accounting: Buyer's Guide & Directory, Warren Gorham & Lamont, 1 Penn Plaza, New York, NY 10119; 1989.

DATABASES

Directory of Online Databases, Cuadra/Elsevier, 655 Avenue of the Americas, New York, NY 10010.

Business Software Database, Information Sources, Inc., 1173 Colosa Avenue, Berkeley, CA 94707.

Menu—The International Software Database, International Software Database Corp., PO Box MENU, Pittsburgh, PA 15241.

Micro Software Directory, Dialog Information Services, 3460 Hillview Avenue, Palo Alto, CA 94304.

SUBSCRIPTION SERVICES

Ratings Newsletter, The Software Digest, One Winding Drive, Philadelphia, PA 19131. One issue each year is devoted to accounting software and covers from five to ten products.

Data Sources, PO Box 5845, Cherry Hill, NJ 08034. Three volumes. There are approximately 750 pages in the 1990 section on application software. Each application heading is subdivided by hardware platform (such as Apple, Macintosh, IBM PC, etc.). Very brief 100–200-word descriptions are supplemented with data such as price, system requirements, inception year, and number of installations. Software is listed under the name of the publisher.

The Faulkner Report on Microcomputers and Software, Faulkner Technical Reports, Inc., 6560 N Park Drive, Pennsauken, NJ 08109. The July 1989 report surveys approximately 50 products with 2,000–3,000-word descriptions plus data on system requirements, first delivery date, and number of installations.

Datapro Directory of Software, Datapro Research, 1805 Underwood Boulevard, Defran, NJ 08075. The section on accounting software comprises approximately 400 pages, with most descriptions ranging from 1,000 to 2,000 words; some descriptions are much longer. The text is divided into sections by application heading regardless of system requirements. Data may include number of users, date of first installation, prices, and system requirements. The coverage of vertical applications is limited.

MAGAZINES

The periodicals listed below occasionally review accounting software.

InfoWorld, PO Box 1018, Southeastern, PA 19398.

Computers in Accounting, One Penn Plaza, New York, NY 10119.

PC Magazine, PO Box 2445, Boulder, CO 80322.

Business Software, 501 Galveston Drive, Redwood City, CA 94063.

Accountants Microcomputer News, 50 S Ninth Street, Minneapolis, MN 55402.

PC World, PO Box 55029, Boulder, CO 80322.

CPA Micro Report, 16800 W Greenfield Avenue, Brookfield, WI 53005.

C

Software Screens with Commentary

Screens and keyboards are the media through which people interact with software. Accounting software screens disclose many significant characteristics of the software, both strengths and weaknesses.

This section of the book displays and comments on screens selected from nationally available accounting software products—seven for PC computers and two for the Macintosh. The objective has been to use the latest version of each product. However, with a steady stream of upgrades and enhancements appearing on the market, some of these screens may be superseded by press time.

	PC	Macintosh
Charterhouse	X	
Computer Associates	X	
Flexware		X
Great Plains*		X
MAS 90	X	
Open Systems	X	
Platinum	X	
Realworld	X	
Solomon III	X	

*Great Plains has versions for both PC and Macintosh.

These screens show a wide variety in visual style and content. The first thing that strikes the eye is the obvious difference between Macintosh and PC screens. The Macintosh is graphic in orientation; the PC is text oriented.

There are noticable visual differences within the PC family, from the very simple text presentations of Realworld and Computer Associates, to the stylized screens of Solomon III.

More important than visual style are the texts and other visual cues that help the user understand the specific purpose of each screen, and the correct manner for making entries and corrections. This is affected by a number of factors in screen design, such as visual appearance, the amount of information requested, the choice of language, and the display of prompts. Some programs provide more comprehensive screens; others try to make the screens easier to understand by limiting the amount of information per screen. Difficulties arise from the lack of standardized terminology and the tendency to use obscure terms. Prompts guide the user in moving the cursor or making other selections.

Comprehension can also be improved through help screens and pop-up windows. Help screens provide explanations of screen functions and codes. Pop-up windows display lists of accounts and other selections. Both help screens and pop-up windows are invoked from special keys or key combinations designated for this purpose by the software.

Careful scrutiny of the screens will disclose the maximum number of characters provided for such crucial matters as account codes and descriptions.

Every accounting program has a unique style that is more appropriate to some business environments than to others. Note the differences in data storage and functions as shown by these screens. Some programs may be too simple for the needs of certain users. Other programs may provide more information and functional capability than required.

INSTALLATION SCREENS

One of the most daunting experiences for the computer neophyte is dealing with screens that require user input before one can start using the accounting software. Generally these screens cover three topics: hardware configuration, file management, and system options. The software may provide very little help in guiding the user to make the selections best suited to his or her needs. The situation is even more confusing when one screen covers more than one topic.

Hardware Configuration

The PC world involves a wide variety of printers and monitors that require their own special instructions (called drivers) in order to function properly.

The accounting software must be given enough information so that it will use the correct drivers.

In most instances, the names of the printers in use can be selected from an on-screen list such as provided by Realworld (Screen 1). The software comes with drivers for each of the displayed printers. This screen also shows that the software can support five printers and that compressed print will be used if a 135-character report must be printed on a narrow printer.

What does one do if the printer does not appear on the printer selection screen? An additional screen must be used in which the operator must enter printer control codes, such as that provided by Charterhouse (Screen 2). The screen selected here is used to enter the codes from enabling and canceling compressed print. In order to do this, the user must understand how to select the proper codes from the printer manuals. (Note the three prompts at the bottom of the screen.)

Users must also tell the software what kind of monitor has been selected. If a color monitor, the software usually provides a range of color choices. The Platinum (Screen 3) screen is an example of such selections. This particular screen includes options about printing the address on reports and about security. (The prompt "Clear Screen" appearing at the bottom means to blank all fields.)

File Management

One of the first tasks when planning an accounting software system is to determine the amount of disk storage that will be required. Some publishers provide printed charts for use in making the necessary computations. Other software, such as Open Systems (Screen 4), performs the computations for the user. The data at the bottom of the screen changes as entries are made on the screen. Note the question, "How many months of history do you wish to keep?" Such questions can be tricky because most users prefer to store as much data as possible. The best answer requires having some idea of how much disk storage is taken up by detail transaction files.

Programs that work with multiple disk drives, such as Platinum (Screen 5), provide a screen that allows the software to assign company and module data files to different drives. Most programs require a step called "initialization" to create data files on the hard disk. The example given here is Realworld (Screen 6). The same screen can be used to assign individual data files to separate drives.

Older programs required the user to periodically check the files to determine whether they should be enlarged. Newer programs use a process called dynamic file sizing to enlarge the files automatically as required.

Programs that store transaction details, such as Computer Associates (Screen 7), provide for summarizing (compressing) the detail transactions if the hard disk is running out of space. This screen allows the user to select a cutoff period for compression.

System Options

Some software provides a number of user selections that affect the overall operation of the system. The example shown here, Computer Associates (Screen 8), provides choices relating to a number of topics. The unusual choice called "verify entries" lets the user decide whether account and journal names are to be displayed when the corresponding codes are entered. Other choices relate to date format and monitor display. The help screen for "show chat line" appears when a function key is pressed.

An important option provided by many software packages, such as Flexware (Screen 9), is the selection of the output "target" for reports. Users can decided whether to send reports to a printer, view them on the monitor, or store them on disk for future use, such as printing at a later time or transferring to other programs. Flexware provides disk storage in three different formats.

MASTER MENU

Learning to navigate through the various program screens may require some patience.

At start-up, most accounting programs will display the current time and date and wait for the user to accept or change this information. Solomon III displays a rather unique sign-on screen (Screen 10). The screen number at the top right provides an easy cross reference to the software manual. The "Database Name" refers to the company data files. Solomon uses a special unlocking routine to prevent unauthorized use of its software. The "Access No" provides a useful control over unauthorized access to the program. If required, a password must be entered before one can go further with the program.

After the preliminaries have been passed, one finally enters the software and a master menu is displayed, a menu that may include all program modules whether they have been installed or not. Two different examples of a master menu follow: Charterhouse (Screen 11), and MAS90 (Screen 12).

Charterhouse uses a split screen that facilitates navigating from screen to screen. MAS90 allows choices along the top of the screen as well as a "pull-down" menu of applications. The company name and date are displayed on both screens. Display of the company name is important when multi-company records are computerized. The name display minimizes the danger of making entries against the wrong company.

Virtually all programs include a menu item called "Utilities." The functions provided under this name vary from program to program. (Contrast MAS90 (Screen 13) and Charterhouse (Screen 14).) Many of these functions cannot be understood without reference to the software manual.

GENERAL LEDGER

The real accounting work begins when an application module has been selected from the master menu. At this point, the main menu is displayed for the selected module. Realworld (Screen 15 and Screen 16) uses two screens for this purpose. The first screen lists the selections for routine processing. Charterhouse (Screen 17) displays all selections on a split screen.

Many programs use the term "maintenance" or "file maintenance" to refer to the functions of setting up, modifying, and deleting data files. Some data files must be set up before work can be processed. The file setup requirements vary from module to module.

In addition to storing transactions, separate general ledger data files are used to maintain such information as the definition of fiscal periods, the chart of accounts, and budgetary and historic data.

Screens for maintaining the chart of accounts disclose a great deal of information about the way the software functions. Note the size of the fields for account and department numbers, as well as account descriptions. Some general ledger software uses an expanded chart of accounts to determine the format of financial statements. This approach requires setting up pseudoaccounts for captions and totals. The example shown comes from Platinum (Screen 18). This pseudoaccount sets up the caption ASSETS for printing on the balance sheet.

Computer Associates (Screen 19) uses a screen requiring few responses, because the chart of accounts does not determine the format of financial statements. The function for adding accounts is on a separate screen from functions for viewing and modifying the accounts. This separation of functions can be useful for control purposes. The screen also displays the number of records in the file.

Open Systems (Screen 20) combines chart of account information with historic and budget data. The software permits the use of memo accounts (notice the prompt DR, CR OR MEMO?) and multiphase closings ("Clear to Account Step#"), features rarely found in micro accounting. The prompt "Inquiry Window" in the upper righthand corner tells the user that a pop-up window is available to look up acccount codes.

Realworld (Screen 21), by using a compression code, provides a choice by account for summarizing transactions. A prompt at the bottom of the screen describes the available choices as one moves from field to field.

Realworld (Screen 22), as shown, provides an example of a report specification screen. The use of report specification screens provides greater flexibility and variety in report design than financial statements derived from expanded charts of accounts. It is often difficult to learn the use of such screens.

Examples of screens for setting up accounting periods are Realworld (Screen 23) and Flexware (Screen 24). Many programs display the current accounting period (as it appears in screens such as this) when one enters each module. The accounting period may be displayed as a range of dates, the period-ending date, or the period number.

The number of accounting periods that can be accessed at any one time varies.

The style for journal entry screens varies from one screen per line entry—Computer Associates (Screen 25)—to multiline screens—Charterhouse (Screen 26). Pop-up windows, when available, ease the task of assigning account codes. The number of journal (or source) codes varies. Some software programs preassign the codes; others allow users to assign them. The amount of description space varies from program to program. Both of these screens provide debit and credit totals.

Different methods are used to assign accounting periods to transactions entered outside of general ledger, such as in accounts payable or accounts receivable. Some software provides a field for accounting period during transaction entry. Computer Associates (Screen 27) assigns the accounting period to each transaction batch at the time of transfer to general ledger, using a screen called "Retrieve Transactions from Other Systems." Other software may assign the accounting period from the transaction date (Great Plains) or the system date (MAS90).

Journals can be printed by source journal (source code) and one or more accounting periods.

Some software, such as Platinum (Screen 28), provides functions for computing gross profit inventory and tax accruals.

Reports may be selected from a menu such as Flexware (Screen 29) or from the selection of a statement identification code such as Computer

Associates (Screen 30). Format options may be offered, such as Platinum (Screen 31) and MAS90 (Screen 32).

Realworld (Screen 33) provides an example of a screen for year-end processing.

ACCOUNTS RECEIVABLE

Accounts receivable and accounts payable modules of the same program frequently are similar in design. If one becomes familiar with one of these modules, it usually is quite easy to learn the other. Both modules use special data files for establishing codes and descriptions that are accessed for processing transactions.

In accounts receivable, such files might be used for coding and describing customer class, tax class, territory, sales terms, and salesperson. Even if the general ledger module has been installed, most receivable software requires keying in certain account codes into a GL account code file. Codes and descriptions must be entered into the system before customer accounts can be set up.

Sample screens that list these data files are Charterhouse (Screen 34) and Flexware (Screen 35). Charterhouse requires setting up files two through seven before customer accounts. User options are presented in a screen entitled "System Control." A similar file in Flexware is called "A/R Parameters."

The design of the screens for assigning these codes and descriptions are clues to the way the software will process transactions. The size of the code fields may indicate the maximum number of entries that are permitted. Computer Associates' screen "Edit Company Profile—General Ledger Data" (Screen 36) shows that five cash accounts and five accounts receivable control accounts can be used. Platinum (Screen 37) provides for separate general ledger accounts by customer class. Charterhouse (Screen 38) accumulates and displays sales and commission data in the screen that is used for entering salesperson codes and names.

Option screens must also be processed before customer accounts can be entered. The nature of these options varies from program to program and can offer a variety of choices such as whether or not one wishes to store detail transactions, or integrate data with other modules. Selections can be made regarding the factors to use for computing discounts and finance charges, the time periods for agings, and whether commissions should be computed at sale or cash receipt date. Some options may be difficult to change after processing begins, although the software may not provide a clear warning about this.

The options may be clearly marked as such or displayed under such titles as "Edit Company Profile," "System Control File," or "Control Data." Compare the option screens for Computer Associates (Screen 39), Platinum (Screen.040), and Realworld (Screen 41, Screen 42, and Screen 43). Realworld, in option 33, allows the user the choice of detail or summary posting to the general ledger.

The screens that accept and display customer data are the core of the module. There is wide variation in the number of screens that display customer data and the amount of data displayed. Flexware (Screen 44) and Open Systems (Screen 45) use a single screen. Great Plains (Screen 46 and Screen 47) requires two screens. Some software displays or prints customer data under different menu choices. In some cases, the information can be obtained only by printing a report.

The style for invoice or cash entry screens varies in much the same manner as the journal entry screens in general ledger. Running batch totals vary from no totals—Realworld (Screen 48)—to separate totals by deposit and customer—MAS90 (Screen 49). Both of these programs allow the processing of non–accounts-receivable cash. Solomon III (Screen 50) provides batch controls, assignment of the accounting period, and a number of running totals. Realworld displays one open customer invoice at a time. MAS90 and Solomon III display many items.

Requirements for the application of cash, the matching of customer credits to open invoices, and the processing of unauthorized deductions vary from business to business. Users who have complex requirements should look for software that can handle these transactions in a straightforward manner.

Very few accounts receivable modules can print cash receipts or sales journals after transactions have been posted. One program that will print these journals is Platinum (Screen 51).

Programs that print sales orders and sales invoices may be very rigid in output format or may allow users some control over the printed forms, such as MAS90 (Screen 52 and Screen 53). Notice that the second screen prompts for 55 lines, although only 15 are visible at any one time. The additional lines are called up by scrolling through the screen.

Screens for selecting and printing forms and reports provide a clue about the output built into the program. Flexware provides two report screens; one example is given here (Screen 54). Selecting "Sales History" in Open Systems brings up a screen offering a number of options (Screen 55). Realworld (Screen 56) and Solomon III (Screen 57) offer a variety of choices for printing customer statements.

ACCOUNTS PAYABLE

Accounts payable usually requires less preliminary file work than accounts receivable. MAS90 (Screen 58) and Flexware (Screen 59) provide samples of accounts payable master menus. Note that scanning the MAS90 menu choices quickly tells the reader that the software can process recurring invoices (such as monthly service and rent bills) as well as checks prepared off the system.

Examples of option screens are Realworld (Screen 60) and Charterhouse (Screen 61). Both of these screens display examples of module requirements for entering general ledger account numbers. Realworld is limited to one cash account. Charterhouse, by using the phrase "default," suggests that different account numbers can be entered and also allows for different time periods for aging the accounts and projecting cash requirements.

Vendor data files form the core of accounts payable. As in accounts receivable, the number of screens and amount of data displayed for each vendor varies from product to product. Examples shown here are one of the Platinum screens (Screen 62) and Realworld (Screen 63).

Most accounting software processes transactions in batches. Some software can handle only one transaction batch per module. The batch must be posted and then erased before another batch can be started. Other software products can store many batches in each module. Great Plains (Screen 64) provides an example of a multibatch system screen that displays all unprocessed batches. In this example, a "pop-up screen" is displaying the options available for "Batch Type."

Screens for entering vendor invoices and debits vary. Some software limits the number of general ledger account distributions and provides little room for entering transaction descriptions. Some integrate with job cost. The number of screens required to enter a single vendor invoice varies. Computer Associates provides one screen (Screen 65). Platinum provides as many as four screens to accommodate entries that affect lot inventories and job cost. Two examples (Screen 66 and Screen 67) are given here. The two additional screens are used for serial/lot inventories and job cost entry.

Cash planning requires a listing of obligations. One example of a screen for this is Solomon III (Screen 68).

The method for selecting invoices for payment also varies from product to product. A method that is easy for a cash-rich company may be very clumsy for a company that must keep close watch on its cash flow. Most software provides for a review of the invoices selected for payment and the ability to make changes before checks are printed. Great Plains (Screen 69) displays the screens required to process computer checks. Most software, such as MAS90 (Screen 70), provides a type of preliminary selection of vendor invoices for payment. This selection usually is scanned for items that are not to be paid. Solomon III (Screen 71) is an example of a screen for entering payment exceptions.

Flexware (Screen 72) is a sample display of accounts payable reports provided by the software. Notice that vendor statistics are available from two reports: vendor activity and vendor purchase history.

INVENTORY

When inventory is significant to a business, the chances are that the inventory files will be the largest files in the accounting system. A great deal of care is required to choose appropriate software and select the codes and other options for using the system because wrong choices can result in wasted time and effort.

The inventory modules offered by publishers of general-purpose accounting software generally are most suitable to distributors and retailers and offer limited support for manufacturing operations. Some will handle simple bills of material as well as serial or lot inventories. Most will handle multiple warehouses.

A representative inventory main menu is provided by Solomon III (Screen 73).

Realword (Screen 74) and Platinum (Screen 75) provide examples of inventory option screens. Many users have problems with accounting software that requires some input regarding cost of sales. Realworld option 6 permits users to ignore this matter. Platinum permits users to run their inventories without posting to general ledgers.

Inventory costs based in FIFO and LIFO require storing layers of inventory cost. Open Systems (Screen 76) displays 12 layers of receipts for inventory costing. Computer Associates (Screen 77) provides a separate screen for defining the format of the item code (16-character total length).

Field sizes can be more critical in this module than in any other. One must pay careful attention to the maximum allowable length of item codes and descriptions. In some instances, the restriction on the number of decimals permitted in quantities and prices may be too limited.

Inventory is usually tied in with sales orders and invoices. Pricing structure is an important attribute of inventory software. Most software offers pricing levels related to item or customer classes. The capability of defining price, discount, and sales commission by inventory item varies with each software product.

The following examples of inventory item screens provide some idea of the wide variation in information that can be stored for inventory items: Platinum (Screen 78 and Screen 79), Realworld (Screen 80 and Screen 81), and Great Plains (Screen 82 and Screen 83). Platinum provides for serial and lot inventories. The field for item weight is useful for computing freight charges. Great Plains provides a separate screen for displaying item pricing (Screen 84) and source vendors.

Pricing methods can be complex and based on such criteria as customer type, quantity purchased, and other pricing variables. Some examples of pricing screens are Open Systems (Screen 85), Computer Associates (Screen 86 and Screen 87), and Solomon III (Screen 88).

MAS90 (Screen 89) and Solomon III (Screen 90) provide representative transaction entry screens. Platinum (Screen 91) provides a number of codes that can be useful for analyzing inventory transactions.

Some users need to make simultaneous price changes for a range of products (so-called global changes). Open Systems (Screen 92) and MAS90 (Screen 93) are examples of screens that can be used for this purpose.

There is no fixed rule as to where one can find such basic reports as item purchases by customer or customer purchases by item. In some instances, the reports are provided in accounts receivable. In other cases, the reports can be found in order entry or inventory control. The inventory reports provided by Solomon III (Screen 94) provide a represenative choice.

Reports that are entitled "Sales Analysis" or "Sales History" may be quite different as one goes from product to product. A report called a "listing" can range from a single line per record to a separate page that shows every piece of information in the record. If the wrong report is selected, the ability to interrupt printing can save a lot of time.

Great Plains (Screen 95) provides a representative selection of inventory reports. Open Systems (Screen 96) and Platinum (Screen 97) provide interesting options for sales analysis.

SALES ORDER ENTRY AND INVOICING

The final set of screens depicted here deal with entering and invoicing sales orders. While some programs place the sales invoice function in the accounts receivable module, most include invoicing with sales order entry.

Sales order entry and invoicing usually must call upon files in other modules. Accounts receivable provides customer information. The sale of merchandise requires item data in the inventory module. Construction billing might link to job cost. The ability to link with other modules and to deal with differing sales terms, pricing methods, commission structures, shipping methods, and line item descriptions distinguishes the various programs.

Solomon III (Screen 98) provides a sample menu for the order entry and invoicing module. Computer Associates (Screen 99) and Great Plains (Screen.100) provide examples of options available in order entry.

In most cases, three screens are used to process each order or invoice; one screen for header information, one for the body of the order, and a final screen for sundry charges and totals. Credits are usually processed as negative invoices using the same screens.

Header screens such as Charterhouse (Screen 101) and Realworld (Screen 102) combine basic customer data from accounts receivable with variable information such as order numbers and dates. Some of the displayed information, such as credit information and customer telephone numbers, are processing aids. Other information will print on the order/invoice or statement.

The number of different order types, such as quotes and standing and recurring orders, varies with the software. In most instances, a separate order/invoice must be prepared for each warehouse. Some software is able to process drop-ships, although drop-ships may not be properly reported in sales statistics.

Item screens call on data in inventory for item descriptions, units of measure, and prices and display item quantities such as amount on hand, on order, committed to sales, and so on. Charterhouse (Screen 103) displays one item per screen and four item quantities. Open Systems (Screen 104) displays two items per screen and two item quantities (at the selected warehouse). Other software, such as Platinum (Screen 105) and Flexware (Screen 106), provide multiple item listings on the screen. Platinum squeezes a lot of information onto one line of the monitor screen by allowing the description field, when the cursor is in that field, to overlap the next field.

Examples of the totals screen are Realworld (Screen 107) and Great Plains (Screen 108). Realworld provides for both an item and an order discount.

The final screen comes from Solomon III (Screen 109) and shows selections for printing open sales orders.

Maintain company data   SC Consultants - Alt

                    Compressed ?   Type   Printer device name
    14. Printer-1   Y   3   LPT1

    15. Printer-2

    16. Printer-3

    17. Printer-4

    18. Printer-5

===============================PRINTER TYPES===============================

    1) IBM   7) Diablo   13) IDS
    2) Epson   8) C. Itoh   14) Smith Corona
    3) Okidata   9) Star Micronics   15) Commodore
    4) NEC   10) Digital (DEC)   16) Silver Reed
    5) Anadex 9501A   11) Qume   17) Apple
    6) Anadex 9620A   12) Texas Instruments   18) Other

Field number to change ? ___

Screen 1: RealWorld Version 5.0

                    *** PRINTER CONFIGURATION ***

    Editing file: compress

    ┌───┐
    │ Printer Setup Codes: │
    │   │
    │ Ø29   Ø..   Ø..   Ø..   Ø..   Ø..   Ø..   Ø..   Ø..   Ø..   Ø..   Ø.. │
    │   │
    │ Ø..   Ø..   Ø..   Ø..   Ø..   Ø..   Ø..   Ø..   Ø..   Ø..   Ø..   Ø.. │
    │   │
    │ Ø..   Ø..   Ø..   Ø..   Ø..   Ø..   Ø..   Ø..   Ø..   Ø..   Ø..   Ø.. │
    ├───┤
    │ Printer Cancel Codes: │
    │   │
    │ Ø24   Ø..   Ø..   Ø..   Ø..   Ø..   Ø..   Ø..   Ø..   Ø..   Ø..   Ø.. │
    │   │
    │ Ø..   Ø..   Ø..   Ø..   Ø..   Ø..   Ø..   Ø..   Ø..   Ø..   Ø..   Ø.. │
    │   │
    │ Ø..   Ø..   Ø..   Ø..   Ø..   Ø..   Ø..   Ø..   Ø..   Ø..   Ø..   Ø.. │
    └───┘

        F1 -Write Data to Disk   F2 -Clear   Esc -Return to Menu

---

Screen 2: Charterhouse Version 2.1

```
╔══════════════════════════════════════════════════════════════════╗
║                    SYSTEM CONFIGURATION                            ║
╚══════════════════════════════════════════════════════════════════╝

┌─────────────────────────────────┐   ┌─────────────────────────────────┐
│ COLORS:   Foreground        2   │   │ Reserved for future use      N  │
│           Background        0   │   │                                 │
│           Border            0   │   │ NETWORK: No. of retries      5  │
│           High Intensity   14   │   │          Delay loop        5000 │
│           Flash - normal   28   │   │                                 │
│           Flash - inverse  28   │   │ Fast Color Display · (Y/N)   Y  │
│           Underline        15   │   │                                 │
└─────────────────────────────────┘   └─────────────────────────────────┘

┌─────────────────────────────────┐   ┌─────────────────────────────────┐
│ CURSOR: Top    scan line     5  │   │ HELP COLOR : Foreground     11  │
│         Bottom scan line     7  │   │              Background      0  │
│                                 │   │ NOTES COLOR: Foreground      0  │
│ Screen delay  (1-9000)    3000  │   │              Background      3  │
│ Print address on reports (Y/N) N│   │                                 │
│ PAGE LENGTH: Screen output   20 │   │ Security or Password (S/P)   S  │
│              Disk   output   66 │   │                                 │
└─────────────────────────────────┘   └─────────────────────────────────┘
```

<F1>=Process, <F2>=Clear Screen, <Esc>=Return to Menu

Screen 3: Platinum Version 6.0

                    INVENTORY for Company T

How many different inventory items do you stock?   -----

How many items are serialized?   0

On the average, how many serial numbers do you
have for each serialized item?   0

Do you wish to keep serialized history?

How many months of history do you wish to keep?   0

Based on previous experience, how many serialized
items do you expect to sell in one month?   0

How many warehouses do you wish to track?   0

                    WORK SPACE: 0.010 Megabytes
                 SIZE OF FILES: 0.000 Megabytes
              SPACE REMAINING: 4.943 Megabytes

Screen 4: OPEN SYSTEMS Version 3.2

```
┌─────────────────────────────────────────────────────────────┐
│              MULTI-COMPANY FILE MAINTENANCE                  │
│      Add   Change   Delete   Inquire   First   Last   Next   Prior   │
└─────────────────────────────────────────────────────────────┘


              ┌─────────────────┐
              │  COMPANY KEY     │
              │  COMPANY NAME    │  Your Company
              └─────────────────┘

                      Drive                            Drive
                    ┌─Specs─┐                        ┌─Specs─┐
                    Data┬Work┐                       Data┬Work┐
┌────────────────────────┬───┬───┐   ┌────────────────────────┬───┬───┐
│ ACCOUNTS RECEIVABLE     │ D │ D │   │ JOB COST               │ D │ D │
│ ORDER ENTRY            │ D │ D │   │ GENERAL LEDGER         │ D │ D │
│ INVENTORY              │ D │ D │   │ BANK BOOK              │ D │ D │
│ MANUFACTURING          │ D │ D │   │ FIXED ASSETS           │ D │ D │
│ ACCOUNTS PAYABLE       │ D │ D │   │ NETWORK LOCKING        │ D │ ─ │
│ PURCHASE ORDER         │ D │ D │   │ RESOURCE               │ D │ ─ │
│ PAYROLL                │ D │ D │   │ SPREADSHEET INTERFACE  │ D │ D │
└────────────────────────┴───┴───┘   └────────────────────────┴───┴───┘
```

<F1>=Process, <F2>=Clear Screen, <F9> <F10>=Select Action, <Esc>=Return to Menu

---

Screen 5: Platinum Version 6.0

Initialize G/L files

          Please enter for each file:

                            Disk   Disk

 1. Company file   _   12. Gen ledger lock file
 2. G/L control file   13. Cross ref work file
 3. Accounting period file   14. Layout file
 4. Text file   15. Layout reseq work file
 5. Chart of accounts file   16. SAF layout file
 6. Chng chart of accts file   17. Stmnt specification file
 7. Gen journal trans file   18. Statement pass file
 8. Gen journal lock file   19. Statement work file
 9. Std journal trans file
10. Std journal lock file
11. Gen ledger trans file

Screen 6: RealWorld Version 5.0

THE UNIVERSAL CORPORATION   Date: Nov 30 86
Purge Posted Transactions

```
                        * WARNING *
                        -----------
              Back up General Ledger Data
              before proceeding to this function.

              This function will delete all G/L transaction
              details that have been posted to accounts.

              Type YES to proceed, ESCAPE to exit. [    ]


              Purge up to and including fiscal period  [  ].



          Purging Account:          Department:
```

Screen 7: © 1989, Computer Associates International, Inc. Version 5.x

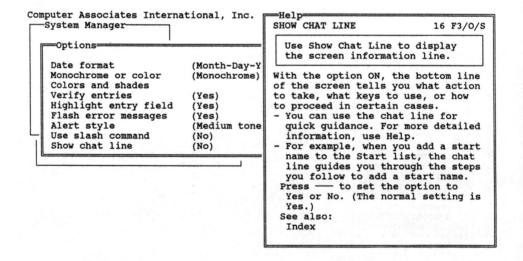

Screen 8: © 1989, Computer Associates International, Inc. Version 5.x

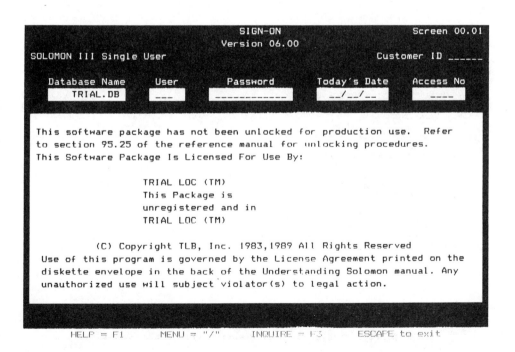

Please select output location

○ Screen-S
⦿ Printer-P
○ Spreadsheet (SYLK)-Y
○ Text (Tab delimited)-T
○ Merge (Comma delimited)-C

[OK-Ret] [Cancel-⌘Q]

Screen 9: Flexware Version 6.02

```
                        SIGN-ON                    Screen 00.01
                      Version 06.00
SOLOMON III Single User                          Customer ID _____

   Database Name    User      Password      Today's Date   Access No
    TRIAL.DB        ___    _____      __/__/__        ____


This software package has not been unlocked for production use.  Refer
to section 95.25 of the reference manual for unlocking procedures.
This Software Package Is Licensed For Use By:

           TRIAL LOC (TM)
           This Package is
           unregistered and in
           TRIAL LOC (TM)

      (C) Copyright TLB, Inc. 1983,1989 All Rights Reserved
Use of this program is governed by the License Agreement printed on the
diskette envelope in the back of the Understanding Solomon manual. Any
unauthorized use will subject violator(s) to legal action.



    HELP = F1      MENU = "/"      INQUIRE = F3      ESCAPE to exit
```

Screen 10: Solomon III Accounting Software Version 6.0

```
┌─────────────────────────────────────────────────────────────────────┐
│ Solo User                    *** MASTER MENU ***              v2.1   │
│ DEMO                    PROCESSING Sample Company          03/18/88   │
└─────────────────────────────────────────────────────────────────────┘

    ┌──────────────────────────────┐    ┌──────────────────────────────────┐
    │   *** PROCESS SELECTION ***  │    │  *** APPLICATION SELECTIONS ***  │
    │                              │    │                                  │
    │ <F1> - Application Selections │    │ 1 - Order Entry                  │
    │ <F2> - Utilities             │    │ 2 - A/R, Billing and Inventory   │
    │ <F3> - Initialize Data Files │    │ 3 - Accounts Payable             │
    │ <F10>- HELP                  │    │ 4 - Payroll                      │
    │ <Esc>- to End the SESSION    │    │ 5 - General Ledger               │
    │                              │    │ 6 - Purchase Order Entry         │
    │                              │    │ 7 - Manufacturing Inventory      │
    │                              │    │ 8 - Job Costing                  │
    └──────────────────────────────┘    └──────────────────────────────────┘



              ┌────────────────────────────────────────────┐
              │  PLEASE ENTER YOUR SELECTION    ..           │
              └────────────────────────────────────────────┘
```

Screen 11: Charterhouse Version 2.1

```
ABC DISTRIBUTING AND SERVICE CORP. (ABC)                      08/07/89
M.A.S 90 MASTER ACCOUNTING SERIES                             12:02 AM
| MAIN | REPORT MASTER | SECURITY | UTILITIES | PREFS | COMPANY | DATE | END |
    ┌─M.A.S 90 Applications Menu──────────────┐
    │   1.   GENERAL LEDGER                    │
    │   2.   ACCOUNTS RECEIVABLE               │
    │   3.   ACCOUNTS PAYABLE                  │
    │   4.   PAYROLL                           │
    │   5.   INVENTORY MANAGEMENT              │
    │   6.   SALES ORDER PROCESSING            │
    │   7.   PURCHASE ORDER PROCESSING         │
    │   8.   JOB COSTING AND ESTIMATING        │
    │   9.   BANK RECONCILIATION               │
    ├──────────────────────────────────────────┤
    │   ENTER YOUR OPTION: ···············     │
    └──────────────────────────────────────────┘



        F1=help, F2=company, F3=date, F4=print, F5=status, ESC=exit
```

Screen 12: MAS90 EVOLUTION/2 Version 1.1x

```
ABC DISTRIBUTING AND SERVICE CORP. (ABC)                      08/07/89
M.A.S 90 MASTER ACCOUNTING SERIES                             12:08 AM
| MAIN | REPORT MASTER | SECURITY | UTILITIES | PREFS | COMPANY | DATE | END |
                           ┌─System Utilities──────────────────────┐
                           │  1.   COMPANY MAINTENANCE              │
                           │                                        │
                           │  2.   DATA BACKUP/RESTORE UTILITY      │
                           │                                        │
                           │  3.   FILE SIZING WORKSHEET            │
                           │  4.   RESIZE DATA FILES                │
                           │  5.   SYSTEM ACTIVITY LOG              │
                           │  6.   FILE ANALYSIS AND REPAIR UTILITIES│
                           │  7.   REMOVE HELP TEXT FILES           │
                           │                                        │
                           │  8.   DEVICE CONFIGURATOR              │
                           │  9.   ALTERNATE DIRECTORY MAINTENANCE  │
                           │ 10.   DATA DIRECTORY TRANSFER          │
                           │ ───────────────────────────────────── │
                           │                                        │
                           │ ENTER YOUR OPTION: ·············       │
                           └────────────────────────────────────────┘


          F1=help, F2=company, F3=date, F4=print, F5=status, ESC=exit
```

Screen 13: MAS90 EVOLUTION/2 Version 1.1x

```
┌────────────────────────────────────────────────────────────────────┐
│ Solo User              *** MASTER MENU ***                    v2.1  │
│ DEMO                 PROCESSING Sample Company             03/18/88  │
└────────────────────────────────────────────────────────────────────┘

┌──────────────────────────────────┐  ┌──────────────────────────────────┐
│     *** PROCESS SELECTION ***     │  │       *** UTILITIES ***          │
│                                   │  │                                  │
│ <F1> - Application Selections     │  │  1 - Change System Date          │
│ <F2> - Utilities                  │  │  2 - Select Another Company      │
│ <F3> - Initialize Data Files      │  │  3 - Company Maintenance         │
│ <F10>- HELP                       │  │  4 - Company Listing             │
│ <Esc>- to End the SESSION         │  │  5 - Computer Definition         │
│                                   │  │  6 - Format Diskette             │
└───────────────────────────────────┘  │  7 - Copy Diskette               │
                                        │  8 - Backup Hard Disk Data       │
                                        │  9 - Restore Hard Disk Data      │
                                        │ 10 - Install Application / Data  │
                                        │ 11 - Printer Configurations      │
                                        └──────────────────────────────────┘


              ┌──────────────────────────────────────────┐
              │ PLEASE ENTER YOUR SELECTION   ..          │
              └──────────────────────────────────────────┘
```

Screen 14: Charterhouse Version 2.1

```
RealWorld - General Ledger                    The Software Consultants
Version 5.0, Serial # 0089004945


                   Please select

                        1. Chart of accounts
                        2. General journal
                        3. Standard journal
                        4. Trial balance
                        5. General ledger worksheet
                        6. View accounts
                        7. Source cross reference
                        8. Financial statement layouts
                        9. Financial statements
                       10. Get distributions



F2 = more selections    F8 = Help
```

Screen 15: RealWorld Version 5.0

```
RealWorld - General Ledger                    The Software Consultants
Version 5.0


              Please select

                       11. Company information
                       12. Accounting periods
                       13. Control information
                       14. Texts
                       15. Set-up procedures
                       16. Summarize general ledger
                       17. Calculate loan payments
                       18. Close a year
                       19. Data integrity check
                       20. Print reports from disk
```

Screen 16: RealWorld Version 5.0

```
┌─────────────────────────────────────────────────────────────────────────┐
│ Solo User          *** GENERAL LEDGER SYSTEM MENU ***          v2.11      │
│ DEMO                    PROCESSING Sample Company              03/18/88    │
└─────────────────────────────────────────────────────────────────────────┘

  ┌──────────────────────────────┐   ┌──────────────────────────────────┐
  │   *** PROCESS SELECTION ***  │   │    *** FILE MAINTENANCE ***      │
  │                              │   │                                  │
  │ <F1> - Journal Processing    │   │  1 - Chart of Accounts           │
  │ <F2> - Special Journal Processing│ 2 - Budget                       │
  │ <F3> - Financial Reporting   │   │  3 - Schedule                    │
  │ <F4> - Year-End Processing   │   │  4 - Division Name               │
  │ <F5> - File Maintenance      │   │  5 - Department Name             │
  │ <F6> - File Listing          │   │  6 - Journal Name                │
  │ <F7> - AutoPilot             │   │  7 - Statement Titles & Comments │
  │ <F8> - Utilities             │   │  8 - G/P Inventory Adjustment    │
  │ <Esc>- to Return to Master Menu │ 9 - Tax Accrual Adjustment       │
  │                              │   │ 10 - Journal Transaction         │
  │                              │   │ 11 - Account Balances            │
  │                              │   │ 12 - System Control              │
  └──────────────────────────────┘   └──────────────────────────────────┘

            ┌───────────────────────────────────────────┐
            │  PLEASE ENTER YOUR SELECTION   ..          │
            └───────────────────────────────────────────┘
```

Screen 17: Charterhouse Version 2.1

```
┌─────────────────────────────────────────────────────────────────────────┐
│       CHART OF ACCOUNTS FILE MAINTENANCE - STANDARD FINANCIALS            │
│       Add   Change   Delete   Inquire   First   Last   Next   Prior       │
└─────────────────────────────────────────────────────────────────────────┘


              ┌──────────────┐
              │ ACCOUNT NO.  │   1000 - 0000
              └──────────────┘


              ┌──────────────┐
              │ DESCRIPTION  │   ASSETS
              │ ACCOUNT TYPE │   CEN    CENTERED TITLE
              └──────────────┘

              ┌─────────────────────────────────────────────┐
              │ NO. OF BLANK LINES BEFORE ACCOUNT           │  1
              │ PRINT: DEPT,COMBINED,BOTH,NEITHER (D/C/B/N) │  B
              └─────────────────────────────────────────────┘



    <F1> = Process,  <F2> = Clear Screen,  <Esc> = Return to Menu
```

Screen 18: Platinum Version 6.0

```
THE UNIVERSAL CORPORATION                          Date: Nov 30 86
Add Accounts

                                          Number of G/L Accounts
                                          Currently : 91


        Account       [       ]   Department [       ]


        Description   [                                    ]

        Account Type  [ ]     I - Income / Expense
                              B - Balance Sheet
                              R - Retained Earnings


        Opening balance  :
        Current balance  :



Press ESCAPE to exit.
```

Screen 19: © 1989, Computer Associates International, Inc. Version 5.x

```
═══════════════════════ Add/Change G/L Accounts ═══════════Inquiry Window═
 Company        H      Account ------------
 Description                            DR, CR, OR MEMO   1
 Clear To Account              Step Ø
 Consol To Account             Step Ø
│Period         Actual         Budget         Last Year
│Begin          .ØØ            .ØØ            .ØØ
│   1           .ØØ            .ØØ            .ØØ
│   2           .ØØ            .ØØ            .ØØ
│   3           .ØØ            .ØØ            .ØØ
│   4           .ØØ            .ØØ            .ØØ
│   5           .ØØ            .ØØ            .ØØ
│   6           .ØØ            .ØØ            .ØØ
│   7           .ØØ            .ØØ            .ØØ
│   8           .ØØ            .ØØ            .ØØ
│   9           .ØØ            .ØØ            .ØØ
│  1Ø           .ØØ            .ØØ            .ØØ
│  11           .ØØ            .ØØ            .ØØ
│  12           .ØØ            .ØØ            .ØØ
│  13           .ØØ            .ØØ            .ØØ
│End            .ØØ            .ØØ            .ØØ
```

Screen 20: OPEN SYSTEMS Version 3.2

```
Maintain chart of accounts                      The Software Consultants
Change/Inquire


                 * 1. Account number        1000-000

                   2. Description           Cash Account #13557

                   3. T/B subtotal level

                   4. Fin statement type    B

                   5. SAF type              C

                   6. Paren control code    C

                   7. Compression code      P



N = no compression   D = by date   P = by period
```

Screen 21: RealWorld Version 5.0

```
Maintain financial statement layouts            The Software Consultants
Change/Inquire
Layout #: 005   Statement of Revenue

Seq   Acct-# or
 #    function


____
0010  LIT                                        XYZ Company
0020  LIT                                   Statement of Revenue
0030  LEG
0040  LIT                                          Sales
0050  LF
0060  4010-100   Sales - Tools               Prt/Accum ?   P
0070  4010-200   Sales - Tools               Prt/Accum ?   P
0080  4020-100   Sales - Parts               Prt/Accum ?   P
0090  4020-200   Sales - Parts               Prt/Accum ?   P
0100  UL
0110  SUB1           Total Sales             Paren cntrl   D
LF

Press F1 for next page or F2 + seq # to see a page from a specific position
```

Screen 22: RealWorld Version 5.0

```
Maintain accounting periods                    The Software Consultants

                        Period   Start      End

                          1.    1/01/99    1/31/99
                          2.    2/01/99    2/28/99
                          3.    3/01/99    3/31/99
                          4.    4/01/99    4/30/99
                          5.    5/01/99    5/31/99
                          6.    6/01/99    6/30/99
                          7.    7/01/99    7/31/99
                          8.    8/01/99    8/31/99
                          9.    9/01/99    9/30/99
                         10.   10/01/99   10/31/99
                         11.   11/01/99   11/30/99
                         12.   12/01/99   12/31/99
                         13.

                         14.  Current period #  3
                                3/01/99    3/31/99
                         15.  Reporting period
                                3/01/99    3/31/99

Do you wish to re-enter periods ?   N
```

Screen 23: RealWorld Version 5.0

 ⌐ **File Edit System General Ledger Selections**   **11:05:07 AM**

Demo System Only- G/L Parameters (Co - 99)

Fiscal Year........ `87`	Fiscal Begin Month.. `1`
Current Year........ `87`	Current Month/period `1`

Ret Earn Acct#...... `305.00` `RETAINED EARNINGS`

Next Recur JE #..... `1`
Next Seq No......... `1`   Number Of Periods... `12`
Next Batch Number... `1`   Last Per End Seq No.

Monthly R&E Closing? `N`   Entry Period........ `1`
Job Cost Interface ? `N`   Entry Year......... `87`

[Change-C] [Cancel-⌘Q]

Chart of Accounts file lookup

Screen 24: Flexware Version 6.02

```
THE UNIVERSAL CORPORATION                              Date: Nov 30 86
Enter/Edit Batch of Transactions


     Batch Number [30 ] has 15   Transactions.
     -------------------------------------------------------------------

     Transaction Number [1   ]

     Period      [3 ]
     Source      [2]                    Cash Disbursements
     Date        [09/15/86]
     Reference   [JE67 ]
     Description [Curry and Co. Ck#520    ]

     Account    [    800]  Dept.[    ]   Accounting & audit
     Amount   Dr.[     1,250.00 ]   Cr.[                ]


     Totals : Dr.     14,017.06       Cr.     14,017.06

Press ESCAPE in first field to exit.
```

Screen 25: © 1989, Computer Associates International, Inc. Version 5.x

```
         * * *   J O U R N A L   T R A N S A C T I O N   E N T R Y   * * *
       ┌──────────────────────────────────────────────────────────────┐
       │  PROCESSING JOURNAL 92 - RECURRING JOURNAL        FOR PERIOD 02 │
       └──────────────────────────────────────────────────────────────┘

    Date    Description          Ref    G/L Acct      Debit       Credit


 ../../..  ....................  .....  .... ‾ ....  ...........  ...........
 ../../..  ....................  .....  .... ‾ ....  ...........  ...........
 ../../..  ....................  .....  .... ‾ ....  ...........  ...........
 ../../..  ....................  .....  .... ‾ ....  ...........  ...........
 ../../..  ....................  .....  .... ‾ ....  ...........  ...........
 ../../..  ....................  .....  .... ‾ ....  ...........  ...........
 ../../..  ....................  .....  .... ‾ ....  ...........  ...........
 ../../..  ....................  .....  .... ‾ ....  ...........  ...........
 ../../..  ....................  .....  .... ‾ ....  ...........  ...........
 ../../..  ....................  .....  .... ‾ ....  ...........  ...........

Verify= Y       Decimal= N       Session Totals          0.00         0.00
                                         Difference
Processing Entry:   1            Status: Ready

   F1 -Proc   F2 -Clear   F3 -Up   F4 -Down   F5 -Search   F6 -More   Esc -Options
```

Screen 26: Charterhouse Version 2.1

```
THE UNIVERSAL CORPORATION                                    Date: Aug 05 89
Retrieve Transactions from Other Systems

                Enter the System Code [  ] of batch being retrieved.

---------------------------- Enter File Name ----------------------------
    [                                                                    ]


                Enter information for the new transactions.
                    G/L Source Code  [  ]
                    Fiscal Period    [  ]


                Assigned batch number




Press ESCAPE to exit.
```

Screen 27: © 1989, Computer Associates International, Inc. Version 5.x

```
┌──────────────────────────────────────────────────────────────────────┐
│               GENERAL LEDGER STATUS FILE MAINTENANCE                   │
└──────────────────────────────────────────────────────────────────────┘


  ┌──────────────────────────┐          ┌──────────────────────────┐
  │ POSTED FROM: A/R    N     │          │ NO ERROR EDIT LIST    N  │
  │             A/P    N     │          │ VERIFIED CHART        N  │
  │             P/R    N     │          └──────────────────────────┘
  │             B/B    N     │
  │             I/V    N     │
  │             J/C    N     │
  │             F/A    N     │
  │            OTHER   N     │
  │                          │
  │ AUTO:    FED TAX   N     │
  │        STATE TAX   N     │
  │     GROSS PROFIT   N     │
  │        RECURRING   N     │
  │     REALLOCATION   N     │
  └──────────────────────────┘


        <F1> = Process, <F2> = Clear Screen, <Esc> = Return to Menu
```

Screen 28: Platinum Version 6.0

Selections

COA List ⌘1	Alphabetical COA ⌘2	Journal Type List ⌘3	Journal Entries ⌘4	Entries by Source ⌘5	Entries by COA ⌘6	Unposted Journal ⌘7
Inbalanced Batches ⌘8	Summary Gnrl Ledger ⌘9	Dtl General Ledger ⌘A	Comparative GL 1-6 ⌘B	Comparative GL 7-13 ⌘C	Budget – Per 1-6 ⌘E	Budget – Per 7-13 ⌘F
'Rough' Inc Stmnt ⌘I	'Rough' Bal Sheet ⌘S	Income Statement ⌘T	Balance Sheet ⌘U	S/Sheet Interface ⌘X	Help ⌘W	

Please make menu selection or choose icon

Screen 29: Flexware Version 6.02

THE UNIVERSAL CORPORATION   Date: Nov 30 86
Maintain Specifications

```
┌─Specifications─┐              ┌─Active Specifications──────────┐
│                │                                          File
│  TITLE         │
│  UNIV1         │                Financial Statement      UNIV1
│  UNIV2         │              └────────────────────────────────┘
│  UNIV3         │
│  UNIV4         │
│  UNIV5         │
│  UNIV6         │
│  UNIV7         │
│  UNIV8         │
└────────────────┘
```

Make active	Edit	Copy	Delete	Align	Print	Retrieve	Import

Screen 30: © 1989, Computer Associates International, Inc. Version 5.x

```
┌─────────────────────────────────────────────────────────────────────┐
│           FINANCIAL REPORTING OPTIONS FILE MAINTENANCE                │
└─────────────────────────────────────────────────────────────────────┘

┌─────────────────────────────────────────────────────┬───┐
│ BRACKET CREDITS OF: ASSETS          (Y/N)            │ Y │
│                     LIABILITIES  (Y/N)               │ N │
│                     EQUITY          (Y/N)            │ N │
│                     REVENUE         (Y/N)            │ N │
│                     EXPENSES        (Y/N)            │ Y │
│                                                      │   │
│ ROUND TO NEAREST DOLLAR             (Y/N)            │ Y │
│ PRINT COMMAS IN NUMBERS             (Y/N)            │ Y │
│ FIXED POSITION DOLLAR SIGNS         (Y/N)            │ Y │
│ PRINT PAGE ON TOP,BOTTOM,NONE (T/B/N)                │ N │
│ MAX DIGIT POS. - BALANCE SHEET (6-20)                │ 15│
│                - INCOME STMNT  (6-20)                │ 15│
│ LONGEST PRINTABLE DESCRIPTION (20-30)                │ 30│
│ SINGLE UNDERLINE ASCII CODE                          │ 45│
│ DOUBLE UNDERLINE ASCII CODE                          │ 61│
│ ALTERNATE 100% COMPARISON VALUE                      │ 0 │
│ NEXT DEFAULT REFERENCE NUMBER                        │ 0 │
└─────────────────────────────────────────────────────┴───┘

        <F1> = Process, <F2> = Clear Screen, <Esc> = Return to Menu
```

Screen 31: Platinum Version 6.0

```
ABC DISTRIBUTING AND SERVICE CORP. (ABC)        PRINTER LP           05/31/90
FINANCIAL STATEMENTS                                                 12:31 AM
```

```
            PRINT FINANCIAL STATEMENTS FOR:

            ACCOUNTING PERIOD:                          05    05/31

            PRINT LINES WITH ZERO BALANCE? (Y/N):       N

            PRINT DEPARTMENTAL INCOME STATEMENTS:       N
            BEGINNING DEPARTMENT:
            ENDING DEPARTMENT:

            PRINT THE FOLLOWING INCOME STATEMENT DATA:  1
               1.  PERIOD TO DATE ACTUAL / YEAR TO DATE ACTUAL
               2.  P-T-D & Y-T-D ACTUAL, BUDGET & VARIANCE
               3.  P-T-D & Y-T-D ACTUAL & PERCENT/BUDGET & PERCENT
               4.  P-T-D & Y-T-D ACTUAL, PRIOR YEAR & VARIANCE
               5.  Q-T-D & Y-T-D ACTUAL & PERCENT
               6.  P-T-D & Y-T-D ACTUAL, ANNUAL BUDGET & VARIANCE
               7.  P-T-D & Y-T-D ACTUAL, ANNUAL BUDGET & PERCENT

        IS THE ABOVE CORRECT? (Yes, No, Printers, Video, END): [Yes     ]
```

Screen 32: MAS90 EVOLUTION/2 Version 1.1x

Process end of year   The Software Consultants

        This program sets all profit and loss accounts to zero

        and brings the balance forward for balance sheet accounts.

        It adjusts last year comparatives and the period dates.

Are you sure you want to do this ?   N

Screen 33: RealWorld Version 5.0

```
┌──────────────────────────────────────────────────────────────────────┐
│ Solo User *** A/R, BILLING AND INVENTORY CONTROL SYSTEM MENU ***  v2.1 │
│ DEMO                   PROCESSING Sample Company           03/21/88    │
├──────────────────────────────────────────────────────────────────────┤
│  ┌─────────────────────────────────┐  ┌──────────────────────────────┐│
│  │    *** PROCESS SELECTION ***     │  │  *** A/R FILE MAINTENANCE ***││
│  │                                  │  │                              ││
│  │ <F1> - Daily Processing          │  │  1 - Customer                ││
│  │ <F2> - Physical Inventory        │  │  2 - Salesman                ││
│  │ <F3> - Monthly Processing        │  │  3 - Territory               ││
│  │ <F4> - A/R File Maintenance      │  │  4 - State                   ││
│  │ <F5> - Inv'ty File Maintenance   │  │  5 - Revenue                 ││
│  │ <F6> - A/R File Listings         │  │  6 - Sales Tax               ││
│  │ <F7> - Inv'ty File Listings      │  │  7 - G/L Accounts            ││
│  │ <F8> - AutoPilot                 │  │  8 - Invoice/Payment Detail  ││
│  │ <F9> - Utilities                 │  │  9 - Cash                    ││
│  │ <Esc>- to Return to Master Menu  │  │ 10 - FOB                     ││
│  │                                  │  │ 11 - Terms                   ││
│  │                                  │  │ 12 - System Control          ││
│  └─────────────────────────────────┘  └──────────────────────────────┘│
│                                                                        │
│           ┌────────────────────────────────────────┐                  │
│           │   PLEASE ENTER YOUR SELECTION   ..      │                  │
│           └────────────────────────────────────────┘                  │
└──────────────────────────────────────────────────────────────────────┘
```

Screen 34: Charterhouse Version 2.1

```
┌─────────────────────────────────────────────────────────────────────┐
│ □                            Selections                               │
├────────┬────────┬───────────┬──────────┬────────┬─────────┬──────────┤
│  🎩    │  ✏️    │   👤      │   👤     │  📧    │  📨     │   🗺️     │
│  Tax   │  Term  │Salesperson│ Customer │ Credit │ Dunning │  A/R     │
│ Types  │ Types  │  Codes    │  Types   │ Types  │Messages │Parameters│
│  ⌘1    │  ⌘2    │   ⌘3      │   ⌘4     │  ⌘5    │  ⌘6     │   ⌘A     │
├────────┼────────┼───────────┼──────────┼────────┼─────────┼──────────┤
│  📕    │        │           │          │        │         │          │
│  Help  │        │           │          │        │         │          │
│  ⌘W    │        │           │          │        │         │          │
└────────┴────────┴───────────┴──────────┴────────┴─────────┴──────────┘

┌───────────────────────────────────────────────────────────────────────┐
│ Please make menu selection or choose icon                               │
└───────────────────────────────────────────────────────────────────────┘
```

Screen 35: Flexware Version 6.02

```
THE UNIVERSAL CORPORATION                              Date: Nov 30 86
Edit Company Profile - General Ledger Data

              ─────────── Receivable Control Accounts ───────────

          Acct.        Dept.           Description
      1. [200    ]  [       ]  [                                ]
      2. [       ]  [       ]  [                                ]
      3. [       ]  [       ]  [                                ]
      4. [       ]  [       ]  [                                ]
      5. [       ]  [       ]  [                                ]


              ─────────────── Bank Accounts ───────────────

          Acct.        Dept.           Description
      1. [   104]  [       ]  [                                ]
      2. [       ]  [       ]  [                                ]
      3. [       ]  [       ]  [                                ]
      4. [       ]  [       ]  [                                ]
      5. [       ]  [       ]  [                                ]


Press ESCAPE to proceed.
```

Screen 36: © 1989, Computer Associates International, Inc. Version 5.x

```
┌─────────────────────────────────────────────────────────┐
│            CUSTOMER CLASS FILE MAINTENANCE                │
│      Add   Change  Delete  Inquire  First  Last  Next  Prior │
└─────────────────────────────────────────────────────────┘


        ┌──────────────────────────────┐
        │ CUSTOMER CLASS KEY           │   00001
        │                              │
        │ DESCRIPTION                  │   RETAIL
        │ FINANCE CHARGE %             │   1.5
        │ FINANCE CHARGE ACCOUNT       │   8300 - 0000
        │ SALES         ACCOUNT        │   5100 - 0000
        │ CASH          ACCOUNT        │   1010 - 0000
        │ A/R           ACCOUNT        │   1300 - 0000
        │ FREIGHT       ACCOUNT        │   6400 - 0000
        │ DISCOUNT TAKEN ACCOUNT       │   5150 - 0000
        │ DISCOUNT GIVEN ACCOUNT       │   5150 - 0000
        │ LATE CHARGE    ACCOUNT       │   8250 - 0000
        │ LATE CHG ON INV or CUST (I/C)│   C
        │ LATE CHG AMOUNT              │   10
        └──────────────────────────────┘
```

          <F1> = Process, <F2> = Clear Screen, <Esc> = Return to Menu

Screen 37: Platinum Version 6.0

```
        ┌────────────────────────────────┐
        │  *** SALESMAN MAINTENANCE ***   │
        └────────────────────────────────┘
    ┌──────────────────────────────────────────────┐
    │ ACTION: <A>dd <C>hange <D>elete <I>nquire  .  │
    │                                               │
    │   Salesman ID:        . . . .                 │
    │                                               │
    │   Name:               . . . . . . . . . . . . │
    │                                               │
    │   Commission Rate:    . . . . . . .           │
    │              ┌─────────────────────────────────────┐
    │         S    │ Commission - MTD:  . . . . . . . . . .│
    │         Y    │ Commission - YTD:  . . . . . . . . . .│
    │         S    │                                      │
    │         T    │ Sales - MTD:       . . . . . . . . . .│
    │         E    │ Sales - YTD:       . . . . . . . . . .│
    │         M    │                                      │
    └──────────────┴─────────────────────────────────────┘
```

F1 -Process   F2 -Clear   F3 -Prev   F4 -Next   Esc -Return to Menu

Screen 38: Charterhouse Version 2.1

THE UNIVERSAL CORPORATION   Date: Nov 30 86
Edit Company Profile - System Options

```
        Statement default                  [Y]   Y/N
        Interest default                   [Y]   Y/N
        Balance forward default            [N]   Y/N
        Retain batch history               [N]   Y/N
        Suppress zero balance statements   [N]   Y/N

        Standard aging - 0 to [30 ] to [60 ] to [90 ] days and over.

        Interest charged on accounts over [30 ] days
        Minimum finance charge             [          0.00 ]   Round up [N]   Y/N
        Interest rate                              [ 2.00]
        Interest identification - Common part      [INT-]
                               - Next sequence number [0   ]
```

Press ESCAPE to proceed.

Screen 39: © 1989, Computer Associates International, Inc. Version 5.x

```
                        NAME & OPTIONS FILE MAINTENANCE


    COMPANY NAME        DEMONSTRATION, INC.
    STREET ADDRESS      1000 ANY STREET
    CITY                SOMEWHERE                Pull from CUST or INVENTORY:
    STATE               CA
    ZIP                 75000                    DEFAULT REV. ACCOUNT (C/I)    C
                                                 DEFAULT TAX RATE (C/I/B/b/X)  C


    INTERFACE TO INVENTORY        (Y/N)   N
    INTERFACE TO BANK BOOK        (Y/N)   N      AGE BRACKET  1 LIMIT      30
    RETAIN A/R TRANS HISTORY      (Y/N)   Y                   2 LIMIT      60
    RETAIN A/R LINE ITEM HISTORY  (Y/N)   Y                   3 LIMIT      90
    INTERFACE TO G/L              (Y/N)   N
    COMMISSIONS PAID or BOOKED    (P/B)   B      TAX LEVEL  1 NAME       STATE
    NAME ON INV/STMNT/BOTH        (I/S/B) B                 2 NAME       COUNTY
    LONG or SHORT INVOICE FORM    (L/S)   L                 3 NAME       EXCISE
    LONG or SHORT STATEMENT FORM  (L/S)   L                 4 NAME
```

             <F1> = Process, <F2> = Clear Screen, <Esc> = Return to Menu

---

Screen 40: Platinum Version 6.0

312

```
Maintain A/R control data                    The Software Consultants

            1. Age by invoice or due date    D
            2. # age days in period 1        30
            3. # age days in period 2        60
            4. # age days in period 3        90
            5. # age days in period 4        999
            6. Aging period 1 description    30 days
            7. Aging period 2 description    60 days
            8. Aging period 3 description    90 days
            9. Aging period 4 description    over 90

           10. Finance charge pct - level 1  .00
           11. Level 1 cut-off amount
           12. Finance charge pct - level 2  .00
           13. Age past due by what date ?   D
           14. # days past-due for F/C
           15. Minimum finance charge        .00
           16. Calc fin chgs on fin chgs ?   N

           17. Print company name on stmt ?  Y
           18. Current period end date       3/31/90

Field number to change ?  ___
```

Screen 41: RealWorld Version 5.0

```
Maintain A/R control data                    The Software Consultants

           19. Accts receivable acct #    1100-000  Accounts Receivable
           20. Distribute sales ?         Y
           21. Default sales acct #       4010-000  Equipment Income/Expense

           22. Distribute misc chrgs ?    Y
           23. Default misc chrgs acct #  4000-000  Revenue from Jobs

           24. Distribute freight ?       Y
           25. Default freight acct #     4050-000  Discounts Allowed

           26. Discount acct #            4050-000  Discounts Allowed
           27. Finance chgs acct #        4060-000  Sales Allowances
           28. Default allowance acct #   4070-000  Finance Charges

           29. Are salesmen used ?        Y
           30. Are commissions used ?     Y
           31. Default commission pct     5.00
           32. Are costs-of-sales used ?  N
           33. Summary post distribs ?    N
           34. A/R statement format       1

Field number to change ?  ___
```

Screen 42: RealWorld Version 5.0

```
        35. Cash account # 1  1000-000   Cash Account #13557
        36. Cash account # 2
        37. Cash account # 3

        38. Calc disc on misc chgs ?      N
        39. Calc disc on freight ?        N
        40. Calc disc on sales tax ?      N

        41. Calc sls tax on misc chgs ?   Y
        42. Calc sls tax on freight ?     N

        43. Over 30 days dunning notice


        44. Over 60 days dunning notice


        45. Over 90 days dunning notice



Field number to change ?   ___
```

Screen 43: RealWorld Version 5.0

```
 ┌                                                                    ┐
    ⌘  File  Edit  System  Accounts Receivable  Frequent Items  1:54:03 PM
 └                                                                    ┘
 ┌──────────────────────────────────────────────────────────────────┐
 │▒▒▒▒▒▒▒▒▒▒▒▒▒  Demo System Only- Customer (Add,Inq) (Co - 99) ▒▒▒▒▒ □▒│
 │ Customer Id..  [BEST    ]                                        ⇧ │
 │ Bill Name....  [BEST HOMEBUILDERS ]    Ship Name....  [BEST HOMEBUILDERS ] │
 │ Address......  [1122 E. HWY 111 ]      Address......  [1122 E. HWY 111 ]   │
 │ -...........                           -...........                │
 │ City........   [PALM DESERT ]          City........   [PALM DESERT ]       │
 │ State.......   [CA] Zip [92911]        State.......   [CA] Zip [92911]     │
 │ Country......                          Country......                │
 │                                                                    │
 │ Usual Slsprsn  [JJ] [JOHN JONES ]          Price Level........  [1] │
 │ Customer Type  [BU] [BUILDER ]             Dunning Type.......  [1] │
 │ Tax Code.....  [NO] [NON TAXABLE ]         Finance %....    [   .]  │
 │ Term Code....  [30] [NET 30 ]              Bal Fwd         [     .] │
 │ Date Entered.  [6/07/87]               Contact......  [PHIL BEST ]  │
 │ Resale Number                          Telephone....  [  /  ]       │
 │ Current......  [    ,   .]   Hold Orders?             Last Invoice [  /  /  ] │
 │ 30 Days......  [    ,   .]   Cred Rating.  [A]        Last Payment [  /  /  ] │
 │ 60 Days......  [    ,   .]   Credit Limit [10,000.00] Open Inv/Credits.. │
 │ 90 Days......  [    ,   .]   Balance.....  [    ,   .]Last Stmnt.. [  /  /  ] │
 │ 120+ Days....  [    ,   .]   Highest Bal.  [    ,   .]On Order..  [    ,   .] │
 │                                                                    │
 │ (Ageing Graph-G) (Return-R) (Cancel-⌘Q)                          ⇩ │
 │ ⇦                                                                ⇦⇨ │
 │ Term Code found                                                    │
 └──────────────────────────────────────────────────────────────────┘
```

Screen 44: Flexware Version 6.02

```
═══════════════════ Add/Change Customers ═══════════ Normal Entry ┐
Cust ID GRE001    Copy From

»Name    GREATER NEW YORK DOMES, INC.    Run Code      1
 Addr 1  1001 AVE OF THE AMERICAS         Stmt Code     B  Both Stmt & Inv
 Addr 2  NEW YORK CITY, NY 10012          Tax Code      1    4.000%
 Addr 3                                   Price Code    0
 Phone   (100) 555-0011                   Account Type  B  Balance Forward
 Salesperson 04                           Terms Code    4   15 days    1.0%
 Credit Limit       150000                Finance Code  Y  Yes

 New Fin Chg          .00        S A L E S    H I S T O R Y
 Unpaid Fin Chg       .00                  MTD           YTD
 Current Due          .00     Sales          .00    1843808.76
 Balance 31-60     1103.28     Profit         .00     868387.20
         61-90        .00     # Invoices      0          30
         91-120       .00
         120+         .00
                              Last Sales Date  11/10/84
 Total Due         1103.28
```

Screen 45: OPEN SYSTEMS Version 3.2

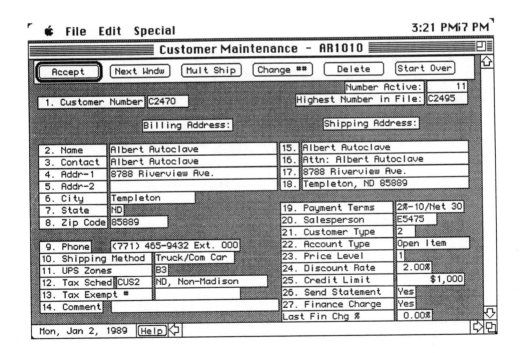

Screen 46: Copyright © Great Plains Software, Incorporated, 1989 Version 5.x. All rights reserved.

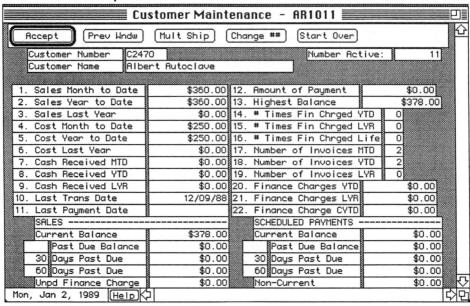

```
Process cash receipts                           The Software Consultants
Add

          1. Cust #          1        Moniques Boutique          Open item
                                      Terms: Net 30 days
          2. Check #         3456
          3. Receipt date    3/31/88
          4. Amount recd     100.00
          5. Cash acct code  1  1000-000 Cash Account #13557
          6. Bank route #
          7. Credit A/R ?    Y        Amount remaining:  100.00

  Apply-to  Type  Doc date  Due date     Orig amt        Balance    Valid disc


  _____

             Terms:
          8. Amt paid
          9. Discount
         10. Allowance
             Account #
         11. Reference
Press F1 for next outstanding document with non-zero balance
Press F2 for previously entered applications for this check
```

Screen 48: RealWorld Version 5.0

```
ABC DISTRIBUTING & SERVICE CORP (ABC)              LIST MODE      05/31/90
CASH RECEIPTS ENTRY                                RECORDS: 2     12:24 AM
─────────────────────────────────────────────────────────────────────────
 BANK CODE: A      Security Pacific Checking    DEPOSIT DATE: 05/31/90
 DEPOSIT NO: 00024     DEPOSIT AMOUNT:    1000.00 DEPOSIT BALANCE:    675.00
─────────────────────────────────────────────────────────────────────────
CUSTOMER NO: 01-ABF    American Business Futures   A/R BALANCE:      5238.24
    CHECK NO: 45687    AMOUNT REC'D:      325.00 POSTING BALANCE:     325.00

  ┌──────┬──────────┬───────────┬────────────┬───────────┬────────────┬────────────┐
  │ LINE │ INV DATE │ INV NUMBER│ INV AMOUNT │ DSC AVAIL │ AMT POSTED │ INV BALNCE │
  ├──────┼──────────┼───────────┼────────────┼───────────┼────────────┼────────────┤
  │  1   │ 01/31/90 │ 0000101-IN│        .00 │       .00 │        .00 │        .00 │
  │  2   │ 02/28/90 │ 0000122-IN│     850.00 │       .00 │        .00 │     850.00 │
  │  3   │ 03/31/90 │ 0000141-IN│    1178.69 │       .00 │        .00 │    1178.69 │
  │  4   │ 04/30/90 │ 0000190-IN│      85.00 │       .00 │        .00 │      85.00 │
  │  5   │ 04/30/90 │ APR0001-FC│      43.89 │       .00 │        .00 │      43.89 │
  │  6   │ 05/15/90 │ 0100033-IN│     613.05 │       .00 │        .00 │     613.05 │
  │  7   │ 05/15/90 │ 0100034-IN│    2467.61 │       .00 │        .00 │    2467.61 │
  │  8   │ 05/23/90 │ 0100009-IN│        .00 │       .00 │        .00 │        .00 │
  └──────┴──────────┴───────────┴────────────┴───────────┴────────────┴────────────┘
  ENTER LINE NO:

   Use UP/DOWN cursor control keys, PAGE-UP/PAGE-DN keys, HOME/END keys to move
      highlighted selection, <ENTER>=select, F1=help, F3=search, ESC=end
```

Screen 49: MAS90 EVOLUTION/2 Version 1.1x

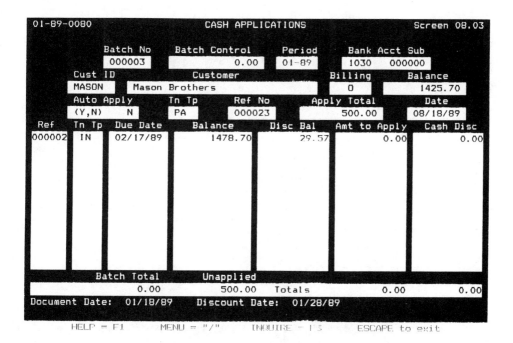

Screen 50: Solomon III Accounting Software Version 6.0

```
┌─────────────────────────────────────────────────────────────────┐
║                       SALES JOURNAL                               ║
║      Add   Change   Delete   Inquire   First   Last   Next   Prior     Output  ║
└─────────────────────────────────────────────────────────────────┘

              ┌─────────────────────┐
              │ PARAM KEY           │
              │ DESCRIPTION         │
              └─────────────────────┘


              ┌──────────────────────────────────┐
              │ BEGINNING  TRANSACTION DATE       │    /  /
              │ ENDING     TRANSACTION DATE       │    /  /
              └──────────────────────────────────┘

              ┌──────────────────────────────────────────┐
              │ PRINT INVOICES, RECEIPTS, OR BOTH (I/R/B) │
              └──────────────────────────────────────────┘
```

───

<F1>=Process, <F2>=Clear Screen, <F9>-<F10>=Switch Action, <Esc>=Return to Menu

───

Screen 51: Platinum Version 6.0


```
ABC DISTRIBUTING AND SERVICE CORP. (ABC)          PRINTER LP              08/29/88
INVOICE PRINTING                                                          12:48 AM
─────────────────────────────────────────────────────────────────
                          FORM HEADER INFORMATION
─────────────────────────────────────────────────────────────────

              PRINT ANY DESCRIPTIONS: Y
                   PRINT COMPRESSED: N
                     LENGTH OF FORM: 066
                      WIDTH OF FORM: 080

─────────────────────────────────────────────────────────────────
                     INVOICE DETAIL LINE GROUPING
─────────────────────────────────────────────────────────────────

          NUMBER OF LINES IN GROUPING: 031
                LINES PER LINE GROUP: 001
        STARTING LINE OF LINE GROUPING: 024




        IS THE ABOVE CORRECT? (Yes, No, Print, RESET, END): [Yes       ]

─────────────────────────────────────────────────────────────────
```

Screen 52: MAS90 EVOLUTION/2 Version 1.1x

```
ABC DISTRIBUTING & SERVICE CORP (ABC)           PRINTER LP            05/31/90
INVOICE PRINTING                                                     12:31 AM

 LN FIELD DESCRIPTOR          PRINT? LINE TAB   PRINT? DESCRIPTION    LINE TAB

  1 TITLE OF INVOICE            Y    002  030    N
  2 PAGE NUMBER                 Y    002  076    Y  PAGE:             002  070
  3 INVOICE NUMBER              Y    006  064    Y  INVOICE NUMBER:   006  048
  4 INVOICE DATE                Y    008  064    Y  INVOICE DATE:     008  050
  5 COMPANY NAME                Y    006  007    N
  6 COMPANY ADDRESS LINE 1      Y    007  007    N
  7 COMPANY ADDRESS LINE 2      Y    008  007    N
  8 COMPANY ADDRESS LINE 3      Y    009  007    N
  9 COMPANY ADDRESS LINE 4      Y    010  007    N
 10 COMPANY PHONE NUMBER        Y    011  007    N
 11 CUSTOMER NAME               Y    015  007    N
 12 CUSTOMER ADDRESS LINE 1     Y    016  007    N
 13 CUSTOMER ADDRESS LINE 2     Y    017  007    N
 14 CUSTOMER CITY               Y    018  007    N
 15 CUSTOMER STATE              Y    018  029    N


    ENTER LINE NUMBER TO MODIFY (1-65, HEADER, <ENTER> to end): [        ]
```

Screen 53: MAS90 EVOLUTION/2 Version 1.1x

Customer List ⌘1	Misc Cust Info List ⌘2	Customers By Slsmn ⌘3	Ship Location List ⌘4	Invoice Summary ⌘5	Invoices By Number ⌘6	Commission/ profit ⌘7
Inv/Payment Summary ⌘8	Detailed Inv Rpt ⌘9	Ageing ⌘A	Credit Report ⌘B	Tax Code List ⌘C	Term Code List ⌘D	Credit Type List ⌘E
A/R To G/L Audit ⌘G	A/R Line B/Order ⌘H	Unapplied Credits ⌘I	Credits/ How Appld ⌘J	Invoices By Date ⌘K	Invoices/ How Paid ⌘L	Cust Sales History ⌘M
Customer	Salesperson	Help				

File   Edit   System   Accounts Receivable   Selections   12:48:11 PM

Selections

Screen 54: Flexware Version 6.02

```
┌────────────────── Sales History ══════════════ Normal Entry ─┐
│ Pick Customer ID    from   ------            Sort by:          │
│                     thru                     1.  Customer ID   │
│      Salesperson    from                     2.  Salesperson ID│
│                     thru                     3.  Job or Inventory No│
│      Job or Inv No  from                     4.  Product Category│
│                     thru                                       │
│      Prod Category  from                                       │
│                     thru                                       │
│      Invoice Date   from                                       │
│                     thru                                       │
│                                                                │
│      1.   Full detail                                          │
│      2.   Summary only                                         │
│                                                                │
│                                                                │
│      1.   Quantity in base units                               │
│      2.   Quantity in selling units                            │
│                                                                │
│                                                                │
├────────────────────────────────────────────────────────────┤
│                                                                │
└────────────────────────────────────────────────────────────┘
```

Screen 55: OPEN SYSTEMS Version 3.2

Print statements   The Software Consultants
FORMAT 1

            Please enter:

                 1. Statement period   _____
                 2. Statement comments

                 3. Use dunning messages ?
                 4. Print aged totals ?
                 5. Show payment detail ?
                 6. Cut-off balance due
                 7. Cut-off aging period

                 8. Starting customer #
                 9. Ending customer #

                10. Stmnt cycles to print
                11. Print zero bal customers ?
                12. Print CR bal customers ?

Screen 56: RealWorld Version 5.0

320

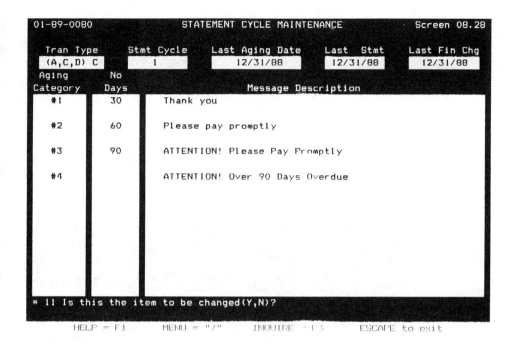

```
01-89-0080              STATEMENT CYCLE MAINTENANCE            Screen 08.28

  Tran Type    Stmt Cycle   Last Aging Date   Last  Stmt   Last Fin Chg
  (A,C,D) C        1            12/31/88        12/31/88      12/31/88
Aging        No
Category     Days                    Message Description
   #1         30      Thank you

   #2         60      Please pay promptly

   #3         90      ATTENTION! Please Pay Promptly

   #4                 ATTENTION! Over 90 Days Overdue








* 11 Is this the item to be changed(Y,N)?

    HELP = F1       MENU = "/"      INQUIRE - F3       ESCAPE to exit
```

Screen 57: Solomon III Accounting Software Version 6.0

```
ABC DISTRIBUTING & SERVICE CORP (ABC)                         05/31/90
ACCOUNTS PAYABLE                                              12:34 AM
| MAIN | CHECK PRINTING | REPORTS | PERIOD END | SETUP | DATE | END |

   ┌Accounts Payable Main Menu────────────────┐
   │   1.   VENDOR MAINTENANCE                 │
   │   2.   VENDOR INQUIRY                     │
   │   3.   REPETITIVE INVOICE ENTRY           │
   │   4.   REPETITIVE INVOICE SELECTION       │
   │   5.   INVOICE DATA ENTRY                 │
   │   6.   INVOICE REGISTER                   │
   │   7.   MANUAL CHECK ENTRY                 │
   │   8.   MANUAL CHECK REGISTER              │
   │   9.   DAILY TRANSACTION REGISTER         │
   │                                          │
   │   ENTER YOUR OPTION: ···············     │
   └──────────────────────────────────────────┘



       F1=help, F2=company, F3=date, F4=print, F5=status, ESC=exit
```

Screen 58: MAS90 EVOLUTION/2 Version 1.1x

```
┌─────────────────────────────────────────────────────────────────────────┐
│ □                            Selections                                   │
├──────────┬──────────┬──────────┬──────────┬──────────┬──────────┬────────┤
│          │          │          │          │          │          │        │
│ Vendors  │ Invoices │New Batch │ Add to   │Distribution│Calc What│See What│
│          │          │ of Invcs │Old Batch │   Only   │ to Pay   │Will Pay│
│   ⌘1     │   ⌘2     │   ⌘3     │   ⌘4     │   ⌘5     │   ⌘6     │  ⌘7    │
├──────────┼──────────┼──────────┼──────────┼──────────┼──────────┼────────┤
│          │          │          │          │          │          │        │
│Change What│  Write  │  Scan    │ Change   │Vndr Purch│  Help    │        │
│ to Pay   │ Checks   │Check Reg │Check Params│History  │          │        │
│   ⌘8     │   ⌘9     │   ⌘A     │   ⌘B     │   ⌘H     │   ⌘W     │        │
└──────────┴──────────┴──────────┴──────────┴──────────┴──────────┴────────┘

┌───────────────────────────────────────────────────────────────────────────┐
│ Please make menu selection or choose icon                                   │
└───────────────────────────────────────────────────────────────────────────┘
```

Screen 59: Flexware Version 6.02

```
Maintain A/P control data                        The Software Consultants

           1. A/P account number              2000-000
           2. Cash account number             1000-000
           3. Default disc account number     5050-000

           4. Age by inv or due date          Due date
           5. number age days in period 1     30
           6. number age days in period 2     60
           7. number age days in period 3     90
           8. number age days in period 4     999
           9. Aging period 1 description      Current
          10. Aging period 2 description      Over   30
          11. Aging period 3 description      Over   60
          12. Aging period 4 description      Over   90
          13. Last voucher number             1002
          14. Last check number               100

          15. Print company name on checks ?  N
          16. Print check number on ?         Both stub and check
          17. Keep vendor history file ?      Y

Field number to change ?    ___
```

Screen 60: RealWorld Version 5.0

322

```
┌────────────────────────────────────────────────────┐
│         *** SYSTEM CONTROL FILE MAINTENANCE ***      │
└────────────────────────────────────────────────────┘

┌──────────────────────────────────────────────────────────────────────┐
│  Period Ending Date:        10 / 31 / 85                               │
│                                                                        │
│  Next Voucher Number:       10026                                      │
├──────────────────────────────────────────────────────────────────────┤
│  Aging Periods:  0 to  30.     Cash Requirements Periods:  0 to  14.   │
│                    to  60.                                   to  30.   │
│     (Days)         to  90.              (Days)               to  45.   │
│                  over                                      over        │
├────────────────────────────────────┬─────────────────────────────────┤
│  Print Company Name                 │  Default G/L Accounts:           │
│  on Checks (Y/N)       N            │                                  │
│                                     │  Cash:                1020 - 0000 │
│  Accounting Method:                 │  Accounts Payable:    3020 - 0000 │
│  <C>ash  <A>ccrual     A            │  Discounts Taken:     7021 - 0000 │
├────────────────────────────────────┴─────────────────────────────────┤
│  Post to General Ledger in Detail or Summary ? (D/S) D                │
│  Maintain a Vendor History File ?                    (Y/N) Y          │
│  Interface to Job Costing ?                          (Y/N) .          │
└──────────────────────────────────────────────────────────────────────┘
     F1 -Write Data to Disk      F2 -Clear      Esc -Return to Menu
```

Screen 61: Charterhouse Version 2.1

```
┌──────────────────────────────────────────────────────────────────────┐
│                 VENDOR ACTIVITY FILE MAINTENANCE                       │
│        Add   Change   Delete   Inquire   First   Last   Next   Prior   │
└──────────────────────────────────────────────────────────────────────┘


              ┌──────────────┐
              │  VENDOR KEY  │    00100   IDM CORPORATION
              └──────────────┘


                                             ┌─MTD AMT──────YTD AMT─┐
┌─────────────────────────┐    ┌─────────────┼──────────┬──────────┤
│ LAST INVOICE DATE │ 02/28/86 │  TOT PURCH.  │ 84478.75 │ 132878.75 │
│ LAST PAYMENT DATE │ 02/15/86 │  DEBIT MEMO  │  8655.75 │   8655.75 │
│ LAST AGING   DATE │ 01/01/86 │  DISC TAKEN  │    0     │    0      │
│ AGING  BRACKET 1  │ 29425    │  NET PURCH.  │ 75823    │ 124223    │
│ AGING  BRACKET 2  │ 0        │  DISC LOST   │    0     │    0      │
│ AGING  BRACKET 3  │ 0        │  1099 AMOUNT │ 89798    │  94798    │
│ AGING  BRACKET 4  │ 0        │  CASH PAID   │ 89798    │  94798    │
└─────────────────────────┘    └─────────────┴──────────┴──────────┘


       <F1> = Process, <F2> = Clear Screen, <Esc> = Return to Menu
```

Screen 62: Platinum Version 6.0

```
Maintain vendor data                              The Software Consultants
Change/Inquire
                    * 1. Vendor #    1

                      2. Name        The Software Consultants
                      3. Address 1   1 Stoneleigh Close
                      4. Address 2   Scarsdale N Y
                      5. Address 3   10583

                      6. Phone #     914-725-3602
                      7. Contact 1   Irwin Winsten
                      8. Contact 2   Jay Butler


      9. Type       REG           15. Last invoice date   9/20/87
     10. Terms                    16. Purchases YTD        12,500.00
     11. Due days   30            17. Purchases 1st yr     45,000.00
     12. Disc days  10            18. Discounts YTD        250.00
     13. Disc pct   5.00          19. Discounts 1st yr     500.00
     14. Status     _             20. Dflt distrib acct #  5010-000
                                      Purchases - Misc. Items

  Blank = normal   A = always take discount   H = hold payment   N = no purchases
```

Screen 63: RealWorld Version 5.0

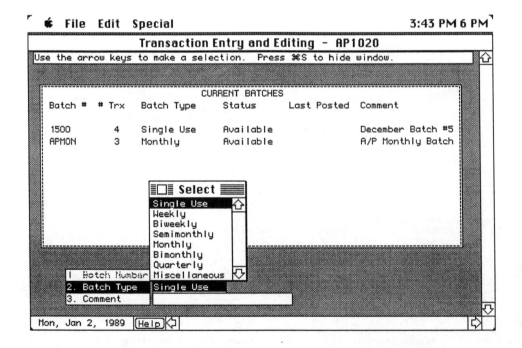

Screen 64: Copyright © Great Plains Software, Incorporated, 1989 Version 5.x. All rights reserved.

```
THE UNIVERSAL CORPORATION                        Date: Mar 21 88
Enter / Edit Invoice Batches

    Batch number      [6  ]        No. of transactions: 0
                                        Batch total: 0.00
    Entry number      [1   ]
    Vendor number     [   200]      Chloride Systems
    Invoice number    [      34]
    Invoice date      [03/21/88]
    Due date          [04/20/88]    Terms:  2.00 % / 10   Net 30
    Reference         [45678     ]
    Total payable     [         0.00 ]



    Acct        Dept      Job-Ph-Cat           Amount
   [502   ]    [     ]    [   -  -    ]    [              ]



Press ESCAPE when distribution is complete.
```

Screen 65: © 1989, Computer Associates International, Inc. Version 5.x

```
┌─────────────────────────────────────────────────────────────┐
│                 VOUCHER ENTRY - Screen 1 of 4                 │
│        Add   Change   Delete   Inquire   First   Last   Next   Prior │
└─────────────────────────────────────────────────────────────┘
─────────────────VENDOR:─────────────────
KEY      ◄│00100                    │
 NAME     │IDM CORPORATION
 ADDR  1  │123 FOURTH STREET
       2
       3
 CITY     │DENVER           STATE:CO
 ZIP      │65000            COUNTRY:
 ATTN.    │ACCOUNTS RECEIVABLE

VOUCHER◄│000021      │DUE  DATE│ 01/26/89 │RECUR  KEY  │ 000
APPLY TO│            │DISC DATE│ 12/26/88 │INVOICE NO.
STATUS  │            │AGE  DATE│ 12/26/88 │BRANCH      │00001 WAREHOUSE
TERMS   │ N NET 30   │CHECK NO.│          │RESPONSIB.  │00000
─────   │            │CHECK AMT│          │VENDOR CLASS│00001 COST OF SA
DISCOUNT│ 0%         │CHECK DT │  /  /    │CASH ACCOUNT│1010-0000
INV DATE│ 12/26/88   │DSC TAKEN│          │P.O. NO.

 FREIGHT:      0.00              INVOICE TOTAL:        9,270.50

<F1>=Process, <Alt-2>=Line Items, <Alt-3>=Serial/Lot, <Alt-4>=J/C, <Esc>=Menu
```

Screen 66: Platinum Version 6.0

ITEM KEY	DESCRIPTION	LOC	QTY	AMOUNT	ACCOUNT
000000000000000100	IDM PERSONAL COMPUTER MX	00001	2	2885.25	6100-000
	512K 20 MG. HARD DISK				0000-000
000000000000000200	MONOCHROME VISEO DISPLAY	00001	10	350	6100-000
					—
					—
					—
					—
					—
					—
					—
					—

VEND: IDM CORPORATION	EXTENSION:	0.00	SUB TOTAL:	9,270.50
LOC:	FREIGHT:	0.00		
			INV TOTAL:	9,270.50

<Alt-1>=Header Screen, <Alt-3>=Serial, <Alt-4>=J/C, <PgUp>,<PgDn>,<Home>,<End>

Screen 67: Platinum Version 6.0

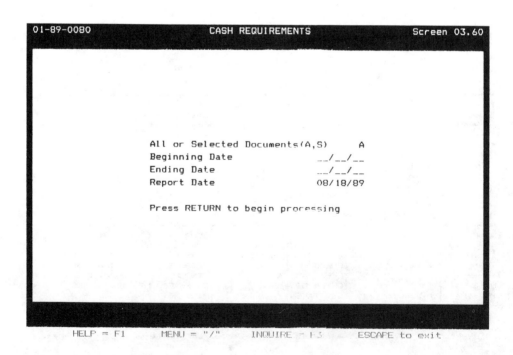

```
01-89-0080              CASH REQUIREMENTS              Screen 03.60




              All or Selected Documents(A,S)     A
              Beginning Date              __/__/__
              Ending Date                 __/__/__
              Report Date                 08/18/89

              Press RETURN to begin processing




     HELP = F1      MENU = "/"     INQUIRE = F3      ESCAPE to exit
```

Screen 68: Solomon III Accounting Software Version 6.0

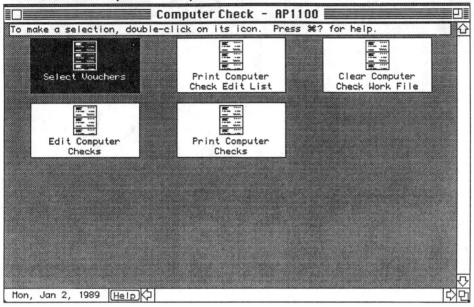

```
EDWARDSON ELECTRICAL CONTRACTORS (EEC)                        05/30/90
INVOICE PAYMENT SELECTION                                     12:58 AM
───────────────────────────────────────────────────────────────────────

                 VENDOR RANGE TO PAY:
                    STARTING VENDOR:        ALL VENDORS
                    ENDING VENDOR:

                 JOB NUMBER TO SELECT:      ALL JOBS

                 PAY RETENTION BALANCE? (Y/N):  N

                 ONLY SELECT INVOICES WITH AVAILABLE DISCOUNT? (Y/N):  N

                 ALWAYS TAKE DISCOUNTS? (Y/N):  N

                 INVOICE DUE DATE:              05/30/90

                 DISCOUNT DUE DATE:             05/30/90




             IS THE ABOVE CORRECT? (Yes, No, END): [Yes   ]
───────────────────────────────────────────────────────────────────────
```

Screen 70: MAS90 EVOLUTION/2 Version 1.1x

Ref No	Tn	Stat(A,H) Pay Date	Ven ID Disc Bal	Ven Stat/ Document Bal	Disc Date/ Disc Taken	Due Date/ Amount Paid
000006	VO	A 02/17/89	TARTAN 0.00	A 15000.00	01/18/89 0.00	02/17/89 15000.00

HELP = F1   MENU = "/"   INQUIRE = F3   ESCAPE to exit

Screen 71: Solomon III Accounting Software Version 6.0

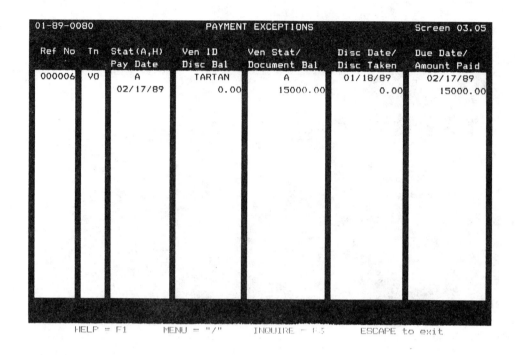

Screen 72: Flexware Version 6.02

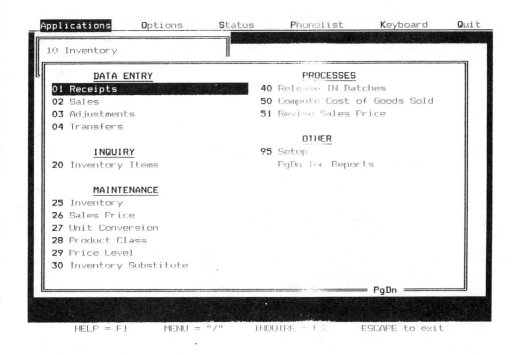

Applications   Options   Status   Phonelist   Keyboard   Quit

```
┌─ 10 Inventory ─────────────────────────────┐
║                                            ║
║    DATA ENTRY                 PROCESSES    ║
║ ┌────────────────────────┐ 40 Release IN Batches
║ │01 Receipts             │ 50 Compute Cost of Goods Sold
║ 02 Sales                   51 Revise Sales Price
║ 03 Adjustments
║ 04 Transfers                  OTHER
║                            95 Setup
║    INQUIRY                    PgDn for Reports
║ 20 Inventory Items
║
║    MAINTENANCE
║ 25 Inventory
║ 26 Sales Price
║ 27 Unit Conversion
║ 28 Product Class
║ 29 Price Level
║ 30 Inventory Substitute
║                                  PgDn
└────────────────────────────────────────────┘

  HELP = F1      MENU = "/"     INQUIRE = !5      ESCAPE to exit
```

Screen 73: Solomon III Accounting Software Version 6.0

Maintain I/C control data   The Software Consultants

        1. Inventory valuation method ?   F
        2. Multi warehousing ?   Y
        3. Using Purchase Order ?   Y

        4. How many prior periods of qty-sold
           do you wish to track (1 to 12) ? 12
        5. Are these periods monthly ?   Y

        6. Are cost of sales used ?   N
        7. Back order control ?   Y

        8. Default profit center   100
        9. Default sales account   4010
       10. Default expense account   5070
       11. Credit memo account   5000
       12. B/S inventory account   1200-000
       13. B/S liability account   2000-000
       14. Cost correction account   7050-000

       16. Current period ending date   3/31/99

Field number to change ? ___

Screen 74: RealWorld Version 5.0

```
┌────────────────────────────────────────────────────────────────────┐
│                  NAME & OPTIONS FILE MAINTENANCE                     │
└────────────────────────────────────────────────────────────────────┘


  ┌──────────────────┐   DEMONSTRATION, INC.
  │ COMPANY NAME     │   1000 ANY STREET
  │ ADDRESS          │   SOMEWHERE
  │ CITY             │   CA
  │ STATE            │   70000
  │ ZIP              │
  └──────────────────┘

  ┌────────────────────────────────────────────────────┐  F
  │ LIFO, FIFO, WEIGHTED, STANDARD COSTING (L/F/W/S)    │  Y
  │ RETAIN HISTORY TRANSACTIONS (Y/N)                   │  Y
  │ RETAIN HISTORY RECAP (Y/N)                          │  N
  │ G/L INTERFACE (Y/N)                                 │  01/31/86
  │ LAST G/L POSTING DATE                               │  N
  │ INTERFACE TO J/C  (Y/N)                             │
  └────────────────────────────────────────────────────┘


        <F1> = Process, <F2> = Clear Screen, <Esc> = Return to Menu
```

Screen 75: Platinum Version 6.0

```
═══════════════════ Inventory Costs ═══════════════ Normal Entry ═╗

  Warehouse ID CA0001              OAKLAND WAREHOUSE
  Inventory No 100                 ELECTRICAL PACKAGE

                Quantity        Cost           Value
     First In     .0000         .0000          .0000    Month to Date
     Mid 1 In     .0000         .0000          .0000    Cost of Goods
     Mid 2 In     .0000         .0000          .0000    Adjustment
     Mid 3 In     .0000         .0000          .0000
     Mid 4 In     .0000         .0000          .0000        .00
     Mid 5 In     .0000         .0000          .0000
     Mid 6 In     .0000         .0000          .0000
     Mid 7 In     .0000         .0000          .0000
     Mid 8 In     .0000         .0000          .0000      Average
     Mid 9 In     .0000         .0000          .0000       Cost
     Mid 10 In    .0000         .0000          .0000
     Last In      .0000         .0000          .0000        .0000
                 ─────────────────────────────────────
     T o t a l    .0000                        .0000

   » << 'P' if OK, 'S' to Start over, 'X' to Restart, 'M' for Menu >>
```

Screen 76: OPEN SYSTEMS Version 3.2

```
        Sample item number XX-XXX/X

                Segment name      Length
        1.      [CLASS      ]        2
        2.      [STYLE      ]        3
        3.      [COLOR      ]        1
        4.      [          ]         0
```

```
┌──────────────────────────────────────────────┐
│                                                │
│       Edit    Previous    Next    Cancel       │
│                                                │
└──────────────────────────────────────────────┘
```

Screen 77: © 1989, Computer Associates International, Inc. Version 5.x

```
╔══════════════════════════════════════════════════════════════╗
║               ITEM MASTER FILE MAINTENANCE                     ║
║     Add   Change  Delete  Inquire  First  Last  Next  Prior    ║
╚══════════════════════════════════════════════════════════════╝
```

```
┌────────────────────┐
│ ITEM KEY           │    000000000000000100
│ DESCRIPTION 1      │    IDM PERSONAL COMPUTER MX
│            2       │    512K 20 MG. HARD DISK
└────────────────────┘
```

```
┌──────────────────────────┐      ┌──────────────────────────────┐
│ PURCH. UNIT DESCR.       │      │ SERIAL NO. (Y/N/L)     │ Y    │
│ CONVERSION FACTOR    │ 0  │      │ TYPE (R/W/F/L/O)       │ F    │
│ WEIGHT               │ 45 │      │ MANUFACTURER           │ IDM  │
│ PHYS. CYCLE (DAYS)   │ 30 │      │ ALTERNATE ITEM KEY     │      │
└──────────────────────────┘      └──────────────────────────────┘
```

```
        <F1> = Process, <F2> = Clear Screen, <Esc> = Return to Menu
```

Screen 78: Platinum Version 6.0

```
┌─────────────────────────────────────────────────────────────────────┐
│                   ITEM LOCATION FILE MAINTENANCE                      │
│         Add   Change   Delete   Inquire   First   Last   Next   Prior │
└─────────────────────────────────────────────────────────────────────┘

                                     IDM PERSONAL COMPUTE

┌──────────────────────────┐              ┌──────────────────────────────┐
│ ITEM KEY     000000000000000100          │ BASE PRICE         4500      │
│ LOCATION KEY 00001   STORE #1            │ AVERAGE COST       2887.05   │
│                                          │ LAST COST          2885.25   │
│                                          │ STANDARD COST      0         │
                                           └──────────────────────────────┘

┌──────────────────────────┐
│ INV CLASS       00100   COMPUTERS        │
│ BIN NO.                                  │
│ VENDOR 1 KEY    00100                    ┌──────────────────────────────┐
│   VENDOR 1 ITEM NO  5150-567             │ QTY ON-HAND          24       │
│ VENDOR 2 KEY    00000                    │ QTY ON-ORDER         0        │
│   VENDOR 2 ITEM NO                       │ QTY TRAN-IN  -COMING 0        │
│ REVENUE  ACCOUNT  5100 - 0000  Sales -   │ QTY TRAN-OUT -GOING  0        │
│ PURCHASE ACCOUNT  6100 - 0000  Purchas   │ QTY COMMITTED -SALES -1       │
│ COMMISSION KEY   01                      │ QTY COMMITTED -PROD  0        │
│ DEFAULT TAX                              │ MINIMUM QUANTITY     10       │
│ LEAD TIME (DAYS)  15                     │ MAXIMUM QUANTITY     20       │
└──────────────────────────┘              │ REORDER QUANTITY     5        │
                                           └──────────────────────────────┘

        <F1> = Process, <F2> = Clear Screen, <Esc> = Return to Menu
```

Screen 79: Platinum Version 6.0

```
Maintain item data                        The Software Consultants
Change/Inquire
   1. Item #          1
   2. Description     Drill, 1/4" Power Hand
                      Extra Chuck
   3. Category        TLS
   4. Vendor          TEST

   5. Stocking unit   EACH              16. Taxable ?      Y
   6. Pricing unit    EACH              17. ABC code
   7. Conv factor     1                 18. B/O code       B

   8. Pricing code    01 Quantity Discount
   9. Commis code     01 Regular

  10. Price-1         23.00             19. Sls acct #    4010
  11. Price-2         21.00             20. Exp acct #    5070
  12. Price-3         19.75

  13. Average cost    .00               21. Qty on hand   0
  14. Std cost        (Not applicable)  22. Qty commit    100-
  15. Rplcmnt cost    .00               23. Qty on ord    0
Make changes, or press F1 for next item
Field number to change ?  ___
```

Screen 80: RealWorld Version 5.0

```
Maintain item data                      The Software Consultants
Add/Change status data                     Current period: March, 1999
            Item #: 1               Drill, 1/4" Power Hand
                                     Extra Chuck

    1. Warehouse      1   First WH
    2. Location code  2                Vendor #: TEST      Category: TLS
       Stocking unit: EACH
                                       ----- Prior periods qty sold -----
    3. Qty on hand    0               14. February  1999  0
    4. Qty committed  100-            15. January   1999  0
    5. Qty on order   0               16. December  1998  0
    6. Maximum qty    20              17. November  1998  0
    7. Reorder level  5               18. October   1998  0
                                      19. September 1998  0
    8. Qty sold PTD   100             20. August    1998  0
    9. Qty sold YTD   1,000           21. July      1998  0
   10. Sales PTD      2,100.00        22. June      1998  0
   11. Sales YTD      19,500.00       23. May       1998  0
   12. Costs PTD      1,200.00        24. April     1998  0
   13. Costs YTD      11,000.00       25. March     1998  0

Make changes, or press F1 for status in next warehouse
Field number to change ?  ___
```

Screen 81: RealWorld Version 5.0

```
 🍎  File  Edit  Special                         3:25 PM!8 PM

 ═══════════════ Item Maintenance - IV1010 ═══════════════
 (Next Wndw) (Accept) (Pricing) (Vendors) (Change ##) (Delete) (Start Over)

    1. Item Number      IV5035        13. Commission Type  % of Price
    2. Description                    14  Commission Amt          $0.00
       Deluxo Microwave               15. Commission Pct   10.0%
    3. Item Type        Sales Inventory
                                      16. Ship Weight      49.0
    4. Bin                            17. Ship by UPS      No
    5. Prod Category    APP
    6. Generic Descr    WAVER         18. Inventory Acct   FURNIT
    7. Substitute 1     IV5040        19. IV Offset Acct
       Cheapo Microwave               20. Cost Of Goods
    8. Substitute 2                   21. Sales
                                      22. Sales Discount
                                      23. Sales Returns
    9. Serial Numbers   Yes
   10. Retain History   Yes
   11. Sales Tax Sched  FRN1          24. Primary Vendor   V1570
       Main Furniture Sched              Wessington Kitchens
   12. Back Order       Yes           25. Reorder Number   TW9095

                                      26. Item Avg Lead Time   0.0
   Finished Product    No             27. Total Receipts         0
 Mon, Jan 2, 1989  (Help)
```

Screen 82: Copyright © Great Plains Software, Incorporated, 1989 Version 5.x. All rights reserved.

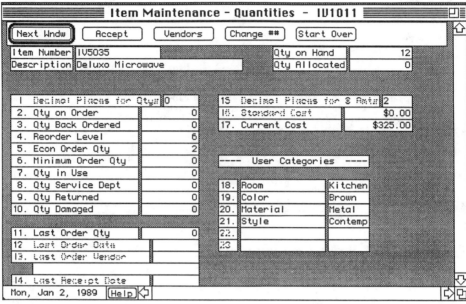

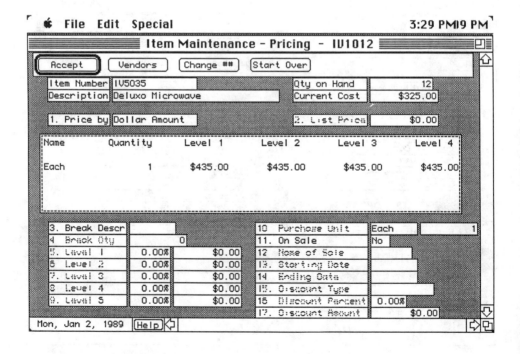

334

```
Warehouse ID CA0001              OAKLAND WAREHOUSE
Inventory No 100                 ELECTRICAL PACKAGE

              *** Quantity Break Prices ***

         Break 1      Break 2      Break 3      Break 4      Break 5
Qty      8.0000       .0000        .0000        .0000        .0000
Price   475.6860      .0000        .0000        .0000        .0000

            **** Alternate Units of Measure ****

    Unit of Measure       Conversion        Price      ---- Penalties ----
                            Factor                      Type(%$)    Amount
Default          PKG       1.0000          528.5400     %            .0000
1st Alternate              .0000            .0000        %            .0000
2nd Alternate              .0000            .0000        %            .0000
3rd Alternate              .0000            .0000        %            .0000
4th Alternate              .0000            .0000        %            .0000
```

Screen 85: OPEN SYSTEMS Version 3.2

```
THE UNIVERSAL CORPORATION                              Date: Aug 04 8
Add/Modify/Delete Items - Modify Item

Item number A1-103/0 Fluorescent Desk Lamp
 — Units of Measure ────────────────────────────────────────
Stocking unit:    EA
Alternative units     [        ] [              ] EA       Conversion factor
                      [        ] [              ] EA
                      [        ] [              ] EA
                      [        ] [              ] EA
Pricing unit     (EA       )      Base price:          33.75  EA
Costing unit     (EA       )      Standard cost:       27.00  EA
                                  Most recent cost:    27.99  EA


Selling price based on (Discount).
Discount on price by   (Percentage).
Pricing determined by  (Customer type     ).
                  Discount percent
               A    [   0.00 ]
               B    [   2.00 ]
               C    [   3.00 ]
               D    [   4.00 ]
               E    [   0.00 ]
```

Screen 86: © 1989, Computer Associates International, Inc. Version 5.x

```
THE UNIVERSAL CORPORATION                                    Date: Aug 04 8
Edit Company Profile - Default Pricing Policy

   Selling price based on (Discount).
   Discount on price by   (Percentage).
   Pricing determined by  (Customer type      ).

                              Discount percent
                         A   [   0.00 ]
                         B   [   0.00 ]
                         C   [   0.00 ]
                         D   [   0.00 ]
                         E   [   0.00 ]


   Discount/markup rounding method (Round up    )
   Rounded to nearest [  0.05 ]

   Default tax status [1]

           ┌─────────────────────────────────────────────┐
           │     Edit    Previous    Next    Cancel       │
           └─────────────────────────────────────────────┘
```

Screen 87: © 1989, Computer Associates International, Inc. Version 5.x

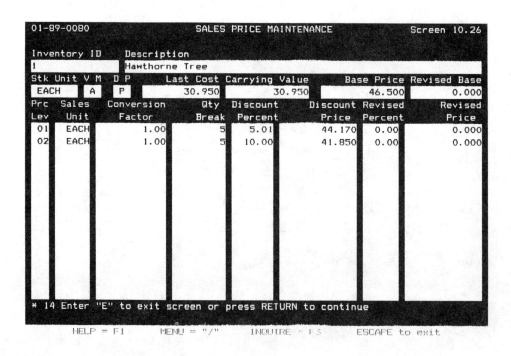

Screen 88: Solomon III Accounting Software Version 6.0

336

```
ABC DISTRIBUTING & SERVICE CORP (ABC)                        05/31/90
TRANSACTION DATA ENTRY                        RECORDS: 1      12:40 AM

 ADJUST. ENTRY NO:    00012345      DATE:   05/31/90    ADJ TOTAL:      45.21

LINE    ITEM NUMBER       DESCRIPTION
                                             QUANTITY     UNIT COST      EXTENSION

   1  4886-18-14-3     PAPER CADDY 18"W 14"D 3"H     U/M:   EACH    WHSE:  000
       AVG COSTING                      .....2.00           22.604          45.21




              ON HAND QUANTITY IN THIS WAREHOUSE IS 94 EACH
```

Screen 89: MAS90 EVOLUTION/2 Version 1.1x

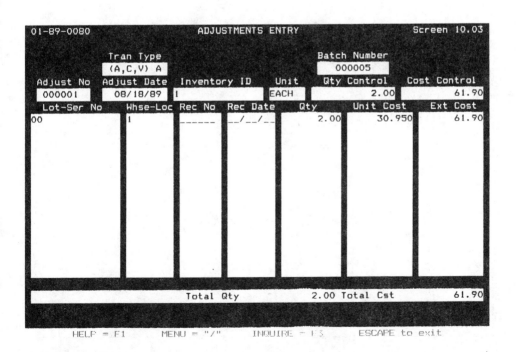

Screen 90: Solomon III Accounting Software Version 6.0

ITEM KEY	LOC	DATE	T	DOC	QUAN	UNIT COST	UNIT SALE	T-LOC
		/ /						
		/ /						

```
┌─Move──────────────────────────────────────────────────────────┐
│ Page 160.0 from D:\PLATINUM\HELP\IVHELP                        │
│                                                                │
│ All entries to the Inventory not made through other modules are made at│
│ this screen.                                                   │
│ <F7><F8> index at ITEM KEY, LOC(ation), and T(ransaction Type).│
│                                                                │
│ Tranasction Type                                              │
│     A  Adjustment                S  Sales Invoice             │
│     C  Credit Memo               T  Transfer Going Out        │
│     D  Debit Memo                U  Transfer Coming In         │
│     I  Inventory Commitment      R  Receipt of Transfer        │
│     O  On Order                  N  Notification of Receipt    │
│     P  Purchase                  X  Production Commitment      │
│                                                                │
└────────────────────────────────────────────────────────────────┘
```

<F1>=Process, <F9>,<F10>=Select mode, <Cursor keys>=Move window, <Esc>=Exit

Screen 91: Platinum Version 6.0

```
┌──────────────────────────────────────────────────────────────────┐
│┌────────────────── Inventory Category Price Change ──────────────┐│
││                 Warehouse ID From  ──────                       ││
││                             Thru                                ││
││          Pick  Inventory No From                                ││
││                             Thru                                ││
││                Category     From                                ││
││                             Thru                                ││
││                                                                 ││
││          Change All Prices By              %                    ││
││                                                                 ││
││          Round Prices To Nearest--                              ││
││                                                                 ││
││                  1.   $1.00                                     ││
││                  2.   $ .10                                     ││
││                  3.   $ .01                                     ││
││                  4.   $ .001                                    ││
││                  5.   $ .0001                                   ││
││                                                                 ││
││                                                                 ││
│└─────────────────────────────────────────────────────────────────┘│
└──────────────────────────────────────────────────────────────────┘
```

Screen 92: OPEN SYSTEMS Version 3.2

338

```
              APPLY COST/PRICE CHANGES TO:

              STARTING ITEM NUMBER: [                    ]
              ENDING ITEM NUMBER:    ZZZZZZZZZZZZZZZ

              PRODUCT LINE:          ALL PRODUCT LINES
              PRICE CODE:            ALL PRICE CODES
              VENDOR NUMBER:         ALL VENDORS

              COST CHANGE METHOD:    1   INCREASE BY % OF COST
              COST CHANGE RATE:          .000%

              PRICE CHANGE METHOD:   1   INCREASE BY % OF PRICE
              PRICE CHANGE RATE:         .000%
              PRICE TYPE TO CHANGE:  S   STANDARD PRICE


                   ENTER ITEM NUMBER (F2=list)
```

Screen 93: MAS90 EVOLUTION/2 Version 1.1x

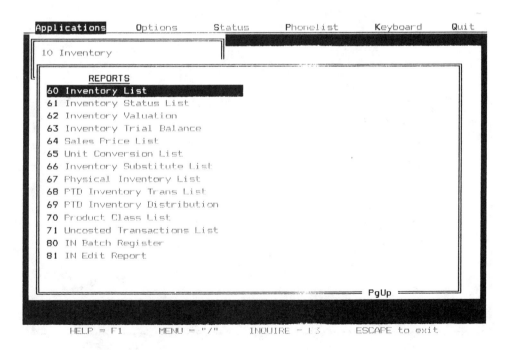

Screen 94: Solomon III Accounting Software Version 6.0

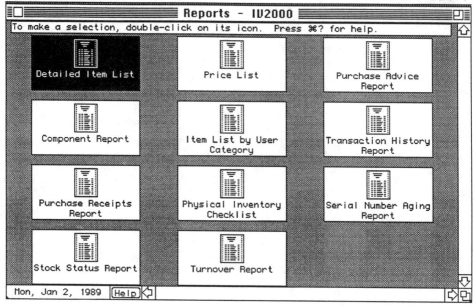

```
======================= Inventory Sales Analysis =======================
Pick    Warehouse ID  from ------              1. Year to Date History
                      thru                     2. Month to Date History
        Inventory No  from                     3. Both
                      thru
        Category No   from
                      thru
        Bin No        from
                      thru

Sort   1. Warehouse ID              Sort by:
Keys:  2. Inventory Number          Primary   -
       3. Category                  Secondary -
       4. Date of Last Sale                      Inventory Number
       5. Sales Dollar Volume (Descending)       Warehouse ID


                     Calculate Turns as of
```

Screen 96: OPEN SYSTEMS Version 3.2

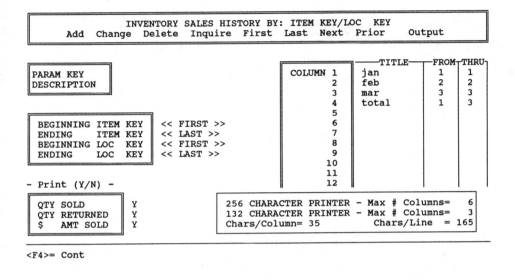

```
┌──────────────────────────────────────────────────────────────────────┐
│              INVENTORY SALES HISTORY BY: ITEM KEY/LOC  KEY             │
│    Add   Change  Delete  Inquire  First  Last  Next  Prior    Output   │
└──────────────────────────────────────────────────────────────────────┘
```

```
                                          ┌────────────TITLE──────FROM─THRU┐
┌─────────────────┐                       │ COLUMN 1   jan         1    1  │
│ PARAM KEY       │                       │        2   feb         2    2  │
│ DESCRIPTION     │                       │        3   mar         3    3  │
└─────────────────┘                       │        4   total       1    3  │
                                          │        5                       │
┌───────────────────────────────────────┐│        6                       │
│ BEGINNING ITEM KEY   << FIRST >>       ││        7                       │
│ ENDING    ITEM KEY   << LAST  >>       ││        8                       │
│ BEGINNING LOC  KEY   << FIRST >>       ││        9                       │
│ ENDING    LOC  KEY   << LAST  >>       ││       10                       │
└───────────────────────────────────────┘│       11                       │
                                          │       12                       │
- Print (Y/N) -                           └────────────────────────────────┘
┌─────────────────────┐   ┌──────────────────────────────────────────────┐
│ QTY  SOLD        Y  │   │ 256 CHARACTER PRINTER - Max # Columns=    6   │
│ QTY  RETURNED    Y  │   │ 132 CHARACTER PRINTER - Max # Columns=    3   │
│ $    AMT SOLD    Y  │   │ Chars/Column= 35          Chars/Line  = 165   │
└─────────────────────┘   └──────────────────────────────────────────────┘
```

<F4>= Cont

Screen 97: Platinum Version 6.0

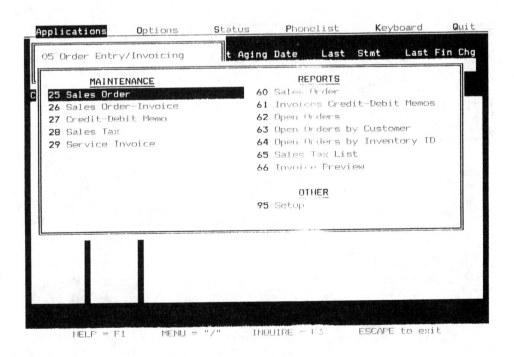

Screen 98: Solomon III Accounting Software Version 6.0

```
THE UNIVERSAL CORPORATION                                    Date: Aug 04 89
Edit Company Profile        - Option Data

  Data Tracking Options
     Retain sales data for analysis            [Y]
     Retain commission data for analysis       [Y]
     Retain order history for analysis         [Y]

  Processing Options
     Allow invalid customer numbers? (Y/N)     [Y]
     Calculate backorder quantity? (Y/N)       [Y]
     Allow credits on invoices? (Y/N)          [Y]
     Calculate commission on (Sales  )
     Delete completed order/invoice/credit note data after [ 30] days.

  Printing Options
     Allow direct invoice printing? (Y/N)      [Y]
     List miscellaneous charges last? (Y/N)    [N]
     Stop printing after each page? (Y/N)      [N]
     Age orders into ┌─────────────────────────────────┐ays.
                     │                                 │
     A/R clearing G/ │   Edit   Previous   Next   Cancel │
                     └─────────────────────────────────┘
```

Screen 99: © 1989, Computer Associates International, Inc. Version 5.x

```
 ┌
   🍎  File  Edit  Special                          3:32 PMi9 PM ┐
╔══════════════════ Order Entry Setup  -  OE3020 ═══════════════╗▯
║ ┌──────────┐  ┌──────────┐  ┌──────────┐  ┌──────────┐        ⇧
║ │Next Wndw │  │  Accept  │  │Change ## │  │Start Over│        │
║ └──────────┘  └──────────┘  └──────────┘  └──────────┘        │
║     1. Post Commissions                          │Yes│        │
║     2. Base Commissions on Actual Cost           │Yes│        │
║     3. Post Transaction Detail                   │Yes│        │
║     4. Integrate With Accounts Receivable        │No │        │
║     5. Automatically Post Transactions Through Other Modules│No││
║     6. Keeping Detail Sales History              │Yes│        │
║     7. Keeping Serial Number History             │Yes│        │
║     8. Keeping Sales Summary                     │Yes│        │
║     9. Default Invoice Number To            │Order Number│     │
║    10. Allow Override Of Default Invoice Numbers │Yes│        │
║    11. Track Voided Transactions                 │Yes│        │
║    12. Edit Invoice Password                                  │
║    13. Credit Limit Password                 │ACCESS│         │
║    14. History Removal Password              │ACCESS│         │
║    15. UPS Identification Number             │ND092-605│      │
║    16. Next Order Number                         │  27│       │
║    17. Next Invoice Number                       │  27│       │
║    18. Next Order Entry Sales Journal Number     │   2│       │
║    19. Non-Inventory Items - Decimal Places For Qtys │2│      ⇩
║    20. Non-Inventory Items - Decimal Places For $ Amts│2│   ⇦⇪
║ Mon, Jan 2, 1989  │Help│◁                                     │
╚═══════════════════════════════════════════════════════════════╝
```

Screen 100: Copyright © Great Plains Software, Incorporated, 1989 Version 5.x. All rights reserved.

342

```
┌─────────────────────────────────────────────────────────────────────┐
│        * * *  E N T E R   O R D E R   H E A D E R   D A T A  * * *    │
├─────────────────────────────────────────────────────────────────────┤
│   TRANSACTION ID:     *00001          ORDER DATE:    03 / 21 / 88     │
├──────────────────────────────────┬──────────────────────────────────┤
│  Customer ID: .....      (or)     │  Ship-to ID: .....               │
│  Name: ........................   │  Name: ........................  │
│                                   │                                  │
│  Addr:                            │  Addr: .........................  │
│                              .    │        .........................  │
│                                   │        .........................  │
│  City:                            │  City: ..................         │
│  ST:      Zip:                    │  ST:    ..  Zip:  ..........      │
├──────────────────────────────────┴──────────────────────────────────┤
│  P-O Number:    ...........       Requested:  03 / 21 / 88           │
│  Buyer:         ..............                                        │
│  Department:    ..........        Terms:      ....                   │
│  Ship Via:      ..........        Territory:  ....                   │
│  # of Labels:   ....              Salesman:   ....                   │
│  FOB:           ....              Commission: ........  (% or $): .  │
├─────────────────────────────────────────────────────────────────────┤
│   CREDIT STATUS:          Limit:         In Use:        Avail:        │
├─────────────────────────────────────────────────────────────────────┤
│  F1 -Process   F2 -Clear   F3 -Prev   F4 -Next   F5 -Cr Memo   Esc -Options │
└─────────────────────────────────────────────────────────────────────┘
```

Screen 101: © 1989, Computer Associates International, Inc. Version 5.x

```
Process orders                        The Software Consultants
Add
           * Order #     2
           1. Order date  4/01/88
           2. Order type  O
           3. Customer #       4.
                               5.
                               6.
                               7.

           8. Ship to          9.
                              10.
                              11.
                              12.

          13. Salesman
          14. Cust PO #        19. Warehouse
          15. Ship via         20. Pft cntr
          16. Ship date
          17. Terms
          18. Tax code

O = order   I = invoice   C = CR memo
```

Screen 102: RealWorld Version 5.0

```
┌─────────────────────────────────────────────────────────────┐
│  ┌────────────────────────────────────────────────────────┐ │
│  │   * * *   E N T E R   L I N E   I T E M S   * * *       │ │
│  └────────────────────────────────────────────────────────┘ │
│ ┌──────────────────────────────────────────────────────────┐│
│ │ Item ID:              .....................                ││
│ │                                                            ││
│ │ Description:          ....................................  ││
│ │                       ....................................  ││
│ │                       ....................................  ││
│ ├──────────────────────────────────┬───────────────────────┤│
│ │ Unit Price (per    ):  .......    │ Cost (avg):           ││
│ │ Qty Ordered:           .......    │                       ││
│ │                                   │ Qty Onhand:           ││
│ │ Revenue G/L Account:   .... - ....│ On Order:             ││
│ │                                   │ Committed:            ││
│ │                                   │              _____ ││
│ │ Taxable (Y/N):             .      │ Projected:            ││
│ └──────────────────────────────────┴───────────────────────┘│
│            ┌───────────────────────────────────┐             │
│            │  Entering line item        1      │             │
│            └───────────────────────────────────┘             │
└─────────────────────────────────────────────────────────────┘

  F1 -Process   F2 -Clear   F3 -Prev   F4 -Next   F6 -Discount   Esc -Review
```

Screen 103: Charterhouse Version 2.1

```
┌═══════════════════ E N T E R   O R D E R S ═══════ Normal Entry ═┐
│  Our Order # 0013432  Date 03/25/88 │ Whse ID  MN0001    Status  New
│  Sold to:    ACE001                 │ Ship to:
│  ACE BUILDERS
│─────────────────────────────────────┼───────────────────────────────
│      Previous Entry                 │        Entry    001
│   ------------------                 │        -------------
│ Item/Job No                         │ Item/Job No  100
│                                     │ ELECTRICAL PACKAGE
│                          Units       │
│ Qty Ordered    .0000                │ Cat: P1    Sales Acct # 4010
│ Qty Shipped    .0000                │ Tax: 1     COGS Acct #  5010
│ Qty Bkord      .0000                │ G/L:       Inv Acct #   1044
│ Ext Price        .00     Tax 0      │                        Units
│                                     │»Qty Ordered       .0000  PKG
│ T O T A L S   Subtotal      .00     │ Qty Shipped       .0000  PKG
│               Tax           .00     │ Qty Bkord         .0000  PKG
│               Freight       .00     │
│               Misc          .00     │ Unit Price        .0000
│                         ----------- │ Unit Cost         .0000
│               Total         .00     │ Ext Price           .00
│                                     │
└─────────────────────────────────────┴───────────────────────────────
         Quantity on hand = 7   Available for sale = 7
```

Screen 104: OPEN SYSTEMS Version 3.2

344

ITEM KEY	DESCRIPTION	UNIT PRICE	QTY ORD	QTY REMN	TAX	ACCOUNT
0000000000000100	IDM PERSONAL COMPUTE	4500	1	1	0001	5100-000
	Non-inventory item	25.375	200	200	0010	5100-000
	Long description of item					—
						—
						—
						—
						—
						—
						—
						—
						—
						—

CUST: BANK OF BOSTON	EXTENSION:	5,075.00	SUB TOTAL:	9,575.00
CALIFORNIA - BART	FREIGHT:	0.00		
	TAX TOTAL:	355.25	ORD TOTAL:	9,930.25

<Alt-1>=Header Screen, <PgUp>,<PgDn>,<Home>,<End>

Screen 105: Platinum Version 6.0

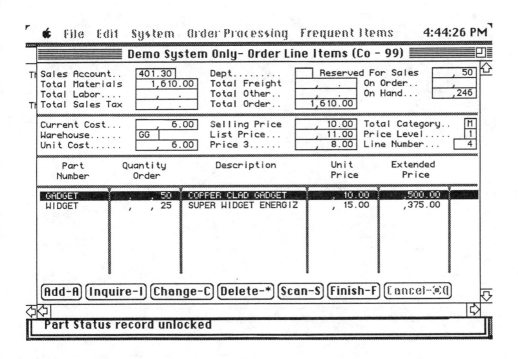

Screen 106: Flexware Version 6.02

```
Process orders                              The Software Consultants
Add
Order #: 2          Customer: 1      Moniques Boutique
  Type: ORDER              CR lim: No limit Bal: 89,900.00

Order total: 161.00      Ship total: 161.00      Txble total: 161.00

      1. Order disc %  _____
      2. Misc charges
      3. Freight
      4. Sales tax

         5. Comm amt              7. Cash received
         6. Comm pct              8. Check #
                                  9. Cash acct


        10. Comment
```

Screen 107: RealWorld Version 5.0

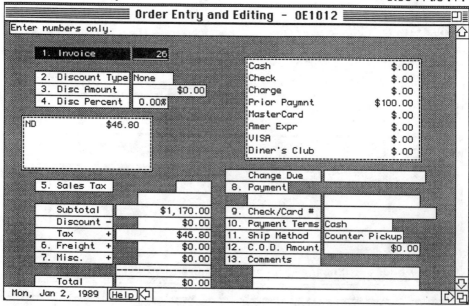

Screen 108: Copyright © Great Plains Software, Incorporated, 1989 Version 5.x. All rights reserved.

```
By Order Type or Order Number(T,N)              T
All or Selected Type(A,S)                       A
Order Type                                      --
All or Selected Order Numbers(A,S)              _
Beginning Order Number                          ------
Ending Order Number                             ------
Report Date                                     08/18/89
```

Screen 109: Copyright © Great Plains Software, Incorporated, 1989 Version 5.x. All rights reserved.

Index